The French Socialists in Power, 1981–1986

The French Socialists in Power, 1981–1986

EDITED BY

PATRICK McCARTHY WITH ESSAYS BY

D. S. Bell and Byron Criddle
Michael M. Harrison
Volkmar Lauber
Patrick McCarthy
George Ross
Martin A. Schain
Vivien A. Schmidt
Michalina Vaughan

CONTRIBUTIONS IN POLITICAL SCIENCE, NUMBER 174

Greenwood Press
NEW YORK • WESTPORT, CONNECTICUT • LONDON

Library of Congress Cataloging-in-Publication Data

The French socialists in power, 1981–1986.

(Contributions in political science, ISSN 0147-1066 ; no. 174)
Bibliography: p.
Includes index.
1. France—Economic policy—1945–   . 2. France—Social policy—1945–   . 3. France—Politics and government—1981–   . 4. France. Parlement (1946–   )—Elections, 1986. 5. Socialism—France. I. McCarthy, Patrick, 1941–   . II. Series.
HC276.2.F699   1987   338.944   86-33569
ISBN 0-313-25407-9 (lib. bdg. : alk. paper)

British Library Cataloguing in Publication Data is available.

Library of Congress Catalog Card Number: 86-33569
ISBN: 0-313-25407-9
ISSN: 0147-1066

First published in 1987

Greenwood Press, Inc.
88 Post Road West, Westport, Connecticut 06881

Printed in the United States of America

∞™

The paper used in this book complies with the Permanent Paper Standard issued by the National Information Standards Organization (Z39.48-1984).

10 9 8 7 6 5 4 3 2 1

Contents

vi   Contents

Figures and Tables

Abbreviations

CDS	Centre des démocrates sociaux
CERES	Centre d'études, de recherches et d'éducation socialistes
CET	Collège d'enseignement technique
CFDT	Confédération française démocratique du travail
CFTC	Confédération française des travailleurs chrétiens
CGC	Confédération générale des cadres
CGT	Confédération générale du travail
CIR	Convention des institutions républicaines
CNIP	Conseil national des indépendants et paysans
CNPF	Conseil national du patronat français
CRS	Campagnie républicaine de sécurité
EMS	European Monetary System
ENA	Ecole nationale d'administration
FEN	Fédération de l'éducation nationale
FN	Front national
FO	Force ouvriére
IFOP	Institut français de l'opinion publique
IUT	Instituts universitaires de technologie
MRG	Movement des radicaux de gauche
OECD	Organization of Economic Cooperation and Development
PCF	Parti communiste français
PFN	Parti des forces nouvelles

PR	Parti républicain
PS	Parti socialiste
PSU	Parti socialiste unifié
Rad	Parti radical
RI	Républicains indépendants
RPR	Rassemblement pour la république
SFIO	Section française de l'internationale ouvrière
SNES	Syndicat national des enseignants du second degré
SMIC	Salaire minimum industriel de croissance
SNPMI	Syndicat national de la petite et moyenne industrie
SOFRES	Société français d'enquêtes par sondages
TUC	Travaux d'utilité collective
UDF	Union pour la démocratie française

Preface

The years 1981 to 1986 mark an important period in French history because for the first time under the Fifth Republic the left was in power. How much of a revolution this was is open to question. It is argued in several chapters of this book that the Socialists frequently did not pursue policies fundamentally different from those of the right and also that their victory in 1981 was in some sense narrow and less epoch-making than the statistics and the rhetoric would indicate. Historians may well decide that 1981 brought no decisive or lasting shift in French life, and yet the fact that the left—or rather the non-Communist left—was able to govern for five years is politically of enormous significance.

This book looks at the way the Socialists governed: their economic and foreign policies and the attempts they made to bring about social change. Although most of the issues of their five years are discussed at some point, choices have inevitably been made, and space has dictated a certain number of omissions. Thus chapters are devoted to education, decentralization and trade unions, which seemed the most important areas of social policy, whereas Robert Badinter's legal reforms, including the abolition of the death penalty, and Jack Lang's cultural innovations do not receive the attention they undoubtedly merit. The very interesting question of how the Socialists ran the state apparatus crops up in several chapters but it is not treated on its own.

Nor is this a book about French politics as a whole. If it were, the UDF-RPR right would not be treated with such unceremonious brevity. The Le Pen phenomenon receives a chapter because the Front national became prominent while the Socialists were in power even if the reasons for its rise are not always linked with their policies. The Communist Party receives a chapter because until 1984 it was a partner in government and because its decline is one factor in the Socialists' success. But the Socialist Party itself is the main object of study.

The years 1981 to 1986 were certainly decisive years for the party, and they have changed it, although the origins of the changes lie earlier and it is difficult to predict how it will change again. In other ways too the five years form a block, separate not merely from the decades when the left was in opposition but from the present period of cohabitation. Mitterrand retains the presidency, but he no longer rules, and his party is back in opposition. It is an intriguing moment in French politics and one that will spawn other but different books.

This analysis of the years of Socialist power is intended first for the specialists concerned with French politics. However, the drama in 1981 was such a fascinating one that college students and general readers should find this book useful. Thus every effort has been made to write clearly and simply and, through the introductory chapter, to provide nonspecialists with background information.

Patrick McCarthy
July 1986

1

Victory in 1981: The Long March of the Socialists

PATRICK McCARTHY

When the Socialists came to power in 1981 they were, as one observer puts it, "a party whose time had come."[1] Yet it will be one of the themes of this chapter that there was nothing inevitable about their triumph, which may be explained in part by strategic errors committed by other parties. Nor may Giscard d'Estaing's seven years as president be viewed as a disaster. The simplest proof is that Prime Minister Raymond Barre's handling of the economy from 1976 to 1981 was good enough to establish him as a major opposition leader and probable presidential candidate in 1988. Giscard's political project, which was to draw together a large centrist group of voters, was followed—albeit with significant differences—by François Mitterrand and Laurent Fabius from the summer of 1984 to the parliamentary elections.

It remains true that the Socialists were aided by the process of economic and social change in France, which includes such factors as movement from the country to the towns and decline in religious attendance, during the more than twenty years of right-wing rule. It is equally clear, although rather more difficult to explain, that the non-Communist left constitutes, in spite of its many splits and defeats, an important political family, whereas the French Communist Party (Parti communiste français, or PCF) was unable to take advantage of these setbacks and to become the dominant force on the left. This is the key difference between Italy and France, and it is in this context that François Mitterrand was able over approximately ten years to rebuild the Socialist Pary (Parti socialiste, or PS).

The way he rebuilt it and the shifts of power within the party during the years of opposition help explain the direction that the PS has taken since coming to power. To offer only one example, the key decision of March-April 1983 which pitted the left-wing CERES against the other *tendances* or currents was a second version of the Pau party congress of 1975 where the CERES was ousted from the leadership.

This chapter has four sections. The first is a review of Giscard's years in office as they appear from a post–1981 vantage point. The second deals with the 1981 elections and presents the thesis that they offered an opportunity rather than a mandate to the Socialists. The third and briefest section sets out the position of the right-wing parties in 1981, while the fourth and longest section deals with the Socialists.

GISCARD'S AMBIGUOUS LEGACY

When Valéry Giscard d'Estaing published his political credo *Démocratie française* in 1976, the key words were "knowledge," "calm," "understanding"and "cohesion," and it is no coincidence that they were very different from the leitmotifs of Charles de Gaulle's memoirs: "glory," "grandeur" and "chaos." The theme of Giscard's book was that in many ways France had already become an advanced industrial society. Its industry was strong, its technology sporadically brilliant and its people prosperous. "Our country has changed," Giscard wrote correctly. "It is more different from the France of 1950 than this was from the France of 1870."[2]

Giscard considered that his task as president was to complete the transformation undertaken by the Fifth Republic. De Gaulle had fostered a belated industrialization and had given France a constitution that provided strong, efficient government. But he had not exorcised the demons of its past: ideological divisions, social inequality, excessive statism and the dialectic of rigid authority and diffuse protest. Giscard promised to create a "liberal" community where class differences would be blunted and free enterprise tempered with social justice. The model for the new France was Germany with its dynamic economy, cohesive society and centrist political parties.

The trouble was that Giscard took power at precisely the moment when France had to face the new economic challenges that emerged from the 1973 oil crisis. This led him to undertake what one commentator called his hard and soft policy: "to reconcile hard economic action—industrial transformation, improved productivity, greater competitiveness—and soft social repercussions—rising standards of living, high unemployment benefits and corrections of social inequalities."[3]

Since the economy had been so long protected, had developed in a period of international prosperity and was coddled by the state, it needed modernization if it was to adapt to a harsher period. Giscard recognized this as clearly as the Socialists have done. However, accustomed since the late 1950s to almost uninterrupted growth, and living under a constitution that seemed to ensure a right-wing majority and to exclude the escape valve of a change of government, the French could be kept in tranquility only, so it was felt, by ever higher standards of living. Vivid in the memories both of Giscard and his predecessor, Georges

Pompidou, were the May 1968 riots, which had been caused in part by de Gaulle's deflationary policies and his determination to keep the franc strong for reasons of foreign policy. Pompidou had devalued the franc and gambled, successfully, on economic growth. Giscard, who could not hope for similar levels of growth, endeavored to steer France "softly" through the 1970s.

Thus he allowed real wages to rise by 4.7 percent in 1974, and buying power went up 24 percent during his seven years in office. As unemployment increased he pumped money into the economy, although this meant taking the franc out of the snake. But, after inflation rose to 12 percent at the end of 1975, Raymond Barre replaced Jacques Chirac as prime minister and a deflationary package was introduced: a three-month price freeze, wage restraint, the money supply fixed at a 12 percent increase.

In place of high growth Giscard tried to offer social reform. Having absorbed Michael Crozier's thinking—or at least his language—he discusses in *Démocratie française* the need to break with remote styles of authority and to engage in face to face confontation. He introduced a fairly generous abortion law and reduced the voting age to eighteen. He also tried to introduce a capital gains tax, and he appointed the centrist Pierre Sudreau to draw up a plan for worker participation in industry. But in neither case was he able to enact significant legislation, partly because he never had the full support of the right. Fewer than one-third of its members of parliament voted for his abortion law and, although he was personally opposed to the death penalty, he was powerless to abolish it.

After Chirac's departure in 1976 the split between Giscardians and the Gaullists, who now became the Rassemblement pour la république (RPR) widened, which was an ominous trend. And yet in the parliamentary elections of 1978 Giscard's gamble seemed to have paid off. The left had obligingly committed suicide in September 1977 when the talks on the Common Program collapsed and the right-center party, the Union pour la démocratie française (UDF), which Giscard had cobbled together, won almost as many votes as the RPR. Now Giscard's hands were freer and he could undertake a bolder economic policy.

Raymond Barre's achievement was to free prices, pushing reluctant French businessmen toward the open market. Supposedly this would help them increase profit margins and strengthen investments. Meanwhile Barre tried to keep down inflation by restricting the money supply while maintaining the sacrosanct level of real wages.

How successful was this policy? "France is doing well," wrote one observer, who was, perhaps significantly, an Englishman.[4] Certainly France was coming through the difficult years better than Britain or Italy, although less well than Germany. Growth was reasonably good: between 1973 and 1980 gross domestic product (GDP) grew at 2.8 percent a year compared with 2.3 percent in Germany and 0.7 percent in Britain. Inflation averaged 11.2 percent a year, while in Italy it was 17.8 percent but only 4.5 percent in Germany. In 1980 unemployment stood at 7.5 percent compared with 9.3 percent in Britain.[5]

Yet, although few academic economists have criticized Barre's performance,

he and Giscard were not able to maneuver round the two reefs of the second
increase in oil prices and the structural weaknesses of the French economy and
society. The 1979 oil price increase made Barre's juggling of his hard and soft
options more difficult. In 1980 inflation, that traditional French scourge, soared
to 13.1 percent, and the trade balance, which had been in the black, showed a
60 billion franc deficit which would turn into a nightmare for the Socialists.
Recession worsened the plight of the manufacturing sector, where steel and
textiles were already in chronic difficulty and would provide further dilemmas
for the left. Nor did French businessmen respond to Barre's proddings. Instead
they launched an "investment strike," reflecting the shortcomings of the capital
markets and the caution of businessmen, both of them rooted in the French past.[6]

In foreign policy Giscard, who had been following a modified Gaullist line,
made his first serious mistake. For most of his presidency relations with the
United States had been better than under Pompidou, while within Europe priority
was given to the alliance with Germany. Inaugurated by de Gaulle and Konrad
Adenauer, it was now revived by Giscard and Helmut Schmidt, who created the
European Monetary System (EMS) in early 1979.

Designed to give an international dimension to the austerity of the Barre Plan,
the EMS was also supposed to shelter the European currencies against the decline
of the dollar permitted or encouraged by the Carter administration. Giscard, who
shared the general European skepticism about President Carter, dragged his feet
after the Soviet invasion of Afghanistan. Seeking to divorce the invasion from
the issue of Western and Eastern European relations, he appeared also to feel
that the administration's weakness offered him an opportunity to act as an intermediary. In May 1980 he became the first Western leader to meet Leonid
Brezhnev since the invasion.

Had the meeting brought results it might have been perceived at least within
France as a successful stroke of Gaullist diplomacy. Since it produced nothing,
it brought on Giscard an onslaught of criticism from Chirac's supporters, who
invoked de Gaulle's support for the United States during the Cuban missile crisis.
Mitterrand, who denounced Giscard as a messenger boy, was able to turn this
mistake into a campaign issue, and he was also careful during his first years in
office to take a strong line on East-West relations and to support the installation
of the cruise missiles.

By 1981 Giscard's position was weaker than the public opinion polls of the
previous autumn had led him to believe. The ostentatiously democratic president
of 1974 who had invited the garbage collectors in for breakfast had been transformed into a remote monarch who was critized (like all presidents before and
after him) for his personal arrogance. Reforms like the abortion law were for-
gotten as the harsh social effects of the Barre Plan grew more apparent. The
deteriorating economic situation allowed the left to rise from its grave, and
unemployment offered Mitterrand another campaign issue.

Indeed, unemployment was becoming a graver issue than inflation. By the
1981 election it was not merely running at 1.5 million and rising but it was

becoming perceived as a structural problem rather than as the temporary down side of the normal economic cycle. In this sense Giscard was a victim of the prolonged recession or, more correctly, depression that has overtaken all the Western European economies. Moreover, unemployment would, after offering the left an opportunity, become a trap, as the left's failure to resolve it become apparent in 1983.

Yet the narrowness of Giscard's defeat suggests that an even more important factor was a strategic political mistake: the failure to neutralize the RPR. Although outpolled by Giscard's UDF in the European elections of 1979, the RPR remained strong enough to mount a challenge in the 1981 elections. The lesson, which would not be lost on Mitterrand, was that opening to the center in France is the correct tactic provided that one can first dominate the right or left.

If the left's first year in office marks a break with Giscard's presidency— Keynesian expansion, nationalizations, a bolder social policy reflected in the abolition of the death penalty or the Auroux laws on industrial relations and a stronger anti-Soviet line—later developments showed the continuity. By 1983 Pierre Mauroy's policy of economic rigor was curiously reminscent of Barre's austerity, and the private sector was once more being exhorted to be more self-reliant, while Mitterrand's own brand of Gaullism has led him recently to improve relations with the Soviet Union. Most of all, the fact that alternation of parties in power could take place and that the left could govern legitimately—albeit with waves of right-wing protest—are signs that the state of "ideological divorce" which Giscard had lamented[7] is less crippling than in the past.

THE LESSONS OF THE 1981 ELECTIONS

One victor in the elections was the institutions of the Fifth Republic. It was not a definitive victory because the relationship between president and parliamentary majority remained unclear and would have to be examined all over again in 1986. But the Constitution did permit the peaceful alternation of parties in power and the accession of the Fifth Republic's first left-wing government. This in turn meant both that the institutions have acquired greater legitimacy and that, when the left altered the system of voting for parliamentary elections in 1985, debate about this and other changes could be conducted in pragmatic rather than theological language.

Much has been written about these institutions,[8] and here one will limit the analysis to the way they worked in 1981. Until then it was widely felt that their effect was to perpetuate right-wing rule. By introducing the two-tiered, single-constituency voting system for parliamentary elections, de Gaulle confirmed the division of France into right and left and ended the centrist coalitions that ruled under the Fourth Republic. He also compelled parties to form alliances on the second round, which was easier in the 1960s for the parties of the right than for the left, where the Communist and non-Communist families were bitterly divided and the Communists were held not to be a party of government. The direct election of the president in a two-tiered vote offered the right the same advantage, while also inhibiting a left that clung to its Republican past and perceived in the office of president a new brand of monarchy. For this reason Pierre Mendès France refused even to be a candidate for president, while in the 1965 presidential campaign Mitterrand attacked de Gaulle in the language French republicans have reserved for kings and emperors.[9] By 1981, however, the left had learned how to use the institutions, while the right's seemingly permanent majority had itself become an issue.

In 1972 the Common Program spoke of "the exorbitant powers which the president exercises unchecked"[10] and promised a return to proportional representation in parliamentary elections. It is interesting, however, that when the Mitterrand government did reintroduce proportional representation in 1985, it was because the alliance of the left was in ruins rather than because of the Common Program. For the existing Constitution had helped bring about the alliance of the left by imposing on the two families the need to unite. As early as 1962 the old Socialist Party (the Section française de l'internationale ouvrière, or SFIO) had seen its number of deputies rise from forty to sixty-five partly as a result of Communist withdrawal on the second round, while in 1965 Mitterrand's surprisingly plausible challenge to de Gaulle and the forty-five percent of the vote he won was the result of an alliance between Communists and non-Communists. It remains true that the Socialists' victory in 1981 came when the alliance was shaky indeed and came in part for that very reason. But the Socialists could not have reestablished themselves as a credible political force in the 1970s if they had not accepted the logic of France's institutions by presenting themselves as a solidly left-wing party that had a privileged relationship with the PCF.

By 1981 the higher voter turnout in presidential elections and Mitterrand's near success in 1974 when he won 49.5 percent of the vote had banished the Socialists' distrust of the directly elected president, although conventional wisdom still held that the left would win more easily in the parliamentary elections, where the role of personal charisma was less strong. However, no Fifth Republic president had yet served two full seven-year terms, and there was a vague but prevalent sentiment that fourteen years was too long. Nor was it merely a matter of the next seven years but also of the previous twenty-three during which the right had been in power.

In *Démocratie française* Giscard had, while lauding alternation, stated that the divisions in French society "prevent France at present from experiencing this harmonious development."[11] Reiteration of this view led to absurd situations, as when President Pompidou called on the country during the 1973 parliamentary elections to vote for the right, for otherwise he would have no parliamentary majority and the government could not function, while the next year candidate Giscard called on the French to vote for the right in the presidential elections, for otherwise the parliamentary majority would have no president and the government could not function. By abusing this tactic at each election the right seemed to be daring the voters to jump off the cliff. By 1981 the French felt—for reasons that will be discussed—that they could jump and land safely.

The presidential elections did not lack the overtones of a religious war, for Giscard's candidacy could be described as ''the election of the king,''[12] and he himself could solemnly declare that the choice lay between him and ''political and economic decadence.''[13] This meant that the Socialists' victory could not be achieved without a counter-mystique. So Mitterrand stood as the candidate of the historic left, which had its roots in nineteenth-century French republicanism and its previous incarnations in Jean Jaurès and Léon Blum. A triumph for him would bring to power ''the people of the left'' who had hitherto been excluded by the Fifth Republic.

All this made a heady brew, and yet it is not too perverse to argue that by bringing the left to power Mitterrand partially resolved the problem of alternation and dedramatized politics. Since then there has been a wave of political extremism on the right in the form of the Front national (FN), but the UDF and the RPR have played by the rules of the institutions. Moreover, the mundane struggle with the trade balance has deflated the counter-mystique about the ''people of the left.''

The only distortion which the Constitution introduced in 1981 was the outright parliamentary majority won by the Socialists. Voters—determined to land safely—refused to face the issue of what might happen with a president and parliament of different political hues. When the newly elected Mitterrand called them to the urns, they gave the Socialists a far more generous endorsement than they had done in the presidential vote. Whereas Mitterrand and the Movement des radicaux de gauche (MRG) candidate, Michel Crépeau, had won 28.05 percent on the first round (see Table 1.1), the PS and the MRG won 37.4 percent (see Table 1.2). This rise of 9 percent, a huge difference by the standards of Western European elections, can be explained only by the dynamic of the presidential result.

This in turn had important consequences. The Socialists would be able to govern without crippling parliamentary opposition from the right, and they would be able in 1984 to dispense with Communist support. However, their victory was artificially large, which was bound to create difficulties for them in 1986, when the dynamic would not be working. The landslide of June 1981 did not reflect the real balance in the country, as a glance at the April presidential elections reveals.

How then did Mitterrand win his narrow victory (51.8 percent to 48.2 percent on the second round)? Both Raymond Aron and Jean-François Revel blamed the right, Revel stating bluntly that ''Giscard has succeeded in losing a contest that could not possibly be lost.''[14] Whereas the opinion polls of September 1980 were giving him 36 percent of the vote on the first round, Giscard obtained just over 28 percent. This was not a high enough springboard to ensure victory on the second round; it was 4 percent less than he had won on the first round in

Table 1.1
Presidential Elections of 1981

Candidate	First Round Percent of Vote
A. Laguiller	2.30
H. Bouchardeau	1.10
G. Marchais	15.34
F. Mitterrand	25.84
M. Crépeau	2.21
V. Giscard d'Estaing	28.31
J. Chirac	17.99
M. Debré	1.65
M.-F. Garaud	1.33
B. LaLonde	3.87

Source: Le Monde, Dossiers et Documents: Les élections législatives du 16 mars, 1986, p. 68.

1974, and it was only 2.5 percent more than Mitterrand gained. To explain this unsatisfactory result one must invoke Giscard's failure to dominate the right but also the PS' success in dominating the left.

As Table 1.1 shows, the first round represents a historic defeat for the PCF, which lost approximately one-quarter of its vote. Except for the 1958 election when de Gaulle returned to power, the PCF had never since the Liberation sunk below 20 percent, and from 1958 to 1973 it had consistently done better than the Socialists. In 1973 it had polled 21.29 percent to the PS' 19.16 percent, and most observers felt that its superior organization and its strength within the trade unions would enable it to remain the dominant party of the left.

By the cantonal elections of 1976 this was not the case, but the margin between the PS and the PCF in the parliamentary elections of 1978 was only 2 percent. Then the delayed impact of the Communists' role in breaking up the union and three years of pro-Soviet policy by George Marchais widened the gap to 10 percent. Mitterrand's strategy from the time he became party leader in 1971 had been to use the union of the left to make the PS the first party of the left. The feature of the 1981 result was that he achieved this because of the breakup of the union.

Table 1.2
Legislative Elections of 1981

Party	Percent of Vote	Seats Won
Extreme Left	1.4	
PCF	16.1	44
PS } MRG	37.4	285
Diverse Left	0.8	4
Ecologists	1.1	
RPR	20.8	85
UDF	19.2	65
Diverse Right	2.8	8
Extreme Right	0.4	

Source: The Europa Yearbook 1985 (London: Europa Publications, Ltd., 1985), p. 463.

This in turn influenced the second round of the election in two different ways. The only conceivable reading of Marchais' 15.4 percent was that it marked a repudiation of the sectarian line which the party leadership had followed since September 1977. Now the PCF had three options: to call on its voters to abstain, to give half-hearted support to Mitterrand while trying to wrest concessions from him, or to offer unconditional support. The first would be a repetition of the mistakes made in the previous three years; the second was too complex a task for a disoriented leadership to undertake (or at least to undertake in public, for there are persistent rumors that in that private Marchais called on the party faithful to vote for Giscard). The third option was the safest, so on April 28 the PCF leadership offered Mitterrand its unconditional support.

This was a crass admission of defeat and would pose problems that are analyzed later in this volume. But the margin of his first-round victory over Marchais brought a second benefit for Mitterrand. For decades the right had argued that a Socialist government would be hostage to the Communists, but Mitterrand's success reassured the voters. Although Aron and Revel kept reminding readers of *L'Express* that Mitterrand would need Communist support in parliament, fear of the PCF no longer outweighed the desire for alternation, and anyway the voters would find a different solution by giving the PS an outright parliamentary majority.

With his left flank safe during the second round, Mitterrand could concentrate his campaign on the floating centrist voter. He downplayed the left-wing *Projet socialiste*, the text which marked his victory over Michel Rocard and which had been partly drawn up by Jean-Pierre Chevènement. Instead he hammered away at Giscard's economic policy without spelling out the controversial measures that he would take and while repeating simple slogans like "Our chief objective is full employment."[15]

The split on the right, which is harder to analyze, was counterpoint to the left's belated unity. It was the latest and greatest episode in a struggle which had gone on throughout Giscard's presidency. His seven years may be divided into three parts: 1974 to 1976 when he appointed Chirac as prime minister and tried to co-opt the Gaullists; 1976 to 1978, when the dismissed Chirac rebuilt the Gaullist party and defeated the Giscardian Michel d'Ornano to become mayor of Paris; 1978 to 1981, when Giscard, exploiting his 1978 victory and convinced that he would win the presidential election, reasserted his power over the Gaullists. Chirac's decision to stand on the first round was a calculated gamble designed to reverse this trend and demonstrate Gaullist strength so that at the very least Giscard would have to contend with the Gaullists after his victory.

During his campaign Chirac stressed supply-side economics. Although the Gaullist family is sympathetic to government intervention in industry, Chirac called for cuts in state expenditure in order to reduce the percentage of GDP going to the government from 42 percent to 36 percent. Business was to be revived by tax cuts and changes in legal procedures that would make it easier to dismiss workers. Significantly, Chirac promised measures to help small businessmen, who had suffered under Barre's austerity and who are frequently Gaullist. He also discounted austerity and spoke instead of a "new growth."[16] His political message was that Giscard had been weak, whereas a Chirac government would in the best Gaullist tradition be stronger. Chirac promised more decisive action in the areas of crime and immigration.

The result of the first round was a half-success. If one adds to Chirac's 18 percent the 3 percent won by the two minor Gaullist candidates, then 21 percent was a reasonable score against an incumbent right-wing president. The logic of a bitter campaign added to the years of hostility then led Chirac to withhold his support from Giscard. On April 27 he declared that "personally I cannot do otherwise than vote for M. Giscard d'Estaing," as if inviting his followers not to follow his example.[17] Opinion polls showed that whereas 90 percent of Communist voters intended to vote for Mitterrand, only 70 percent of Gaullist voters intended to vote for Giscard. In a close race this was likely to be decisive, and one can only agree with Raymond Aron's comment that "it's not so much that the left won as the right committed suicide."[18]

Clearly the RPR leadership did not foresee the outright victory for the PS in the parliamentary elections. Gambling on the traditional caution of French voters, it hoped that they would balance the adventure of a left-wing president with the safety of a right-wing assembly. At worst the RPR would become a bulwark of opposition in a parliament where the Socialists were dependent on Communist votes. However, the elections saw the RPR reduced from 154 to 85 deputies and the UDF from 124 to 65 to the exclusive benefit of the PS. This was to make Chirac's task more difficult, although in the absence of a right-wing president the RPR might expect to become the dominant force on the right.

The 1981 elections confirmed another trend which threatened the left's triumph. If one looks at an electoral map of France it is astonishing how stable it remains from the Third Republic to the 1960s. Except where there were substantial movements of population, and disregarding sudden and short-lived fluctuations, the country remained divided between right and left. The Pas de Calais, the Paris basin and much of the South were red, the West and the Massif Central were white. Then France's belated industrialization began to erode these sharp distinctions even as they were being strengthened by the Constitution. One of the distinctive traits in the rise of the PS was, for example, its ability to penetrate Catholic Brittany.

But this was not merely a trend toward the left for, conversely, the improvement in working-class standards of living and the growth of new industries and of the service sector gave the right its chance. The real trend was toward the erosion of both the red and the white blocs and toward an increase in the number of floating voters.

In 1981 they turned left. In Finistère, where the PS had won 22 percent of the vote in 1978, Mitterrand won 28 percent and the PS 42 percent. Yet the local elections of 1983 demonstrated that the right could penetrate the red bastions. The left lost ground in the Nord and Pas de Calais and was defeated in Nîmes. New voting patterns are emerging in conformity with economic changes. The left will find it increasingly difficult to win in big cities—as Chirac's clean sweep of Paris in 1983 shows—because they are taken over by the middle classes. But certain districts which Chirac won—notably the Thirteenth Arrondissement—had fallen to the left in 1981 and could revert to it.

Voting patterns have lost that eternal aura that they seemed to possess. Rennes was won by the left in the local elections of 1977, lost to the right in the parliamentary elections of 1978, won in 1981 and almost lost again in 1983. As in Britain, where trade unionists no longer automatically—nor even mostly— vote Labour, so the French vote less out of deep-rooted reasons of political culture and more on immediate and economic issues. So there was no reason for the left to feel secure in 1981 and no reason for the right to despair.

THE RIGHT PREPARES TO OPPOSE

The feuding within the right prompts one to ask what the Giscardians and the RPR have in common and what separates them. What sort of a right is this, and what is its relationship with the center? J. R. Frears sees, for example, ''a difference of style and of personal animosities'' between the two parties of the right, but little more.[19] The present author agrees that it is difficult to establish

clear sociological dinstinctions between RPR and UDF voters, although there
may be such distinctions between their militants and between financial backers.
But even if they are not sociologically distinct, the UDF and the RPR represent
different political choices, which explains why each has regrouped and survived
when the other was dominant. Moreover, their choices correspond to a pattern—
however incomplete it may be—which leads one to conclude that these formations
belong to different historical families.

There is of course no reason to assume that the right in any country will
represent a single political viewpoint. There are at least two such viewpoints in
the British Conservative Party: a Tory paternalism alongside a Thatcherite tough-
ness. But historian René Rémond has argued that the French case is different
because there are two separate if overlapping families on the right to which he
gives the names Orleanism and Bonapartism.[20]

Each has its origins in the nineteenth century: Orleanism in the period of
Louis-Philippe and Bonapartism in the reigns of Napoleon I and Napoleon III.
The traits of these periods have been transmitted to the twentieth-century right
because they offer satisfactory and divergent options to the right-wing electorate.
Orleanism is the philosophy of the free market, of individual liberty which
respects hierarchies, and of parliamentary elites; Bonapartism emphasizes the
nation, authority and plebiscitary democracy.

Although Rémond is cautious when he applies these concepts to the Fifth
Republic, they offer insights into the warring allies of the right. Gaullism may
be seen—despite certain unique features—as a manifestation of Bonapartism,
while the Giscardians incarnate the competing Orleanist tradition. Where Giscard
emphasized individual rights, the Gaullists stressed authority; where Giscard was
mildly internationalist, the Gaullists knew only the nation. In economic affairs
the Gaullists were both more interventionist and more adventurist than the
Giscardians.

The RPR is probably better seen as a new manifestation of Bonapartism rather
than as a Gaullist movement. The barons of Gaullism—Jacques Chaban-Delmas
and Michel Debré—are disaffected, and the RPR is essentially a mass party
rebuilt in the mid–1970s with new personnel like Alain Juppé and Michel Noir.
Important features of Gaullism are absent: the distance between leader and movement, de Gaulle's sense of himself as a national leader, the links with World
War II, the primacy he gave to foreign policy and his periodic alliances with
the left. Chirac's is a narrower, more obviously right-wing party.

Yet he was determined not to be forced to the far right of the political spectrum
and strove to portray himself as a populist, once more in the Bonapartist tradition.
As mayor of Paris he was able to offer reduced transportation costs and other
benefits for the elderly, while his 1981 election promises included tax relief for
the lower-income brackets.

Conversely, Giscard's formation was, despite his attempted social reforms,
anchored on the right. The Républicains indépendants (RI), later to become the
Parti républicain (PR), represented that segment of the French right which suc-

cumbed neither to Gaullism nor to the Algérie française movement. Resolute in its defense of free enterprise, the PR contained men like Michel Poniatowsky or Christian Bonnet who were socially conservative. Yet, because Orleanism is flexible, it was able to reach the centrists who disliked Gaullist authoritarianism. This was the alliance which helped Giscard to power in 1974 and which blossomed into the UDF.

The centrist parties—the Centre des démocrates sociaux (CDS) and the Radicals—defended the rights of property but demanded social justice; they abhorred Marxism but distrusted conservatism; they were critical of Gaullist nationalism and enthusiastic about Europe. The CDS was center-right and influenced by the Christian Democrat tradition, while the Radicals were center-left in the lay tradition. Both had tried to play an independent role which right-left division of the Fifth Republic rendered impossible.

As long as Giscard was president his UDF flourished. In the 1978 elections it gained 20.4 percent of the vote, only 2 percent less than the RPR. Next year the UDF had its chance when the European elections were held. It had excellent European credentials, whereas Chirac was obliged to ask the electorate to vote for a party which was traditionally suspicious of Europe. The UDF crushed the RPR, winning 27.5 percent to Chirac's 16.24 percent. But then Giscard's defeat traumatized his followers, who went into the 1981 parliamentary elections with scant hope and emerged with their share of the vote reduced to 19.2 percent.

As already stated, the events of 1981 left the RPR in a stronger position. First, Giscard's defeat weakened his party too. Second, the UDF remained a group without solid structures: it was a coalition rather than an organic party; each element was jealous of its independence, and each possessed different historical roots. This might not have mattered in France twenty years ago, and it did not matter in the presidential elections of 1974. But the trend of the Fifth Republic is toward stronger parties that do not rely on local and personal ties, that can amass financial resources for elections, that mobilize around their leaders and that impose their will on their supposed allies. Proportional representation could conceivably change this, liberating the components of the UDF one from the others and all from Chirac; but in 1981 the organizational strength of the RPR gave it an advantage.

Moreover, the political situation favored Chirac. A fundamental difference between Orleanists and Bonapartists has to do with political strategy. Where *Démocratie française* is ostentatiously tolerant, Chirac prefers the language of combat: freedom versus collectivism. In the early 1980s the Socialists' policy—especially the nationalizations, the presence of Communists in the government and the rhetoric of "the people of the left"—helped to deepen the division between the right and left and suited the RPR's taste for confrontation. By contrast the UDF seemed to be groping for a centrist policy when the center had vanished.

But this struggle was not so easily resolved. The history of the Fifth Republic indicates that any right-wing government will represent a coalition of the two families even if it also indicates that for efficient government one of them must dominate within the alliance. So in the early 1980s the RPR could not do without the UDF, just as the reverse was true during the 1970s.

Animosities and ambitions would indeed create fresh complications, for the right had three candidates for the role of opposition leader, the third being Raymond Barre. He might expect to find support in both families, for he could scrutinize both traditions and offer his own interpretation of them. So he could be an Orleanist with personal ties to the center parties, while he could also rebuke Chirac's pro-American stand on foreign affairs in the name of Gaullist independence.

Between 1981 and 1986 other factors would shake up the right. The first wave of "liberalism"—a liberalism quite different fron that of *Démocratie française*—would cause both the UDF and the RPR to reassess their policies. The second factor was the emergence of another right that is less easy to define in Rémond's terms: the Front national.

At all events, the unpopularity into which the Socialists quickly fell and the victories in the municipal elections of 1983 did not resolve the dilemmas of the RPR and the UDF, which remained unable to rouse popular enthusiasm. As Giscard put it, "The government's loss of credibility does not seem to be helping the right."[21] The right's task was to find a single leader, a strategy that would reconcile firmness and openness and a set of policies.

THE SOCIALISTS PREPARE TO GOVERN

In the 1969 presidential elections the Socialist candidate Gaston Defferre won 5 percent of the vote. This was a defeat of historic proportions, and it came after decades when then Socialists had either participated in Fourth Republic governments as a centrist, coalition party or had struggled unsuccessfully to become a credible opposition party under the Fifth Republic. Some observers concluded that the Socialists were finished.

Revival took the form of importing new elements into the party like the Conventionnels, finding a new leader who had never been a party member—Mitterrand—and adopting a new policy: the Common Program. This would not have been enough without assistance from the party's enemies and in particular from de Gaulle and the Communists. As already stated, de Gaulle's constitution split France into left and right and, while giving enormous advantages to the right, created a space on the left which some party could fill. By their inability to transform themselves into a flexible, Eurocommunist organization the Communists missed the opportunity to become this party.

One suspects, however, that deeper currents in French political life were still more important. Instead of being analyzed as a "Socialist" party, the PS may be perceived as the incarnation of the non-Communist left, a tradition that goes back to the Republican movements of the nineteenth century. The tradition or "family" remained strong enough to survive the mistakes of Guy Mollet's SFIO as it had survived the decline of the Radicals, who had been its incarnation around the turn of the century.

Since they were unable to draw on this ill-defined, contradictory but tenacious strand in French history, the Socialists had a reservoir of sympathy. They inherited the mystique of the Revolution; the struggle of the Republic to rid itself of the Church; a prickly Jacobin nationalism; a distrust of the state in the name of individualism and a concomitant belief in the state as a force to protect the individual; the notion that socialism, whatever it might be, was French; romanticized memories of the Popular Front; and a working-class movement long penetrated by agrarian and middle-class groups. This enabled them—almost in spite of themselves—to recover from their mistakes and to fight off an inept Communist challenge, whereas the Italian Socialists, whose roots in Italian history and culture are less deep, have been reduced to junior partners by their Communist brethren.

Behind the apparent disaster of 1969 lay a certain stability, and it is intriguing that in 1973, with the impetus of the Common Program, the Socialists polled almost the same number of votes as in 1967, when they were a weak coalition: 19.16 percent to 18.96 percent. Yet they could also hope to benefit from the social changes already mentioned. Movement away from the countryside—farmers and farm workers were 28 percent of the population in 1954 and 9 percent in 1975—and a decline in religious practice were two such factors. In Brittany, for example, the Socialist vote in the towns swelled as immigrants from the countryside lost their traditional allegiance to the right and turned to the PS, often via the formerly Catholic union, the Confédération française démocratique du travail (CFDT). The increase in the number of floating voters could help the right too, as de Gaulle demonstrated by winning 45 percent of the manual workers' votes in 1965. But here again these votes could be won back, as Mitterrand showed in 1974 when he cut Giscard's share of them to 27 percent.

In order to take advantage of these opportunities the non-Communist left needed to be reborn, and this is in effect what Mitterrand achieved by the signing of the Common Program in 1972. The specific and lengthy list of nationalizations cut the Socialists off from the centrist alliances that had brought diasters in the 1950s and established the PCF as their natural and indeed only ally. With the inestimable advantage of hindsight one may detect already the problems that would stem from this agreement. The Socialist platform would be situated to the left of many of their potential voters, and there would be disputes with the PCF. At the time most observers felt that trouble would come because the Communists would be too strong; in fact, the reverse was true. However, in the early 1970s the Common Program offered the PS a fairly credible stance of opposition and attracted a generation of new militants. Mitterrand's 49 percent of the vote in 1974 was proof that the reservoir of sympathy was at least being tapped.

The party grew in size: it counted 100,000 members in 1973, 146,000 in 1974 and 250,000 in 1982.[22] It began to draw votes from the right by its expansion into western and eastern France and from the Communists by its comeback in the red belt around Paris. Reestablished as a left-wing party, the PS was flexible and moderate enough not to alienate middle-class voters.

Indeed, it was castigated by a Communist observer as a middle-class party. Jean Elleinstein pointed out that, where the PCF had 8,000 workplace cells, the PS had only 1,000, and that at the PS' Grenoble Congress of 1973 only 3 percent of the delegates were working-class.[23] Interestingly, the PS has made ever greater inroads among working-class voters while remaining, especially in its higher echelons, relentlessly middle- and upper-class. Thus, having won 27 percent of manual workers' votes in 1973 to the PC's 37 percent, the PS won 44 percent in 1981 to the PC's 24 percent. But only 1 percent of the Socialist members of parliament in 1981 were working-class, while 32 percent were professionals or managers and 47 percent were teachers.[24] One might suggest, cynically, that this made it easier for the party to impose austerity in 1982; the British Labour Party, which has closer affiliations to the trade unions and far more working-class activists, had greater difficulty in doing so in the 1970s.

The PS was then a catchall party, described as "an amalgam of conflicting factions" or a "Chinese soup."[25] This too helped, for traditional Socialists were comforted by the figure of Pierre Mauroy, while Catholics were drawn to the Parti socialiste unifié (PSU) contingent and centrists reassured by Mitterrand. But the currents or *tendances* had different backgrounds and policies as well as different funds and organizations, and the battle among them determined the direction that the party would take to come to power and then to rule.

Each of the currents is associated with the name of a leader—Mitterrand, Mauroy, Chevènement, Rocard. Originally, the first might have been called the Conventionnels after the Convention des institutions républicaines, which supported Mitterrand in his first presidential bid of 1965. The disarray of the left in the 1960s spawned a series of clubs which were made up of civil servants, journalists and politicians who had lost their following. Clubs are important in France during times of transition, and they are usually informal. As such they suited Mitterrand, who was then a left-of-center politician with an individualistic temperament.

The relative success of the 1965 elections led Mitterrand not merely to the conclusion that the division between left and right meant that the non-Communist left must ally with the PCF, but to the view that this could be done only if his group were to win the leadership of the non-Communists. His first attempt to achieve this foundered during the May riots of 1968, but the second triumphed at Epinay. The Common Program and the union of the left stemmed from Mitterrand's election as party secretary of the PS, and the role of the Conventionnels—Charles Hernu, Georges Dayan, Louis Mermaz and others—was to form the solid core of his backers in the party.

The current also includes a second generation that entered the PS after Mitterrand had become leader. Promoted rapidly because of their loyalty to him, they include Lionel Jospin, the party secretary, and Laurent Fabius, prime minister from 1984 to 1986. Although the Mitterrandists were not always united, and although the second generation is different in style, a pragmatic strain dominates among them. Mitterrand himself is capable of moving now to the center and now further left, guided by domestic political considerations rather than by economic or ideological considerations. The alliance with the Communists was not to him—as it was to the CERES (Centre d'études, de recherches et d'education socialistes)—the historical reuniting of the working-class movement but a strategy to give the tired Socialists a new image.

The second current was formed from the contingent which Pierre Mauroy brought into the PS. The old SFIO was not dead, for it retained its grip on Marseilles, which was Gaston Defferre's fiefdom, its working-class bastions in Mauroy's Nord and in the Pas de Calais and its clientele of town-hall officials and Force ouvrière (FO) members. Seeing that Guy Mollet would not relax his grip on the SFIO, Defferre and Mauroy went over to Mitterrand and helped form the victorious Epinay alliance. In return they received the freedom to run their federations as they wished. Once the PS took power Defferre was the logical proponent of decentralization, while Mauroy was a reassuring prime minister.

Loyal to Mitterrand from 1972 to 1979, Mauroy's current had supported the Rocardians at the Metz congress of 1979. But Mauroy's role as a party man and a reconciler led him to accept the Metz result. Realizing that Mitterrand had the majority of the party behind him, he dissasociated himself from Rocard's 1980 bid for the presidential nomination. He was thus a man who could claim broad support within the party.

On policy Mauroy's supporters could work with Mitterrand's current, but they were committed to the traditions of the left: Keynesian economics and increased social spending. As such Mauroy was the right man to be prime minister in 1981 when the PS tried to expand the economy, but he seemed unhappy when he conducted the policy of rigor from 1982 on. He was able, however, to win the reluctant party over to such a policy by proclaiming it as a necessary but temporary adjustment. Moreover, the decision to remain within the EMS and not to resort to protectionism suited him, for the SFIO had been enthusiastic about Europe. The difference between Mauroy and his successor, Fabius, is enormous, but it is more a matter of generations and culture than of policy. Mauroy is no technocrat, did not attend the elite institutions of the French education system and is associated with the old industries rather than with new technology.

The Centre d'études, de recherches et d'éducation socialistes is a beguilingly innocuous name for the PS' left wing. Chevènement and his friends joined the SFIO as "stowaways" in 1964, and they drew far-reaching conclusions from its decline.[26] It could be rebuilt only by rejecting Mollet's revisionist policies, which meant an alliance with the PCF, a commitment to public ownership, a reevaluation of Atlanticism and an end to centrist alliances. So at Epinay the CERES threw its decisive 8 percent behind Mitterrand, and as the catalyst of the union of the left it grew rapidly to 25 percent. After 1981 it was enthusiastic about the nationalizations and the Communist participation, but in 1983 it bitterly opposed the choice of rigor and of remaining in the EMS, and Chevènement resigned, to be replaced as minister of industry by Laurent Fabius.

However, the CERES had another strand, and it could—arguably—be described as a manifestation of left-wing Gaullism. Although its analysis of society was Marxist—class was vital, and class divisions were sharpening as capitalism sank into its third historical crisis—it had the Gaullist sense of the nation. "De Gaulle's strategy of grandeur . . . left us by no means indifferent," wrote Chevènement in 1974.[27] Public ownership, for example, was justified as "a means to reconquer independence on the national and European level."[28] So when the alliance with the PCF ceased to be a rallying point Chevènement could rebuild his career around the theme of the Socialists as defenders of the French nation in the best Republican tradition.

The last of the currents, known now as the Rocardians, is the segment of the Parti socialiste unifié that entered the PS along with segments of the CFDT in the autumn of 1974. The political baggage of the PSU had contained diverse elements: first, an updated left-wing analysis derived in part from Pierre Mendès France which stressed planning but not nationalizations, which attached less importance to class, and which was anti-utopian and accepted the need for financial discipline, and second, support for "autogestion," which received great impetus from the May 1968 riots, which the PSU had unreservedly supported.

"The PSU was condemned to live with this explosive mixture," said one unkind observer.[29] The first tendency situated the party on the left-center, while the second pushed it to the far left. This ambiguity has remained to a degree, but the oil crisis gave greater credibility to the PSU's thinking because it cast doubt on the notion of growth. In *L'Inflation au coeur de la crise* (1975) Rocard argued that the pursuit of growth brought the working class nothing but brief gains that were swallowed up by inflation. His thinking appealed to ecologists and antinuclear supporters even as his insistence on discipline and his coolness toward the Communists earned him admiration among centrist voters and distrust among the PS rank and file. The second oil crisis brought further corroboration of his views, and the Rocardians could not look kindly on the Keynesianism which the PS practiced in 1981. The switch of policy in 1982 came exactly as they had forecast it must, but it brought them no greater influence, for their position in the party is determined more by clashes of personality and by intra-party politics than by policies.

To understand why this is so one must examine the jousting among the currents in the 1970s. From 1971 to 1974 Mitterrand used the CERES as a ginger-group to impose on the PS the Epinay choices. But the near-success of 1974 meant that the PS' next task was to win over the floating centrist voter, which called for policy changes like a stronger defense platform, greater discipline within the party and a firmer line with the PCF. As a protest against the last two, the CERES left the majority in the Pau congress of 1975 (anticipating the Bourg-en-Bresse congress of 1983) while the other three currents supported Mitterrand. The split between the CERES and the rest of the party was thus based on issues rather than on personalities, and insofar as Mitterrand needed their support he would have to make concessions to them. But from 1975 to 1978 he did not.

The shattering of the union and the defeat in 1978 brought a new power struggle. They were a severe blow to the CERES, which was identified with the union and which now fell to 15 percent of the party. But Mitterrand was also challenged by Rocard, who attacked the Common Program in the name of "telling the truth." Economic expansion was impossible in this time of economic crisis, while the nationalizations would foster only state capitalism. Rocard reiterated his call for austerity and called on the PS to be "extremely firm with the Communist Party both on the level of economics and of politics."[30]

Despite this his dispute with Mitterrand was not primarily about policies because Mitterrand had been firm with the PCF and was not dogmatic either about nationalism or expansion. Thus observers have written that "Mitterrand had more in common with Rocard than with many of his own allies. The difference is that both men wanted to be President."[31] But in challenging Mitterrand Rocard had to repudiate the bases on which Mitterrand had rebuilt the PS, and in consequence Mitterrand had to stand firm on the Epinay line. Indeed, this was all the more necessary because he was simultaneously being attacked by the Communists, who would have decried any concession to Rocard as a piece of social democratic treachery. So at Metz Mitterrand repeated that the PS would adhere to the union of the left even if the PCF had betrayed it, while nationalization and expansion would remain the cornerstones of economic policy. Logically, Mitterrand reformed the alliance with the CERES and they, he and Defferre fought off the Rocard-Mauroy challenge by approximately 60 percent to 38 percent of the votes. Mitterrand was victorious because of the way his followers had taken control of the party machinery and because the rank and file believed that Rocard had strayed too far to the right. The next autumn Mitterrand easily crushed Rocard's bid to become the Socialists' candidate for the presidency.

Although the victories of 1981 enormously strengthened his position in the party, Mitterrand's first actions were shaped by his previous struggles. Reaffirming his Epinay-Metz stands, he took all segments of the party into the government, although as minister of planning Rocard was allowed little influence; Mitterand invited four Communist ministers, thus recreating the union of the left on his own terms, for the PCF obtained far less than it would have done in 1978 or than it might have demanded had it held the balance of power in parliament. Most important, Mitterrand opted for the nationalizations, economic expansion and sweeping social reforms.

These are analyzed by Volkmar Lauber in the next chapter, but one would like to suggest that the reasoning behind them was partly political. First, the Socialists' narrow victory had turned into a historic landslide and was accompanied, as one observer pointed out, by "high expectations."[32] In this sense the mistakes—if mistakes they were—of the first year were the price France had to pay for a political system that had so long blocked alternation. Pierre Mauroy offers an apologetic explanation of that first year: the left "would not have been credible, would not have been itself . . . if, on coming to power we had taken measures that went against our image."[33] The Socialists had to govern as the party of Epinay and Metz because, although this was not why they had been elected, it was the axis around which they were organized.

The converse, however, is also true. As early as December 1981 Jacques Delors suggested a brake on expensive reforms, and the switch to rigor in 1982 was made with the assent of all groups except the CERES. As the period from 1974 to 1978 suggested, the PS could trim its policies to suit the constraints of government, and among the ruling Mitterrand current men like Fabius and Pierre Bérégovoy were well suited to pursuing rigor in the service of economic modernization.

NOTES

1. D. S. Bell and B. Criddle, *The French Socialist Party* (Oxford: Clarendon Press, 1984), p. 39.

2. Valéry Giscard d'Estaing, *Démocratie française* (Paris: Fayard, 1976), p. 28.

3. Yann de l'Ecotais, "Le Bilan économique du septennat," *Express*, March 28, 1981, p. 45.

4. J. R. Frears, *France in the Giscard Presidency* (London: Allen and Unwin, 1981), p. 136.

5. De l'Ecotais, "Le Bilan économique," pp. 43–47.

6. *Economist*, September 20, 1980, p. 13.

7. Giscard d'Estaing, *Démocratie française*, p. 155.

8. Frears, *France*, pp. 30ff. See also William G. Andrews, *Presidential Government in Gaullist France* (Albany: State University of New York Press, 1982).

9. François Mitterrand, *Politique* (Paris: Fayard, 1977), pp. 71ff.

10. *Programme commun de gouvernement du Parti communiste et du Parti socialiste* (Paris: Editions sociales, 1972), p. 150.

11. Giscard d'Estaing, *Démocratie française*, p. 155.

12. Jean-Denis Bredin, "L'Election du roi," *Le Monde*, November 18, 1980, p. 1.

13. *Express*, March 14, 1981, p. 35.

14. J.-F. Revel, "Etrange défaite," *Express*, May 19, 1981, p. 45.

15. "Mitterrand: ce que je ferais," *Express*, April 14, 1981, pp. 33–38.

16. "Jacques Chirac—Entretien," *Express*, March 21, 1981, pp. 40–42.

17. Chirac did offer a marginally more enthusiastic endorsement on May 6.

18. Raymond Aron, "Le Reconquête," *Express*, March 18, 1983, p. 47.

19. Frears, *France*, p. 53.

20. René Rémond, *La Droite en France* (Paris: Aubier, 1968).

21. Giscard d'Estaing, "Mes scénarios politiques," *Express*, January 21, 1981, p. 50.

22. Criddle and Bell, *French Socialist Party*, p. 198.

23. Jean Elleinstein, *Le PC* (Paris: Grasset, 1976), pp. 106ff.

24. Criddle and Bell, *French Socialist Party*, pp. 133, 202.

25. Vincent Wright and Howard Machin, "The French Socialist Party in 1973,"

Government and Opposition 9 (Spring 1974): 130; J.-F. Bizot, et al., *Au parti des socialistes* (Paris: Grasset, 1975), p. 14.

26. J.-P. Chevènement, *Le Vieux, la crise, le neuf* (Paris: Flammarion, 1974), p. 13.

27. Ibid., p. 22.

28. Ibid., p. 46.

29. Jean Poperen, *L'Unité de la gauche 1965–1972* (Paris: Fayard, 1975), p. 26.

30. "Un entretien avec Michel Rocard," *Le Nouvel Observateur*, October 2, 1978, pp. 52–54.

31. Criddle and Bell, *French Socialist Party*, p. 108.

32. Frank L. Wilson, "Socialism in France: A Failure of Politics Not a Failure of Policy," *Parliamentary Affairs* (Spring 1985): 163.

33. Pierre Mauroy, "Choisir l'Europe, c'est choisir la rigueur," *Express*, April 8, 1983, p. 36.

2

Economic Policy

VOLKMAR LAUBER

When in May and June 1981 the French Socialists came to power and thus assumed responsibility for France's economic policy, they were burdened with several important handicaps. One of them was the poor economic situation. The French economy had not absorbed the oil price shocks yet, and as a result, inflation was running at high levels. Also, French industry had been losing market share for years, with the result that French markets were increasingly penetrated from abroad. Finally, the fact that in many neighboring countries governments had recently shifted to a deflationary policy contributed to an unfavorable economic environment. But the other handicap resided with the Socialists themselves. Having been excluded from power at the national level for over twenty years, they lacked experience of government affairs; due to their surprise victory they had no ready-made teams of high civil servants prepared to serve them. What they did have was a program, an ideology and an economic understanding that were in many respects quite obsolete, despite recent efforts to update them. In addition, the major leader in the effort to modernize the economic program, Michel Rocard, had just been defeated twice within the party. Under these circumstances those leaders and activists who held more traditional views maintained or increased their influence, though there was also a considerable group of pragmatists, especially around Mitterrand. One of their key problems was that they could not come up with an alternative vision of socialism when the need for it arose. This became clear during the years in power, when adjustments in policy became inevitable.

Besides those handicaps the Socialists in 1981 could also count on some assets that were not negligible. The previous government under Raymond Barre had practiced a policy of stabilization and a nearly balanced budget; this gave the new government more leeway than it would otherwise have enjoyed, in particular with regard to going into debt without running into severe obstacles early on. Also, the Socialists disposed of a solid political majority in parliament (in addition to holding the presidency) and thus did not really need the support of the Communists or anyone else to govern. In addition, they had for some time enjoyed the most positive image of any French political party. Immediately upon their arrival in power and for some time afterwards, they also benefited from an immense wave of sympathy which seemed to legitimate whatever measures they took. But this sympathy may have been based to an important extent on the expectations that the Socialists had created while in opposition (to practice ''a new economic logic''), expectations that they could not live up to while in power.

Starting out with a policy which despite some important updates was still at least partially inspired by the Common Program of the left which dated from 1972 (a time of high growth rates and few economic problems), the Socialists had to make important reversals during their tenure in government. Concerning the business cycle, the original policy of reflation by increasing wages and social welfare benefits soon gave way to one of austerity, with wages held down and the growth of social security expenditures brought under control. On industrial and business matters the policy of expanding state control (via nationalizations, credit distribution, selective incentives and disincentives via the tax system, subsidies or regulation) was replaced by a stress on private enterprise, the limits of state power, the importance of profits and of regulatory flexibility. On unemployment, the efforts to stabilize it were abandoned in favor of a policy actively promoting shakeouts and retraining in the name of improving economic efficiency.

Measured by currently prevailing economic criteria, the economic policy practiced by the Socialists must be considered a success, with the important exception of unemployment. But this economic success was only partially recognized by the electorate in 1986. Here again the role of the policy shifts appears decisive. In the first phase, in each policy area the approach chosen was not too far from the positions of the Common Program. This created support for the government by the Communists and ''their'' labor union, the Confédération générale du travail (CGT). By the same token, however, it also contributed to alienating centrist sympathies that the Socialist Party might otherwise have been able to attract, and which it might have expanded. After the policy shifts, Communist support declined and eventually turned into hostility, although the Socialist Party managed to attract many former Communist voters in 1986. But centrist sympathies were lost for good, the innovative current of the Socialist Party around Rocard remained sterilized, and the liberal and technocratic reformists around Prime Minister Laurent Fabius proved unable to come up with a concept that would have allowed creating an electoral basis or alliance sufficiently strong to support a continuation of Socialist policy after 1986 (instead they set their sights on the presidential election of 1988).

This chapter deals with the following subjects: business cycle policy (the evolution from reflation to austerity); industrial and business policy (from nationalization and increased state control to liberalization and restructuring); and unemployment policy (from stabilization to shakeouts and flexibility). At the end the success of these policies shall be assessed and the broader implications of those policy shifts analyzed, in particular from the viewpoint of developing a new Socialist approach to economic policy that might inspire programs and ideologies in the future.

BUSINESS CYCLE POLICY

During the 1970s the Socialists had repeatedly advocated a reflation of the economy. They criticized the reflation carried out by Prime Minister Jacques Chirac in 1975 as insufficient even though it ended up with a massive balance of trade deficit that caused Chirac's downfall and his replacement in 1976 by Raymond Barre, who from then on practiced a fairly continuous policy of austerity that the left condemned as leading to deindustrialization and systematic pauperization. In fact Barre's austerity was moderated by the memory of 1968; he believed that wage increases should be brought down only gradually in order to avoid another explosion of discontent. While he was able to reduce the budget deficit and to significantly improve the balance of trade, inflation levels stayed high (from just below 10 percent in 1975–78 they came close to 12 percent in 1979 and almost reached 14 percent during Barre's last year in office). Wage progression was reduced somewhat but remained significantly above the levels prevailing in other Western industrial countries (a fact for which Barre received little credit from the left).[1]

Against this background the Socialists kept advocating a reflation which, they argued, could still be successful if done correctly. First of all, higher growth rates would improve the use of existing capacities and thus reduce inflationary pressures due to high unit costs. Simultaneous structural reforms (measures to recapture the domestic market and to improve export performance, and eventually "industrial socialism" via the nationalizations) would improve the position of French industry in terms of market share in and outside France, and thus contain the balance of trade deficit. The stimulation of labor-intensive sectors such as construction would produce few imports, and energy imports in turn could be reduced by an aggressive program of energy conservation. In 1981 the Socialists—as did the experts of the International Monetary Fund (IMF) or the European Economic Community (EEC)—also expected an international economic upturn to be imminent; this they thought would ease the pressure until the other measures would show their impact. They further expected that the need for deficit spending by the state would soon be reduced as private investment picked up due to improved growth perspectives. Those were their economic arguments and perceptions. In addition, there was in 1981 the weight of the leftist electorate's expectations, which the Socialists probably felt they could not disappoint. For years the left had promised an improvement in wages and social welfare payments; now it was under pressure to take concrete action.

The main instruments of reflation in 1981/82 were a substantial increase of minimum wage (over 10 percent in real terms in 1981–82), an even stronger increase (about 50 percent) of certain social welfare allocations (family and housing allocations, minimum retirement pensions), the creation of 170,000 new jobs in (central and local) government and the public health care system plus a 57 percent increase (in real terms) of job subsidies in the first two years (25 billion francs by 1983). In addition, aid to investment and subsidies to industry generally increased many times over, particularly in the framework of the nationalizations. The sum total of these measures amounted to 1.7 percent of the GDP of 1981 (0.25 percent in 1981, 1.45 percent in 1982), of which nearly 80 percent was financed by the state, the rest by business firms (minimum wages) and the social security system.[2]

This reflation did save the French economy from stagnation in 1982, but its results were a disappointment in many other respects. The international recession did not end in 1982 but instead became ever more pronounced. As a result of this development, French exports not only did not increase but actually fell, as France's traditional clients (Third World and OPEC countries) were hit particularly hard. Private investment in France declined instead of increasing as the government had expected. In April 1982 the balance of trade showed a sharp deterioration; also, inflation seemed to accelerate again. By late spring, talks of sacrifices became increasingly common among policy-makers, and in June (on the occasion of the second devaluation of the franc) the government imposed a wage and price freeze for several months and decided to streamline the social security system (increasing contributions, reducing payouts).[3] The first U-turn was thus carried out; it angered both business and the unions and led to a pronounced decline of the government's rating in public opinion.[4] The Socialists tried to minimize the damage by claiming that this shift was only a parenthesis, a temporary suspension of principles that remained unchanged and would soon be applied again.

But the new line of austerity (called "rigor" by the Socialists to mark the difference with Barre) was continued in the fall of 1982 with a plan to balance the social security budget by 1983 and the announcement by Prime Minister Pierre Mauroy of the end of automatic wage indexation. It was also admitted now that the new policy would have to last for some time, probably no less than a year and a half, possibly even longer. Even though he denied it at first, the prime minister was thinking of more stringent austerity measures by early 1983. At that time the balance of trade worsened again, with the result that the country was in the process of becoming one of the world's biggest borrowers (its foreign debt doubling in 1982, with an increase in the international debt of $25 billion during that year alone). The situation also required another devaluation of the franc within the European Monetary System (EMS), the third since the Socialists had to come to power. It was on this occasion that intense controversy developed among Socialist leaders about which course to follow.

While Prime Minister Mauroy and Finance Minister Jacques Delors advocated a tightening of austerity after the municipal elections of 1983, there were also those who argued for the opposite course, including Jean Riboud, a successful business executive (Schlumberger) and longtime personal friend of Mitterrand. Those who supported such an alternative also included prominent Socialist leaders such as Pierre Joxe, Christian Goux, Jean-Pierre Chevènement of the CERES faction, and presidential advisors such as Alain Boublil or Pierre Bérégovoy. Riboud proposed that France leave the EMS altogether, float the franc (an idea not entirely foreign to Mitterrand himself, who in the 1970s had criticized the EMS for being a deflationist community), and set up temporary import restrictions under the EEC treaty. Thus protected against a balance of trade deficit, France could continue to give priority to economic growth and an industrial modernization that would assure competitiveness in the future. At least temporarily this might have amounted to the economic protectionism that the right had predicted as the inevitable result of the failure of Socialist policy and that part of the left demanded as a condition of its success.

After considerable hesitation—including plans to replace prime minister and government altogether—Mitterrand confirmed Mauroy and Delors in their positions. Apparently persuaded that France's rapidly growing foreign debt (against the background of very small currency reserves) left no other course open, he accepted their demand for stepped-up austerity, though his demand for it in public was only half-hearted at first. The main element of the new austerity course was a plan to reduce domestic demand by about 2 percent. Nearly half of this was achieved by increasing income taxes for the upper two-thirds of the population and by imposing a forced loan on the top third; the rest resulted from an increase in certain sales taxes, a reduction of social security payouts and a cutback of state expenditure.[5] The idea was to cut the 1983 trade deficit in half. With the help of an expansion of world trade which finally set in and favored French exports, this target could be approached fairly closely (see Table 2.1).

The foreseeable cost of this policy—confirmed by later developments—was also high. The plan could only work if there was no increase in real wages; industrial production would decline, investment be discouraged and unemployment increased; labor leaders and leftist voters would be upset. This led to an attempt by Chevènement to reverse the policy a few months after it had been decided; he was joined in his attack on governmental policy by the Communist leadership. This time Mitterrand had to take a stand. In the summer of 1983 he pronounced himself strongly in favor of Mauroy and Delors' policy and declared that no other approach was feasible. Most dissenters (including the Communists and the labor leaders) now accepted the new course, which in any case was soon confirmed in the fall by the plans for the 1984 budget. Shortly afterwards the government drew the conclusion from its course for industrial policy. This led

Table 2.1
Major Economic Indicators

Indicator	(1980)	1981	1982	1983	1984	1985
Balance of trade (billion francs)	(-56.6)	-54.0	-103.8	-63.9	-39.6	-40.0
Balance of payments (billion francs)	(-17.6)	-25.8	-79.3	-35.7	-6.6	3.0
Growth rate of GDP (percent volume growth)	(1.4)	0.6	2.0	0.7	1.3	1.1
Inflation (retail prices)	(13.6)	13.4	11.8	9.6	7.4	5.8
Disposable household Income (percent)	(-0.1)	2.8	2.6	-0.7	-0.7	0.5
Industrial investment (change in percent; not included are energy, public works, public sector firms)	(7.5)	-5.4	-6.7	-1.6	9.3	9.0
Taxes	(23.5)	23.6	24.0	24.5		
Social welfare contributions	(18.5)	18.5	19.0	19.8		
Total (percent of GDP)	(42.0)	42.1	43.0	44.3	45.5	45.5

Sources: INSEE, cited in Le Monde, sélection hebdomadaire, March 13-19, 1986.
For taxes and social welfare contributions, see Le Monde, January 19,
1984 (for 1980 to 1983) and April 30, 1986 (for 1984 and 1985).

to the important ''restructurings,'' which in practice meant cutting back French
production capacities to more realistic levels, with the inevitable consequence
of letting unemployment rise strongly (subjects to be discussed later on). This
course was stuck to through 1985 even though some Socialist leaders hoped to
revert to a higher growth rate in the year before the 1986 elections (thus Bérégovoy in early 1985—by that time he was finance minister and made tentative
announcements about the possibility of more rapid growth). While on the five-
year average economic growth in France was the same as in the Federal Republic
of Germany and only slightly inferior to the EEC average (1.1 percent and 1.2
percent, respectively), in the years 1984 and 1985 the French rates reached only
slightly more than half those of its main trading partners. But in any case this

was a conscious policy choice: Delors had announced in early 1984 that French growth rates must for some time remain inferior to those of neighboring countries.

Overall the austerity policy achieved most of the goals it was designed for. Demand was brought down for the first time in thirty years and wage progression brought to a halt without major upheaval. The balance of trade deficit was reduced, though it was not cancelled out even in 1985, as hoped for originally, because in that year the international environment was less favorable and French exports showed structural weaknesses again. Inflation declined rapidly and during the last six months of Socialist rule was identical to the low rates prevailing in the Federal Republic of Germany (by the end of February 1986, the rate for the previous twelve months was down to 3.4 percent).[6]

In fact, the government did more than just break the wage-price spiral. By keeping wage and price increases down to roughly identical rates (though price increases authorized for industrial products were sometimes higher than wage increases in that sector) the government reserved gains from productivity investments exclusively for business, whereas in the past those gains had been distributed among business (profits), labor (wages) and the state (taxes).[7] Combined with the labor shakeouts of 1984, this meant a considerable shift of business finances (distribution of value added) in favor of profits and fit in well with the strategy of economic liberalism practiced toward business starting in 1983 (see below).

With regard to public finance, Mitterrand had soon (in early 1982) set a limit of 3 percent of GDP for the budget deficit, a limit not entirely respected but not greatly surpassed. On another point, the Socialists could not fulfill the promise given by Mitterrand in his duel with Chirac in 1981 to stabilize the share of taxes and social welfare contributions (the much-debated *prélèvements obligatoires*). In fact, this share kept rising (as it had done under Barre), from 42.1 percent in 1981 to 45.5 percent in 1984 and 1985 (at least growth was stopped during that last year; see Table 2.1). But then, maintaining this high level of tax pressure did permit reducing the public sector borrowing requirement from 3.1 percent of GDP in 1983 to 2.6 percent in 1985—a performance acknowledged by the report that Renaud de la Genière, former governor of the Bank of France, made at the request of the new government of the right in April 1986. Also in this context, the Socialists submitted, in the fall of 1985, a budget for 1986 that showed a decline in real terms—a unique feat since World War II and one that showed how much economic thinking had changed among the Socialist leadership.

In political terms, the turn toward austerity certainly initiated the decline of support for the government among the leftist electorate, beginning exactly with the U-turn of 1982. Yet it is remarkable to what extent the Socialist leaders were able to secure Communist Party approval, or at least tolerance, of their policy on the occasion of the key decisions in 1982 and in 1983, despite the fact that this ran counter to the Common Program, the clear policy preferences of the Communist leaders and the political line of the largest (Communist-dominated) labor union, the CGT. Part of the decline and demoralization of the unions is undoubtedly due to this acceptance, which for the most part remained without a satisfactory justification in terms of leftist legitimacy.

NATIONALIZATIONS AND PUBLIC SECTOR POLICY

The nationalization of banks and selected industrial companies was an essential part of the Common Program of the left in 1972; it was placed there upon the insistence of the Communists, who had advocated such a measure since 1969. The program clearly defined the firms concerned. However, there were disagreements later on between Socialists and Communists. They concerned, first, the subsidiaries of the big industrial firms (which the Communists, but not the Socialists, wanted nationalized also) and, second, the criteria for management (the Communists wanted a set of criteria that differed from the "logic of profit"). Inability to agree on these points was one of the reasons for the breakup of the Socialist-Communist alliance in 1977.

For some Socialists—including Mitterrand himself—the main reasons for nationalization seemed to be ideological. For others, the reasons were primarily technical: they saw nationalization as the principal means to redress the French economy. This viewpoint was argued most forcefully by Alain Boublil, a Socialist economist who in 1981 became a close advisor to Mitterrand. Boublil reasoned that France's main problem was that the country did not dispose of strong oligopolistic firms dominating entire sections of production. It was these firms, in his view, that managed to concentrate most of the wealth because of their technological leadership (and the technology rent derived from it), their ability to promote the world market, and their insensitivity to trade fluctuations (which do not hit rising sectors so severely).

Liberal capitalism had failed the country, Boublil and others argued, because it was characterized by timid private investors and banks unwilling to take on even normal entrepreneurial risks. Instead of channeling savings into risk capital (such as stock in industrial corporations) they promoted obligations or, worse yet, investment in real estate. The banks thus were more a parasite feeding on industry than a sympathetic supporter or promoter. The problem could not be solved by achieving a higher rate of economic growth and higher profits through increasing demand. First, in an open economy a stepped-up demand could only lead to an import surge that would sooner or later condemn the effort. Second, the Barre years had shown that rising business profits could not be relied upon to induce greater investments at a time when demand stagnated or declined. Nationalization, by contrast, seemed to offer a solution to those problems.

With the help of nationalization the state could build up a limited range of firms to techonological, financial and industrial leadership. This would require massive capital infusions for several years, thus the need to limit the range of the nationalizations (and also the need to take over the banks). In making its selection the government should look for the most promising candidates in order to maximize the desired impact (in terms of technological leadership, employment, etc.). The firms concerned should come to dominate whole sectors of production (or so-called *filières*) from raw materials to final products and thus serve as poles of industrial vitality and leadership for other firms as well, diffusing learning effects, economies of scale, export successes, and so on. The result of such a reconstruction of French industry would be a more prosperous economy capable of providing higher wages and a better welfare system but also more, and more qualified (and better paid), employment. The resulting reindustrialization, Boublil concluded, would allow France to catch up with the main capitalist powers, whereas under the Barre policy of aid to specific, relatively small branches or firms that were already competitive (or at least close to it), France would soon be shifted to the semi-periphery of the world capitalist system. Such were the lessons of industrial (one might also say supply-side) socialism, whose tenets were widely shared by the Socialist leadership, even by Rocard and Delors, who were often considered to be somewhat skeptical with regard to the Socialist program and orthodoxy.[8]

Once Socialists were in power, they accorded very high priority to the nationalization program; however, there were internal disagreements over the organizational statute that should be given the new firms. The approach taken by the first minister of industry (Pierre Joxe) was to reorganize the whole French economy into large branches or *filières*, each of which was to be dominated by a state monopoly along the lines of Electricité de France. This would have amounted to enormous changes and was soon discarded. Joxe was replaced by Pierre Dreyfus, the former chief executive of the Renault car works (nationalized after World War II). Under his guidance the organizational model of Renault (market competition, large managerial autonomy) was adopted. Another question concerned the form of public ownership—should the state take over 100 percent or only acquire a controlling stake of 51 percent, e.g., by converting outstanding state loans into equity capital? The second approach (favored by Rocard and Delors) would have been less cumbersome legally, considerably less expensive, and would have made no difference in terms of effective control.[9] Mitterrand and Mauroy, however, decided for a 100 percent takeover, both for psychological reasons and because it would make the nationalizations more difficult to reverse. After some minor modifications imposed by the Constitutional Council in response to a legal challenge by the rightist opposition, the nationalization of banks and selected industrial corporations became law in February 1982. The two steel firms (quasi-nationalized under Barre) were taken over a little earlier; in some other cases nationalizations were carried out somewhat later after negotiations with (partly foreign) owners.

The new executives appointed in February 1982 (in a few cases they were the previous managers) were instructed to stress normal capital profitability—not just by cutting costs and shedding labor but rather by innovation and expansion of production. Each firm was to come up with a detailed plan laying down its strategy for the near future and to sign a contract with the state consecrating this plan and strategy. When Dreyfus did not push very hard on this issue, he was replaced by Jean-Pierre Chevènement, one of the most outspoken advocates of the expansionist-productivist approach in the Socialist leadership. Most firms then came up with ambitious plans, in accord with the outlook of the minister in charge. But Chevènement irritated many managers by his constant interventions and was replaced in March 1983 by Laurent Fabius, the later prime minister. With Fabius a different approach prevailed: the firms enjoyed greater autonomy, but the minister also stressed the imperious need for management to produce profits (or at least balanced books) by 1985. Fabius' liberalism coincided with the policy of reinforced austerity, which in turn had dramatic consequences for public sector industry.

The most immediate result of austerity was that the state could no longer come up with growing capital provisions for the public sector; this put a lid on the approach of industrial Socialism which provided for massive transfers for several years. As a result, capital provisions by the state peaked quite early (7.9 billion francs in 1982, 12.6 in 1983, 12.8 in 1984, 13.5 in 1985, 11 planned for 1986). In addition, any of the capital provisions granted by the government went to cover losses (particularly in steel) rather than to finance investment as originally intended. Hence the need to achieve profits relatively early on. One way to limit the damage to the ambitious plans of industrial modernization was to allow nationalized industry to draw on private savings for its capital needs. This was achieved by introducing, in early 1983, two financial instruments designed specifically for public sector firms: the *titres participatifs* (similar in status to a bond issue) and the *certificats d'investissement* (similar to stock but without voting rights), both of which knew considerable success on the market in 1984 and 1985 (incidentally showing the confidence of the public in the firms that issued them). The government also considered submitting a bill that would have regulated the sale of subsidiaries of public sector industrial firms in order to raise capital (a Conseil d'Etat holding of 1978 had declared such sales illegal in the absence of legal authorization). However, Fabius as prime minister (after the summer of 1984) was concerned that such a bill might divide the Socialist majority; as a result he never submitted it to the National Assembly. Some corporations sold individual subsidiaries anyhow, drawing the accusation from the Communists of squandering national property and acting against the law.[10]

The curtailment of financial transfers from the state was but one result of the austerity course. The other one resulted from the reduction of demand, particularly for industrial products. It meant that the plans for production expansion were now obsolete (in some cases they were indeed unrealistic from the beginning). The need to achieve profitability meant that some investment programs had to be halted while in progress, and, more dramatically perhaps, that jobs had to be cut again a year or so after hiring had started up. The drama was particularly intense in the declining steel and coal sectors and (later on) in the Renault works. Though these firms were not at the core of the 1982 nationalizations (indeed, the coal mines and Renault had been nationalized much earlier, and the steel industry was close to bankruptcy as a result of mismanagement and the Europe-wide steel crisis), their cases shall be described in some detail, as they illustrate the change in official Socialist thinking. It must be kept in mind, though, that in most of the new public sector corporations things evolved in a much more positive way, with great successes in some.

The coal industry clearly illustrates the Socialist shifts in this area. In 1982 the government had approved a plan to step up coal production by reactivating and modernizing French mines and by additional hiring, in line with the economic analysis of the left during the 1970s. A prominent Communist (Georges Valbon, a member of the Central Committee) was appointed to head the Charbonnages de France (CDF). But very quickly deficits and debts of the coal industry exploded while production and sales (due to the continuing shift to nuclear electricity generation) went down. It looked as though coal alone might soon absorb as much as the entire budget for all of industry taken together. After lengthy hesitation, the government in March 1984 imposed personnel reductions of 5,000–6,000 per year for the next five years (reducing total employment by 50 percent) and demanded balanced accounts by 1988. Valbon resigned in protest, but the new plan was stuck to, and CDF had made considerable progress by 1985, with productivity rising again. A strike launched by the CGT in early 1985 turned out to be a nearly total failure. With Renault (again a firm nationalized not by the Socialists, but under de Gaulle right after World War II) the government, by replacing the chief executive in a rather authoritarian fashion, mandated a similarly tough line in mid–1985, after the firm had suffered considerable losses during the preceding year. Over 20 percent of the jobs were to be suppressed in 1985–86, and the capacities reduced; the new manager's main concern was to lower the threshold of profitability as much as possible.

Steel experienced a similar drama. In the 1970s the Socialists had targeted the two largest firms of this sector for nationalization. They carried it out in December 1981, but in fact it was the Barre government which in 1979 had all but taken over this ailing industry. In July 1982 a steel plan set ambitious production targets with important new investments. It became clear in 1983 that this plan was unrealistic, but the Socialists hesitated to act for fear of Communist opposition (manifested in the CGT). In the fall Mitterrand and Fabius decided to test the cooperation of the Communists by asking them to support a tough plan designed to return the steel industry to profitability by 1987 at the expense of cutting a large proportion of the work force and liquidating investments that in some cases were completely new. To their surprise the Communists—unlike some Socialist deputies from the areas affected, especially Lorraine—did not raise a public protest but accepted the policy shift in March 1984. There was substantial rioting and violence in Lorraine (and Georges Marchais took part in a steelworkers' demonstration in Paris), but the government stood firm. For 1984 the steel industry received only 5.75 billion francs instead of the 12 billion it requested. Here too substantial progress was evident by early 1986 (there were additional complications because of the involvement of the European Community, which had vowed to outlaw all subsidies for steel by 1986).

The corporations nationalized in 1982 did not experience such enormous problems. Some knew spectacular successes—thus Thomson with sale of its RITA surveillance system to the Pentagon. CGE (another electronics firm) showed considerable vitality in its effort to implant itself in the U.S. market in order to take advantage of the breakup of AT&T. In some areas the planning contracts and increased subsidies seemed to effectively reverse decline.[11] Overall, the Socialists transferred some 50 billion francs in public funds to these firms; this was a much better record than that of the previous (private) shareholders. Also, the capital issues of these corporations were a great market success. By 1985 most of these made profits again, and some were profitable as early as 1984; this was obviously helped by generally better economic conditions.

It seems difficult at the present time to assess how much of "industrial socialism" was effectively realized. Time was short; so were funds, partly due to austerity, but also due to the fact that the Socialists (going against Boublil's warning) spent about half of the industrial budget on declining industries. Finally, the strategy of building up *filières* was not really carried out fully anywhere. Instead of focusing technological and commercial development on a few poles, Fabius reverted to the old Barre strategy of building up profits so as to generate investments and, in due course, employment. Industrial socialism as originally intended did not last longer than a year or two.

The Chirac government of 1986 declared its intention to reprivatize all of these corporations (and more). As the Socialists pointed out, the fact that these had been attractive firms for investors (something which was not the case in 1981) was proof that management must have been good. This was a modest claim when compared to the Socialists' original designs but not an unimportant one given earlier fears of likely mismanagement. In this area, as in others, the Socialists had acquired experience on the job.

PRIVATE SECTOR POLICY

By 1981 there was in France a long and solid tradition of mutual suspicion between private sector business and the left, especially a united left that included the Communists. It reached back to such historical episodes as the leftist governments of 1924 and—especially—the Popular Front government of 1936–37. The left used to suspect business of wanting to sabotage any progressive leftist policy; business expected the left to ruin private enterprise and the market economy by a mixture of demagogy and incompetence. The Common Program of 1972 had contributed to some of these fears on the part of business. It proposed a vast increase in wages and social security allocations while at the same time providing for stepped-up taxation on business (on profits, investment, wealth, expense account spending, etc.). Internal financing of industrial investment was to be limited; by contrast the state would increase control over private sector investment via the Plan and a National Investment Bank.[12]

To be sure, there had been many revisions of that program by 1981, but key points survived. Already before the elections of 1978 (when a leftist victory was widely expected) there was an episode of capital flight; this was repeated after Mitterrand's surprise victory in 1981. Many businessmen were highly skeptical of the new government; some were prepared to oppose it systematically. Few Socialists had a positive image with business; of the two exceptions, Rocard and Delors, Rocard had recently been deprived of key functions, and Delors' position was not very clear at first since he had not risen through party ranks and had no real political base of his own.

The first six to nine months after the election of Mitterrand seemed to vindicate some (though not the worst) business fears. The government (but not without negotiations among the social partners) reduced the work week by one hour and then insisted (unilaterally—in fact, Mitterrand overriding Mauroy's preference) that wages be maintained in full; it generalized a fifth week of vacations for all wage earners and increased minimum wage and social welfare allocations heavily financed by employers (more so than in most industrial countries). This created new financial burdens for employers, who in addition were also hit by new taxes on wealth and expense account spending. Financial incentives to business were increased at the same time; however, they met with little response, partly due to the fact that the aid to investment was made conditional on maintaining or increasing personnel, a requirement which effectively precluded most investments in productivity. In the fall of 1981 Socialist activists (including many deputies) indulged in violent antibusiness rhetoric at their party convention; Mitterrand and Mauroy had to make a major effort to calm down the resulting uproar. Simultaneously, though, the top leaders also tried to weaken the power of business organizations by recognizing a breakaway competitor (the Syndicat national de la petite et moyenne industrie [SNPMI]) to the established employers' organization, Conseil national du patronat français (CNPF), and—somewhat later—by threatening to pull the newly nationalized firms out of that organization altogether (this would have hurt because of membership contributions; eventually those firms stayed in, which was original given CNPF's role as champion of free enterprise). CNPF was already weakened by a leadership struggle at the time this was happening; however, the radicalization of businessmen at the grass roots in the course of the following year, due in part to competition between CNPF and SNPMI in their antigovernment protest activities, infused it with new strength.[13]

Businessmen were indeed highly skeptical that they would be able to carry on satisfactorily under the Socialist government, despite reassuring declarations by Finance Minister Delors. The CNPF produced detailed studies showing that business was losing much more, through various reforms, than it was gaining through new aid programs. Businessmen saw themselves reinforced in their hostile views when the government in late 1982 passed the Auroux laws (treated elsewhere in this volume), reforming labor relations in individual firms. They pointed to financial losses, falling profits and falling investments (see Table 2.1), and during the first two years repeatedly took their protest to the streets.

At first the Socialist government did not respond very significantly. It was still counting on reflation and the nationalizations to pull the French economy out of the slump; businessmen would invest because they would not want to miss such an opportunity. There were minor concessions: in April 1982 there was a reduction of taxes (concerning in particular the *taxe professionnelle*, a kind of business and occupation tax) and of some social security contributions paid by employers, with promises of more such reductions to come. The top leaders—above all Mitterrand himself—also practiced symbolic politics by stressing the essential contributions that business enterprises made to the life of the French nation (the emphasis was on "enterprises," a Schumpeterian or—in the French context—Saint-Simonian concept, not on employers or *patrons*, a word which in French has a strong hierarchical connotation).

As in other areas, the big change came in 1983. Reflation was now written off, and it was clear that due to austerity much of the ambitious planning for public sector firms would never be realized. The idea of the National Investment Bank was also scrapped for good. The question arose with ever greater intensity of how business would get the funds it undoubtedly needed. The Socialists also discovered now that it was small and medium-sized firms that had to create employment, develop innovation, and compete for exports—all things for which they needed resources that the state clearly could not provide. From this time on the shift was rapid; the government undertook a whole range of efforts to improve the situation of business. It helped to increase profitability by holding down wage costs, taxes and social welfare contributions (Mitterrand promised to first stabilize and then to reduce them, by 1985) and by initiating a redistribution or value added in favor of business profits at the expense of wages. It took important measures to promote risk capital, which for a long time had been nearly nonexistent in France. By the end of 1983 and through 1984 it actively promoted labor shakeouts, completely reversing its 1981 stand. Finally, during its last two years in power, the Socialist government placed the main emphasis on developing a more flexible legal framework for business, above all in the area of labor relations. These measures shall now be looked at more closely.

With regard to the distribution of value added, the government, with its policy of wage austerity, labor shakeouts and selective price decontrol for manufactured products, managed to reverse a trend that had lasted well over a decade. It increased the share of gross profits at the expense of wages (see Figure 2.1). This contrasted strongly (and paradoxically) with the picture that had prevailed under Barre. At this time the share of wages was briefly reduced, but profits continued to decline anyhow. By contrast, in 1985 gross profits exceeded their level of 1975, and that trend was still unchanged in March 1986. The result of all this was a strong increase in the internal financing of investments: it jumped from about 60 percent in 1983 to 71 percent in 1984 and to over 80 percent in

Figure 2.1
Relative Shares of Wages and Gross Profits in French Business Firms, 1970–1985
(in percent of value added)

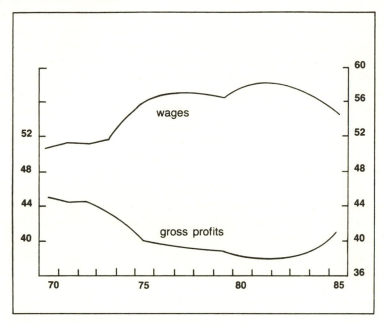

Source: Conjoncture, 15:3 (March 1985), p. 43.
Graphics from Paribas.

1985.[14] In looking at these figures, one must also consider the fact, though, that there was little capital formation in business despite its improved financial position.[15] Only in industry was there marked improvement in 1984–85, after a substantial decline over the three preceding years (see Table 2.1).

Risk capital increased tremendously beginning in 1983. In October of that year Delors launched the *Codevi* formula (accounts for industrial development), which in less than three months attracted over 40 billion francs, most of it out of short-term savings accounts but some of it new, and in any case invested now under a different financial scheme. Earlier that same year the government had introduced risk capital instruments for public sector firms which were also very successful on the stock market (see above). Several measures were taken to make investments in stock more attractive, including tax exemptions and provisions for better protection of the stockholding public through improved auditing procedures and institutions (similar to the reforms carried out in the United States during the New Deal). At the same time traditional forms of investment (gold, real estate, short-term deposits) were made less attractive. The public developed a great interest in the stock market, and the resulting boom was further enhanced by foreign buyers (institutional investors from the United States and Britain, later also from the Federal Republic of Germany), by the former stockholders of the newly nationalized companies looking for attractive opportunities to reinvest their compensation amounts, and finally by the good financial performance of the corporations whose stock was traded. In 1983 the volume of risk captial raised on the capital market (essentially stocks) was about five times as much as during the preceding year.[16] After more than two decades of continuous decline, stock market indicators went up between 50 and 60 percent in 1983, 16.5 percent in 1984, and about 40 percent in 1985, with another strong boom phase in early 1986. It is true that the stock boom was an international phenomenon, but in most of the other countries concerned it was conservative governments that presided over these developments.

It was not an accident that, beginning in late 1983, glowing reports from the stock exchange frequently coincided with yet another increase in unemployment or another dramatic episode of restructuring. One of the prime goals of the famous restructurings was to cut back the redundant work force and thus reduce the financial burden it represented for the firms concerned. Labor flexibility had a similar goal. Because these questions go beyond the immediate scope of private sector policy they shall be treated in a separate section.

UNEMPLOYMENT POLICY

Unemployment in France had increased since the mid–1970s, much as in other Western European countries. Under Giscard two approaches were taken to combat it; Prime Minister Chirac in 1975 tried reflation plus political control of dismissals by a law making them dependent on administrative approval, a regulation unique in Western Europe. Prime Minister Barre viewed employment as dependent on the health of business firms and therefore concentrated his efforts on improving competitiveness; in addition he organized a holding operation in the form of state training and employment programs for the young. He fully accepted the perspective of a continued rise of unemployment, though he played it down; in his view it was primarily due to a demographic and social transition (larger generations, and also a higher percentage of women, arriving on the labor market) that would be largely completed by 1985.

The Socialists in opposition proposed a different course. They promised to stabilize and then reduce unemployment by revitalizing the French economy (reflation, nationalization, etc.), by reducing work time to better distribute employment in the name of greater solidarity (this was to affect weekly, yearly and lifetime work), and by creating additional civil service jobs. Finally, there was also an old Common Program promise still contained in Mitterrand's 1981 election platform: to make dismissals dependent on the consent of works committees.

The proposal concerning works committees' approval never was taken up. With regard to the other points, the Socialists at first proceeded according to their program, avoiding all measures that were painful or unpopular. But in the second phase, starting in late 1983, unemployment policy was turned upside down when it was adjusted to economic policy in other areas. The government now actively promoted labor shakeouts, with only very limited efforts to cushion their impact. Only in 1985 did the situation stabilize again, after more than a year of stark deterioration. In the third phase the government produced new initiatives to realize new forms of solidarity, though that period was governed above all by a concern for greater flexibility.

Back to the first phase: within weeks of the left's accession to power (complete with the National Assembly elections) the work week was reduced from forty to thirty-nine hours after negotiations between business and labor organizations. This was not very much, considering the target of thirty-five hours contained in the election platform; but then this target was maintained for 1985. Many prominent Socialist leaders (Prime Minister Mauroy, Finance Minister Delors, Labor Minister Auroux, Planning Minister Rocard, plus union chief Edmond Maire of the CFDT) argued that the desired effect on employment could only be achieved if this reduction of the work week was accompanied by a partial wage reduction (and some new CFDT labor contracts indeed provided for such concessions). But in February Mitterrand declared that no worker should have to fear for his income on account of the thirty-nine-hour week, and the government made no adjustment in civil service pay. Thus the more traditional leftist views (among their strong supporters were the CGT and FO) prevailed at the expense of job creation; the measure actually generated very few jobs as a result (estimated at 14,000–28,000) and—given the precedent—probably impeded further work time reductions.[17]

Also during this phase, retirement age was reduced from sixty-five to sixty (an overwhelmingly popular measure, though in practice most people could already take advantage of similar regulations earlier on). Finally, the instrument of solidarity contracts was created. By means of this device, firms that introduced part-time work, reduced the work week to thirty-seven hours or less and/or retirement age below sixty, and also created a corresponding number of jobs, received financial incentives from the state. Much aid to private investment was also made dependent on increasing or at least not reducing personnel. Finally, civil service jobs were added much as planned. Taken together, these measures were quite expensive for business, the social security system and the state. But with their help the Socialists managed to first slow down the growth of unemployment and then to stabilize it roughly at the 2 million mark (see Figure 2.2).

With the new economic policy put into place in 1983 (reflation replaced by austerity, stress on business profitability, even in nationalized industry) an entirely different approach was taken. First priority was now given to freeing industry from the burden of redundant labor. It was a hard battle to get this accepted by leftists, particularly among Communist leaders (who in fact never accepted the idea of redundancy but agreed to particular shakeouts after efforts at protecting the labor force). To limit the resulting political damage, Mitterrand favored quick, dramatic action so there would be a period of stability before the

Figure 2.2
Unemployment in Major European Countries, 1981–1985 (in percent of the labor force)

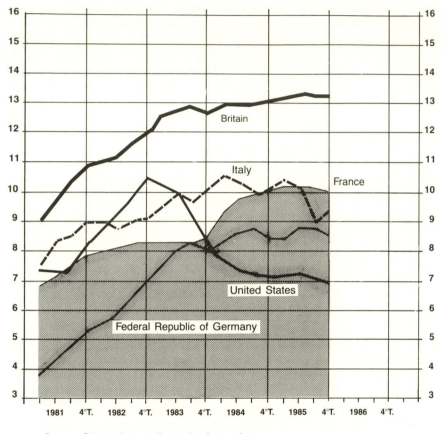

Source: *Observations et diagnostics économiques*
(Revue de l'OFCE No. 15, April 1986), graphics appendix table V/1

1986 elections; in this he was supported by Fabius. (Mauroy and Delors would have favored a more gradual and consensual approach but did not prevail.) Once Communist Party and CGT leaders had given their consent (major test cases were Talbot-Poissy in late 1983 and the steel industry in March-April 1984) the government acted in a decisive and rather authoritarian fashion, giving local unions and personnel little chance to participate in decisions and submit alternative proposals. The effects of these industrial "mutations" and "restructurings" reverberated throughout the French economy; in one firm after another cuts were announced, with the government now requiring personnel reductions as a precondition for aid to business if this was likely to secure a return to profitability. Between late 1983 and early 1985 unemployment increased steeply, by almost 400,000 (see Figure 2.2). During this phase the hard core of qualified industrial workers was hit, no longer primarily those with lesser skills, as had been the case previously. There were a few minor (though expensive) measures to soften the shock: state-subsidized retraining programs, special funds and programs for disaster areas with a concentration of declining industries, and, starting in mid–1984, another holding operation in the form of the TUC (*travaux d'utilité collective*, part-time jobs for the young in public works). But no efforts were made to further reduce work time (here the government waited for a joint European effort). In addition, payments to the unemployed were cut in 1984.[18]

In 1985 a new situation developed. Overall unemployment figures now remained stable and even declined somewhat. The number of full-time jobs not a priori limited in time still declined (though more slowly now), and the duration of unemployment for the long-term unemployed kept increasing. At the same time there was a greatly accelerated turnover in the market for temporary labor, for which the government now loosened the rules after first tightening them in 1982. Precarious and part-time employment experienced a great boom and also became more acceptable to the unemployed.[19] At the same time retraining programs considerably expanded during this year, enjoying a sudden rise in popularity or at least in acceptance.

The major development during this third phase was the discussion of "flexibility." For some time French employers had been unhappy with certain labor regulations: administrative approval for dismissals (introduced in 1975) and the provisions of the Auroux laws (1982) were prominent in this context. During 1984 the CNPF, on the basis of a member survey, concluded that these and other regulations inhibited job creation by as much as 450,000. It therefore proposed a deal to the unions: greater flexibility for 450,000 jobs to be (probably) created in exchange. After producing an agreement the union negotiators were disavowed by their organizations (the CGT never signed, being opposed to the operation from the beginning). After this failure many of the regulations at stake were taken up individually in later agreements and laws. Perhaps the most important bill allowed for the negotiation, between social partners in each branch, of more flexible working hours accompanied by a reduction of the average work week and of yearly overtime hours permitted without authorization. Because of a Communist filibuster the Socialists had to use rather authoritarian methods (article 49/3 of the Constitution), plus the support of opposition members of the Senate, to get this bill passed just two weeks before the legislature ended. The bill showed that the Socialists were capable of something more imaginative than the mere defense of the vested rights of those already holding jobs (a defense which could produce hardships for those seeking employment). They could initiate "modernization" while at the same time not ignoring the imperatives of solidarity and social protection. (The right promised to go much further on flexibility but at the expense of such protection.) Whether labor flexibility would make a big difference in the end was far from clear, incidentally; experts from the Organization for Economic Cooperation and Development (OECD) did not think the likely impact to be very great.[20] In any case, even the Socialists were not prepared to go further than facilitating agreements among social partners. Given the political situation, though, this approach may have represented the best chance to achieve effects that would last beyond the election.

CONCLUSION

In all the four areas of policy described above, the Socialists underwent tremendous change: from assumptions and analyses to practical policy there was little that survived intact. They started out with a predominantly "archaic" understanding of the economy, but recognized its inapplicability fairly quickly and adjusted, particularly as far as practical measures were concerned. But they adjusted reluctantly, having earlier defeated those (like Rocard) who took the lead in the effort to modernize Socialist Party thinking on economics; even Fabius was only a recent convert.[21] Thus they participated in the general shift of French opinion toward liberalism without at first taking a leadership role (a situation which changed later on).

Certain problems, however, remained unsolved. It would undoubtedly have been difficult to explain why ten years of Socialist programs (1972–1982) had so suddenly become obsolete. In fact, this question was at first sidestepped (by reference to the "parenthesis") and never fully addressed later on. It was more difficult still to create a minimal consensus around a new common understanding and approach, to organize—simultaneously with the policy change—the *aggiornamento* of the party itself. This was attempted in 1984, but eventually the leadership hesitated and drew back.[22] It was certainly remarkable how long Communist support for (or at least acceptance of) Socialist economic policies was maintained, since the Communists had endorsed all the major changes (including the restructurings) before leaving the government. But while this further weakened the Communist Party by depriving it of elements of identity, it did not facilitate the Socialists' search for new allies from the center; at the same time the break with the Communist Party became inevitable anyhow.

Perhaps the loss of popularity and the negative image of Socialist economic policy from 1983 onwards was primarily a matter of excessive expectations created during the 1970s, a situation for which the Socialists carry some responsibility: it was never possible to accommodate productivists, bread and butter unionists, ecological Socialists and centrist sympathizers all at the same time. But to some extent evaluations may change as time goes by. It seems likely that it simply takes time to translate the policy changes undertaken by the Socialists into ideological (and eventually into attitudinal) changes. In this context it is striking how, despite some obvious and very remarkable successes in the economic area (at least by conventional criteria), a negative image of Socialist economic policy entrenched itself in 1983 (and it was not simply a question of unpopular austerity; a majority claimed to prefer rigor to additional deficits.[23] In a way it was not unimpressive to see the Socialists continue a policy of rigor the fruits of which they would not be able to harvest, at least not in 1986. But rehabilitation may be under way, initiated in part—and paradoxically—by the new government of the right when it ordered a report by an uncontested expert (Renaud de la Genière, former governor of the Bank of France) on the economic management of the Socialists. The right expected to uncover scandalous mal-practices; to its embarrassment the report was quite positive. The Socialists had acted similarly in 1981, with a similar effect: Barre, who while in power had become the most unpopular prime minister the Fifth Republic had ever known, came back to a popularity achieved by no other figure of the right. In a similar way Socialist management may yet, in due course, come to be viewed as a significant achievement.

NOTES

1. Volkmar Lauber, *The Political Economy of France* (New York: Praeger, 1983), is generally used as a reference for the period 1970–82. Data from p. 102.
2. Alain Fonteneau and Alain Gubian, "Comparaison des relances françaises de 1975 et 1981–1982," *Observations et diagnostics économiques* (Revue de l'OFCE No. 12, July 1985), pp. 123–56.
3. A first devaluation became necessary in the fall of 1981—partly as a result of the previous overvaluation of the franc under Barre, partly due to capital flight, partly as a result of Socialist plans for reflation and an increased budget deficit.
4. Survey by SOFRES, *Le Nouvel Observateur*, August 28, 1982.
5. Alain Vernholes, *Le Monde*, March 28, 1983.
6. *Observations et diagnostics économiques* (Lettre de l'OFCE No. 33, March 26, 1986), p. 4.
7. Alain Vernholes, *Le Monde*, February 5, 1986.
8. Alain Boublil, *Le Socialisme industriel* (Paris: Presses universitaires de France, 1977).
9. The French state holds only 51 percent of the French railroads (SNCF) and still exercises full and unquestioned control. Michel Rocard, *Parler vrai* (Paris: Le Seuil, 1979), pp. 145–46.
10. Claire Blandin, *Le Monde, Dossiers et Documents: Bilan économique et social* (Paris, January 1986), p. 47.
11. For an example of improvements see Martin Rhodes, "French Government Sub-sidies for Information Technology," paper at the ECPR Joint Sessions in Barcelona, March 1985.
12. Lauber, *Political Economy of France*, pp. 35–40, 209–20.
13. Suzanne Berger, "The Socialists and the *Patronat*: The Dilemma of Co-existence in a Mixed Economy," and comment by David Goldey, in Howard Machin and Vincent Wright, eds., *Economic Policy and Policy-Making under the Mitterrand Presidency 1981–1984* (London: Pinter, 1985), pp. 225–54.

14. *Le Monde*, July 31, 1985.

15. *Conjoncture* (published by Paribas) 14, No. 11 (December 1984): 169–74.

16. *Conjoncture* 14, No. 4 (April 1984): 53–58.

17. Debate between Christian Goux and Raymond Soubie, *Le Point*, January 18, 1982; Jacques Julliard, *Le Nouvel Observateur*, February 27, 1982; *Economie et statistique*, No. 154 (April 1983); *Le Monde*, May 28, 1983.

18. OECD Economic Surveys, *Frankreich* (Paris: OECD, July 1985), pp. 79–82.

19. Jean-Luc Heller, *Economie et statistique*, No. 183 (December 1985); Alain Lebaube, *Le Monde*, December 24, 1985.

20. OECD Economic Surveys, *Frankreich* (1985), pp. 65–78; *Observations et diagnostics économiques* (Revue de l'OFCE No. 14, January 1986), pp. 55–56.

21. At the party convention of 1979, Rocard had challenged the party's "archaic" thinking. When he argued that the choice was between either the market or rationing, Fabius broke in with the comment that there was an alternative, namely, socialism. Reports from the convention do not show that Fabius came up with a clearer explanation.

22. Jean-Marie Colombani, *Le Monde*, January 5, 1985.

23. Surveys by SOFRES, cited in SOFRES, *Opinion publique* (Paris: Gallimard, 1986), pp. 233, 243.

3

Foreign and Security Policy

MICHAEL M. HARRISON

The five years of Socialist management of French foreign and security policy—from François Mitterrand's victory in the spring of 1981 until Jacques Chirac's government was installed in the spring of 1986—were an important and perhaps even decisive phase in France's postwar relations with the rest of the world. This is the case not because of any particular dramatic events or controversies that arose during this period, but, on the contrary, because of a dedramatization and even a certain banalization of French foreign policy both at home and abroad. In internal politics, this period confirms the viability of the Gaullist model and legacy as guidelines and constraints for French foreign and defense policy, so that despite differences over particular policies there is a broad consensus on basic French national interests and behavior toward other states and on major international issues.[1] In this respect, the Socialists' abandonment of the irresponsible rhetoric and policies espoused during the 1970s period of opposition was perhaps the most important feature of their time at the helm of France. What they did not do was as important as what they did try to accomplish. While some lingering nostalgia for misguided leftist ideas on Third World affairs was a feature of the early Socialist approach, it is more important that actual policies soon conformed to precedents and the essential conservatism of Mitterrand himself. By the time of the 1986 legislative elections, there were no major disagreements between the Socialist left and the center-right over foreign and defense policy, confirming that a strong and viable national consensus had been established in this arena.

The most important feature of this development for France's partners in the Atlantic system is that this consensus seems to be based on an unprecedented attitude of cooperation with allies. For, although France is doubtless still the most independent-minded and potentially obstreperous country in the West, since

1981 Paris has taken an unusually harmonious approach toward most major European and Atlantic issues, so that the attitude of defiance in principle so common from de Gaulle's era through the period of Giscard d'Estaing's presidency seems unlikely to revive. This new approach was most evident in Franco-American relations which, despite some normal disagreements, were better than at any period in postwar history. A marked pro-European attitude was another feature of Socialist policies, notable for the careful expansion of Franco-German cooperation in defense and security affairs as a complement to the Atlantic Alliance. Finally, France's Socialist rulers capitalized on trends in public and elite opinion to construct a generally critical policy toward the Soviet Union, discarding even the superficial appearance of France as a potential interlocutor between East and West. The clear anti-Soviet orientation of public opinion and the seemingly inexorable decline of the French Communist Party were factors permitting the open and sustained Atlantic orientation that now characterizes both the Socialists and the center-right in France.

A TROUBLED PRESIDENTIAL DOMAIN

A key principle governing foreign and defensive policy under the Fifth Republic has been the presidential domination of decision-making in this arena. Although presidents from de Gaulle through Mitterrand have intervened in virtually any issue when necessary, they have all felt that their domestic image and authority required the appearance of clear and decisive presidential management of foreign affairs. Although this standard was generally adhered to by François Mitterrand, during the early stages of his presidency there was a certain lack of focus and direction that affected the image of the new president. Even after the Elysée began to assert its authority more, major decisions went awry often enough that Mitterrand's generally low public standing was not bolstered by his foreign affairs performance and may have been damaged by it.

As leader of the left opposition from 1971 until 1981, Mitterrand had dominated the left and held it together through a talent for ambiguity and calculated indecision as part of a tactic allowing him to reconcile or divert the clash of factions and viewpoints. This aloof and patrician Socialist for a time employed a similar technique in managing domestic and even foreign policy from the Elysée Palace, where he seemed to allow a variety of voices from his office and various ministries openly to influence and even represent French foreign policy. For example, French policy in Africa and the Third World was marked by openly divergent views expounded by the cautious Quai d'Orsay, the more radical and human rights oriented Ministry of Development and Cooperation under Jean-Pierre Cot until late 1982, and the pragmatic Elysée official responsible for African affairs, Guy Penne. The Socialist Party was sometimes able to push policy in a more radical direction by striking alliances with the more left-ideological elements in the government. The Franco-Mexican Declaration of August 28, 1981, in support of the Sandinistas in Nicaragua was a notable example of this pattern of policy-making in a sensitive area: initially vetoed by the more conservative foreign ministry, it was reportedly revived and awarded the presidential imprimatur through a cabal involving the Socialist Party international affairs bureau and pressure from Régis Debray, for a time an advisor on Third World affairs at the Elysée.

This somewhat untidy pattern of foreign policy-making was visible during the early stages of Mitterrand's presidency, but after 1982 there was clearer assertion of strong presidential authority that reestablished centralized direction and responsibility for foreign policy decisions. Although the Socialist Party remained a locus of radical inclinations in the Third World, this tendency had almost no influence over policy by 1983. At the insistence of African heads of state, France lost much interest in pursuing human rights questions in Francophone Africa after Cot was ousted and, instead, the Elysée asserted its traditionally close surveillance of African affairs and relied on the usual manipulation of political, military and economic power to sustain France's influence in the region. A gradual disillusionment with the Sandinista regime also went hand-in-hand with the process of presidentialization and deradicalization of foreign policy during this period. By 1983 the president's staff at the Elysée was playing the decisive role in determining the direction of foreign policy as a whole, while closely monitoring the implementation of these policies, so that the Quai d'Orsay seemed to play an even less prominent role than usual. The president's key advisors in this area were his resident intellectual and all-around idea man, Jacques Attali, while a professional diplomat, Hubert Vedrine, managed foreign policy with the assistance of Guy Penne on Africa, Christian Sautter on international economic affairs, and, for a while, Régis Debray. The importance of this staff was enhanced partly because Mitterrand's foreign ministers (Claude Cheysson until December 1984; then Roland Dumas) were not exceptional figures, and because many key diplomatic posts were given to political loyalists of varying competence rather than to professionals.

Mitterrand's own performance in foreign affairs amounted to a contradictory mixture of a few solid successes, especially in Atlantic affairs (discussed below), with some major failures in the Third World and the eruption of one of the biggest scandals touching on defense and security in recent French history. Probably the most serious and personally embarrassing embroglio for Mitterrand was France's unsuccessful involvement in the civil war in Chad, a country marked by chaotic politics and repeated French military interventions since the mid–1960s.[2] By 1983 France found itself backing the government of Hissène Habré, based in the south, against the Libyan-backed forces of Goukouni Oueddeye in the north. After direct Libyan interventions against Habré, in August 1983, Mitterrand launched Operation Manta and committed over 3,000 troops to Chad until the opposing forces were pushed back up to the sixteenth parallel. French negotiations with Libyan leader Mummar Khadaffi led to an agreement of September 17, 1984, providing for the simultaneous retreat of French and Libyan forces from Chad, which the French carried out right away. Although Khadaffi's record for unreliability might have led the French to proceed with extreme caution, Mitterrand inexplicably went to Cyprus on November 15 to meet with the Arab world's most disreputable figure and to seal their accord. Intelligence surveillance soon revealed that Tripoli was not withdrawing its forces, so that France and its president were clearly duped in this affair, costing Mitterrand credibility both at home and among African states. By September 1985 Libya was reinforcing its forces in the north and, despite direct warnings from Paris, launched another attack on the south on February 10, 1986, forcing France once again to provide material and air support assistance to the government. Although Mitterrand could scarcely be blamed for failing to resolve the intractable problems of Chad, the lack of elementary precautions in dealing with the Libyan regime revealed serious weaknesses in presidential direction of foreign policy and an inability to safeguard the creditibility of Mitterrand himself.

It is difficult to ascertain whether problems like the Chadian affair stemmed from poor judgment on Mitterrand's part, ill-conceived advice from his counsellors, or (most likely) a combination of such factors. Toward the end of the Socialists' five years in power, two incidents tended to confirm that trust, openness and common sense were too often lacking in the management of France's security affairs by Mitterrand and his key aides. The Greenpeace affair in 1985 was especially damaging to the credibility of the Socialists and left many unanswered questions about the wisdom and integrity of leading officials, including the president.[3] On July 10, 1985, the *Rainbow Warrior*, a ship belonging to the confrontational Greenpeace environmentalist group, was sabotaged with the loss of one life in the New Zealand harbor of Auckland, where it was preparing to mount a challenge to the French underground nuclear testing program at the Pacific atoll of Mururoa. France initially denied any responsibility in the action, even though Prime Minister Laurent Fabius learned on July 16 that the French secret service attached to the Ministry of Defense, the Direction Générale de la Sécurité Exterieure (DGSE), was engaged in some kind of anti-Greenpeace operation in New Zealand, and Mitterrand was apparently informed the next day.

It became increasingly evident that agents of the DGSE were directly involved in the ship sabotage, and public pressure forced the government to appoint an independent investigator, Bernard Tricot, to investigate the affair. A report absolving the government of responsibility for the sinking of the ship was released on August 27. Nevertheless, there was mounting skepticism, and on September 17 *Le Monde* published revelations from within the government implicating the minister of defense, Charles Hernu, and the full scandal was brought out into the open. On September 20, the head of the DGSE, Admiral Pierre Locoste, was dismissed, while Hernu resigned and was replaced by Paul Quilès; on September 22, Fabius admitted official French responsibility in the sinking of the *Rainbow Warrior*, contending that responsibility for approving the operation was Hernu's. Fabius defended France's right to protect its nuclear testing program as an essential aspect of national security, but indicated that political responsibility for the bungled operation and subsequent cover-up within the government lay with Hernu, whose resignation was supposed to put the affair to rest.

Nevertheless, some major questions about the quality of judgment and sense of responsibility at the highest levels of the Socialist-run state remained unanswered. One issue was how much Mitterrand himself may have known about the operation and its scope before July 10, or the extent to which he may have been deceived until late September by Defense Minister Hernu, a close colleague for thirty years and ostensibly one of the most loyal ministers and associates of the president. The general impression created by the Greenpeace affair was that a Socialist president and government, and one of its hitherto most respected ministers, had embarrassed France with an ill-conceived and generally incompetent state security operation. The Socialists then dealt with the matter in a way that discredited the minister of defense and revealed a tissue of duplicity and debilitating political rivalries among senior officials. The principal reason the affair did not do more damage to the Socialists was the opposition's unwillingness to criticize actions in defense of the French nuclear weapons program, or do further damage to the country's defense and security forces.

Mitterrand was not directly tainted by the Greenpeace incident, but both he and his prime minister were later damaged by Mitterrand's curious decision, apparently undertaken without consultations, to receive Polish leader Jaruzelski "unofficially" at the Elysée on December 4, 1985. This was bound to be controversial in France, given the extreme reaction there to the declaration of martial law and suppression of Solidarity in Poland, and the president was unable to give any convincing reason for the meeting or to claim any concessions from General Jaruzelski as a result of it. The incident resulted in an unprecedented declaration by Fabius to the National Assembly on December 4, when he stated that he was "troubled" by the decision and thereby became the first prime minister of the Fifth Republic publicly to disassociate himself from a presidential foreign policy decision. Once again, there were no dramatic long-term repercussions from this incident, but it did confirm a penchant for awkward, even inept, foreign policy decisions while the Socialists were in power.

DÉTENTE AND ENTENTE IN ATLANTIC RELATIONS

The fulcrum of French postwar security policy has been the relationship with the United States and the principal institution linking European and U.S. security interests, the Atlantic Alliance. What the French Atlantic relationship is at any particular time largely organizes French policy on East-West issues and relations with the Soviet Union, in the West European arena, and even in the Third World, where France is the most influential Western power after the United States. Although France has remained within the Atlantic Alliance and has been a basically loyal ally during the period of the Fifth Republic, there were important tensions and discord while Charles de Gaulle was president and carried out France's withdrawal from the NATO military organization in 1966. Although relations generally improved after 1968, disagreements arose frequently enough to sustain the impression of a troubled French-American partnership. Between 1971 and 1977, the Socialist Party adopted its own version of a French antipathy to the Atlantic order, based on a denigration of the Soviet political-military threat and a focus on the danger posed by U.S.-led international capitalism to a future Socialist France. After the 1977 rupture of the Socialist-Communist union of the left, however, this attitude began to change, and at a January 1978 PS meeting on security policy the Socialists declared their loyalty to the Western economic security system. Voicing a newly discovered enthusiasm for the Atlantic security connection, Mitterrand cited with approval the Gaullist precedent of maintaining basic Atlantic ties outside of NATO; he even insisted that "the Americans ought to know that we will be loyal allies, if there is a war and if this war is provoked by the desires of outside powers."[4]

Once in power, Mitterrand and his government initiated a long period of unusual cordiality in French-American ties that has survived some policy conflicts and may mark a fundamental shift in bilateral relations from a norm of conflict to one of somewhat wary cooperation. On the personal level of relations between heads of state, Mitterrand and Ronald Reagan established a friendly working relationship at their first meeting at the Ottawa summit of the leading industrial powers in the spring of 1981, and this has helped the two countries through any rough patches. Moreover, there was apparently a major tactical decision taken early by Mitterrand and his foreign policy advisors to eschew the usual French practice of engaging in public confrontations with the United States, and, instead, to rely on "quiet diplomacy" to try to affect U.S. policies. This was an expansion of the approach followed by Valéry Giscard d'Estaing, who sought a *décrispation* (relaxation) of tensions with Washington, but the Socialists were more consistent and more successful after 1981.

A preoccupation with their audacious domestic economic and social policies was another reason the Socialists sought an entente with the United States, since throughout their period in power France was exceptionally vulnerable to international economic pressures. Mitterrand may also have hoped that French cooperation in the security arena would bring U.S. concessions in the economic one, where significant problems were expected and soon erupted. He was explicit on this point in July 1981, when he exposed an Atlantic linkage doctrine, contending that allies "cannot wish for more political and military homogeneity in the Atlantic Alliance and still indulge in self-centered behavior in economic affairs."[5] Mitterrand's conciliatory Atlantic posture failed to produce any such U.S. concessions, however. France's economic problems under the Socialists meant that Paris became a *demandeur* in the West and was forced to submit to international constraints from a position of weakness. Profligate domestic spending on welfare and social measures helped move France from a virtual equilibrium in the balance of trade in the spring of 1981 to a deficit of 102 billion francs in 1982 and forced three devaluations between October 1981 and March 1983. Despite various austerity measures, the trade deficit remained high, at 64 billion francs in 1983, 35 billion in 1984, and 30 billion in 1985. The new economic policy instituted in March 1983 was showing major salutary effects only in late 1985 and early 1986, so throughout their period in power potential Socialist audacity in foreign affairs was hampered by a debilitated and dependent economy.

The new pro-U.S. and neo-Atlanticist approach pursued by a Socialist France remained predominant throughout Mitterrand's period in charge of French foreign and security policy, even though his own attitudes often seemed obscure and perhaps even confused as he attempted to combine Gaullist, pragmatic, Socialist and Atlanticist policy approaches. An independent and critical Gaullism was evident in statements made as late as 1980, when Mitterrand did not expect to be elected president and felt free to write that he was "no more attached to the Atlantic Alliance than a Rumanian or Pole is to the Warsaw Pact," and that he would be satisfied with a situation which would render "the Alliance" defunct— particularly since it was based on "a fiction" of U.S. intervention in Europe in the case of Soviet aggression.[6] Although criticism of the United States was toned down after Mitterrand moved into the Elysée, he did indicate a continuing dissatisfaction with the "scope and content of the Atlantic Alliance." As late as March 1982, Mitterrand could still "hope that this alliance can be more coherent," but had to admit that "there are no real plans, no preliminary negotiations." With disillusionment as well as resignation, he added that the alliance "is not a living alliance. It is being pulled apart all the time."[7]

By 1983 it was evident that the French Socialists had never had any clear idea of how to revitalize the Atlantic security system and instead were caught up in an ad hoc policy of accommodating the United States by trying to improve the atmosphere of Atlantic ties. Thus, in June 1982, despite rising French-American tensions, Mitterrand found himself able to praise the Atlantic Alliance as one of France's "two pillars of security" along with its nuclear force. He also felt comfortable enough to break tradition and attend a June 1982 alliance dinner held for heads of state in Bonn, to have Premier Pierre Mauroy attend a working meeting of heads of state or government, and to invite the alliance leaders to meet in Paris for the spring 1983 session. Although such developments were important in terms of political symbolism, they fit easily within the parameters of the Gaullist design for continued membership in the Alliance but autonomy from the NATO military organization. Mitterrand's France also remained independent-minded enough to refuse an invitation to attend an ad hoc Western summit organized by Reagan in New York in October 1985, and to oppose the United States on a number of important policy issues involving international trade, Third World affairs, defense policy (SDI), and East-West relations. Perhaps the only firm conclusion to be drawn from the ambivalent pattern of French-U.S. relations under Mitterrand was that they represented a certain normalization of bilateral ties. They may mark the end of a general postwar pattern of conflict despite a formal alliance, while inaugurating a more mature, dedramatized relationship that allows for clashes of interest in the context of a firm partnership recognized as essential and genuinely valued by both allies.

The main source of good French-American relations in the context of the Atlantic Alliance apparently was a convergence of views about the Soviet military threat in Europe that brought France closer to the security views of Washington than at any time in recent years.[8] This consensus can be traced back to a 1977 shift in the Socialist Party's position, which by 1980 led Mitterrand and his colleagues openly to condemn the Soviet occupation of Afghanistan as well as the growth of Soviet military strength aimed at Western Europe—in contrast to slavish PCF support for Soviet interventions and Giscard's seeming diffidence on these issues. Although in 1979–80 the Socialists did not directly support the NATO decision to offset the SS–20 threat by deploying 108 Pershing–2 and 462 Ground Launched Cruise Missiles (GLCM), Mitterrand did focus his criticism on the Soviets and, after his election as president, adopted a firm position by urging France's Atlantic allies to deploy their missiles unless the Soviets agreed to withdraw theirs. This somewhat curious campaign on behalf of a NATO decision that did not directly involve France led to one of the most daring and dramatic incidents of Mitterrand's presidency, his speech of January 20, 1983, to the West German Bundestag urging France's principal European partner to eschew pacifist, neutralist and antinuclear temptations and fulfill its responsibilities as a partner in Western security affairs by agreeing to deploy the missiles.

For about the first two years of Mitterrand's term, French-Soviet relations were exceptionally poor. This was, first, because of France's open criticism of the SS–20 deployment and support for NATO retaliation and, second, because of Afghanistan and later the Soviet-backed imposition of martial law and suppression of the Solidarity movement in Poland. A somewhat antagonistic approach continued throughout the period of Socialist rule and was strongly backed by public opinion as well as all political forces except the Communists. Like most other West European countries, however, French hostility toward the Kremlin remained moderate in comparison with U.S. policies because Paris refused to succumb to the view that détente had collapsed entirely. Different French and U.S. perspectives on this issue led to one of the strongest clashes between the two countries during this period, over contracts tied to a Soviet–West European gas pipeline. The most important lesson of the pipeline dispute was the confirmation of a persistent French and general West European commitment to partial and restrained political-economic détente, despite the intensification of the East-West military confrontation in Europe and elsewhere.

By early 1982 the French and other Western Europeans had proved sensitive to Reagan administration arguments against subsidizing the Soviet economy through low government-guaranteed export credits. Paris had responded by raising the cost of such credits from 7.8 percent to 8.5 percent in October 1981, and finally to 12 percent by the spring of 1982. The United States had also raised the issues of reinforcing restrictions on trade in technology with military applications; some officials in France were reported to be arguing against supplying some of the computer monitoring equipment for the gas pipeline.[9] Soviet-French pipeline negotiations were coming to a conclusion just as the Polish crisis broke out, and there was an intense debate within the government over the wisdom of signing such an important accord just after the Soviet-sponsored coup. Although there was a range of opinions with strong support for postponing the agreement, there was no support for the U.S. sanctions option, and Mitterrand finally decided against even a delay. On January 22, 1982, Paris and Moscow signed an agreement that France would take 8 billion cubic meters of gas a year for twenty-five years after 1984, raising French dependence on Soviet natural gas from 18 percent in 1981 to 31 percent by 1990, or to about 5 or 6 percent of total French energy sources after a decade.[10] As part of the deal, France was granted about $1 billion out of the $10 billion in Soviet contracts with the West to construct the pipeline, financed with credits furnished by French banks.

After the United States imposed an embargo on U.S. firms planning to participate in building the pipeline, Washington tried without success to get its European allies to abandon the project with arguments based on the dangers of dependence on Soviet energy sources, the value to the Soviet Union of long-term hard currency earnings, and possible risks of sharing the technology involved in the pipeline. At the June 1982 Versailles summit, the French and other West Europeans thought they had ended the U.S. campaign with a vague compromise agreement to limit export credits to the Soviet Union and to study all aspects of East-West trade.

Then, amid growing European-American economic controversies over subsidized steel exports, hard-liners in the Pentagon and on the U.S. National Security Council convinced President Ronald Reagan to abandon his accommodating attitude at Versailles, and on June 18 the president extended the embargo to apply to all U.S. companies abroad and to European companies manufacturing under U.S. license. In France, such a ban would have applied to the rotor components manufactured by Alsthom-Atlantique, valves manufactured by Rockwell, and pipeline booster-compressors built by Dressler-France. Although all European countries involved in the pipeline project rejected the claim that the U.S. government would exert this kind of control over American subsidiaries abroad or over American licensing agreements, the French reaction was by far the most determined in terms of countermeasures, as well as in escalating rhetorical attacks on U.S. economic policy. Citing reasons of state and national interest, the Socialist government ordered Alsthom-Atlantique to honor its Soviet contract and furnish the forty spare sets of rotor components. Furthermore, in late August, the government acted under an *ordonnance* of January 1959 and "requisitioned" the activities of Dressler-France, obliging it to disobey its parent U.S. firm and ship its three completed compressors to the Soviet Union and finish work on the eighteen remaining on order.

In addition to an aggressive rejection of Washington's unilateral but international embargo, the French used the dispute as an occasion to vent their pent-up frustration at what they perceived as insensitive and egotistical U.S. economic policies. Embarrassed by the fiasco of the expensive Versailles summit, Mitterrand criticized U.S. actions as "restrictive, oppressive, unfair, and dangerous, creating a veritable disguised protectionism.'' The United States, he added, was guilty of a ''grave breach of solidarity'' in reneging on the Versailles accord on East-West economic relations.[11] Foreign Trade Minister Michel Jobert, Finance Minister Jacques Delors and Foreign Minister Claude Cheysson added that wild fluctuations in the dollar's exchange rate and U.S. interest-rate policies were examples of American insensitivity to the needs of its allies, and examples of an American abidication of ''the responsibilities of international 'leadership.' ''[12] In the face of French resistance bolstered by firm support from the Federal Republic of Germany and other Western European governments, the Reagan administration was gradually forced to retreat from its Atlantic sanctions design and, in November 1982, to accept a face-saving agreement that merely restated existing allied commitments to review a range of East-West trade and financial arrangements, and perhaps adopt more restrictive approaches when technology with military applications was at stake.

The French refusal to participate in the accord symbolized the Mitterrand government's concern for the appearance of independence in an area of economic policy that was especially sensitive for a besieged economy. The U.S. retreat continued until East–West trade issues ceased to play much of a role by the time of the June 1983 Williamsburg summit. This represented a partial victory for France and indicated that Paris was still capable of a stubborn assertion of interest on occasion. The incident also confirmed that most of Washington's allies believed that the disruption of East–West détente in the military arena could be insulated from economic and other relations, even if Paris and the others were willing to tighten up on some trade in sensitive technologies.

From 1983 through 1985 there was a gradual but limited warming trend in French–Soviet relations that was in line with the partial revival of the superpower dialogue and general East-West détente. Bilateral political ties at the top level were restored after a French-imposed hiatus when Cheysson visited Moscow in February 1983 and the Mitterrand went in June 1984 for the only time in the first five years of his presidency. Soviet leader Mikhail Gorbachev made Paris his first foray into the West after assuming his responsibilities in the Kremlin; but the October 1985 visit was notable mainly for Mitterrand's refusal to yield to the Soviet position and allow France's nuclear force to become involved in East–West arms negotiations until the superpowers themselves had made substantial cuts.

The traditional French attitude toward the future of East–West affairs has been organized aound the ''Yalta'' theme of somehow overcoming a division of Europe attributed to the will of the superpowers. The Gaullist approach was to loosen France's ties to the United States within the Atlantic system while capitalizing on France's independence within the West to establish a position as a privileged Soviet interlocutor in the long process of overcoming the division of Europe. The closer identification with the Atlantic system that garnered near-unanimous domestic support after 1981 has led some analysts to conclude that ''the myth of Yalta is at last moribund in France.''[13] As an aspiration for the future, however, Mitterrand has still felt compelled to evoke the image of a post-Yalta system (*"dépassement de Yalta"*) which is necessarily vague but certainly involves the construction of a more viable West European economic, political and military order within the Atlantic system and as a potential bridge to the East. Under the Socialists, however, Mitterrand's European policy was too often sidetracked by the tedious debate over British budget contributions and uninspiring matters such as agricultural compensatory payments. One of the apparent successes of the period, Europe's enlargement to include Spain and Portugal, was essentially an increasingly unwieldy "Europe" lacking social and political harmony or direction. To stimulate European political cooperation, Mitterrand and Chancellor Helmut Kohl launched the idea of a Treaty of European Union at the Milan summit of June 1985, but the notion floundered and finally emerged as a minimalist agreement to abandon the practice of unanimous voting and expand European political cooperation. In general, France's European initiatives during this period provide a mixed and rather ambivalent record, marked more by aspiration and rhetoric than inspiration and accomplishment.

The axis of French European policy has been a special relationship with West Germany, which was institutionalized by the de Gaulle–Adenauer treaty of 1963. The intensification of this relationship at Mitterrand's urging was one of the genuine successes of his presidency. During his first couple of years in office, Mitterrand was preoccupied by the possibility of a weaker West German attachment to the West, after the German public and elements in the Social Democratic Party and the Green movement reacted to the Euromissile debate by flirting with pacificism and neutralism. His reaction was to link the Federal Republic firmly to the West by urging Bonn to make its own contribution to the Atlantic security effort, while France, though still independent, was clearly supportive of NATO security efforts that were in its own as well as others' national interests. While reinforcing the Atlantic connection, France tried to put new life into bilateral security cooperation in the hope that it might lay the groundwork for a more general revival of cooperative West European efforts in a forum such as the West European Union. Thus, in October 1982 Mitterrand and West Germany's new conservative chancellor, Helmut Kohl, made military ties the focus of their first summit meeting and something of a benchmark for future French-German relations. The two leaders decided to revive and intensify their defense discussions under the 1963 treaty, and particularly to discuss the implications of France's development of the new longer-range Hades tactical nuclear weapon and a neutron bomb, both of which would affect their joint security interests. French sources left no doubt that they harbored hopes that discussions might lay the groundwork for a European defense system more independent of NATO and the United States, though it would be complementary to the Atlantic security system and not antagonistic.[14] Progress in this area was necessarily slow, cautious and out of the public eye, but in February 1986 the talks did produce an agreement to consult on the conditions governing the use of French "prestrategic" or tactical nuclear weapons, in the case of aggression against West Germany. This cautious but deliberate "Europeanization" of France's security policy, within a temporarily secure Atlantic framework, was an important development during the Mitterrand presidency, one which opened up new perspectives for fulfilling the grand design favoring a more independent Europe laid down by de Gaulle during the 1960s.

DEFENSE POLICY: INDEPENDENCE AND A EUROPEAN VOCATION

The heart of General de Gaulle's security legacy to France is the *Force nucléaire stratégique* (FNS) and a set of guidelines maintaining French independence from U.S. and NATO defense plans but permitting limited military cooperation in the Atlantic and European arenas. The Socialists adhered to these guidelines and took some important decisions to expand France's nuclear arensal. In terms of formal strategic theory, the Socialists stuck to a fairly strict national defense concept. In practice, however, they expanded France's conditional cooperation with NATO and West Germany, while shifts in force structure and other developments indicated a slow and cautious move toward cooperation with allies on the German central front.

In the spring of 1981, the Socialists inherited responsibility for a triad of nuclear weapons systems based on the original Gaullist design of the 1960s. The oldest component was some thirty-six aging Mirage-IV aircraft dispersed over seven bases. The second component of the FNS consisted of eighteen S–2 IRBMs grouped in two squadrons at hardened sites set amidst the lavender fields of the Plateau d'Albion in Haute-Provence. The third and most important part, designated as the *Force océanique stratégique*, were the five missile-launching nuclear submarines then in service. A submarine was equipped with sixteen missiles, each with a range of 3,300 kilometers and armed with a one-megaton thermonuclear warhead. Plans for modernization called for all but the first submarine to receive MRV-type M.4 missiles with a range of 4,000 kilometers and six warheads of 150 kilotons each. French land and air forces were also equipped with the Pluton tactical nuclear weapons, due to be replaced in the early 1990s with the more advanced long-range Hades system.[15]

After taking control of the government, the Socialists confirmed existing plans for modernizing and expanding France's nuclear armory. One of Mitterrand's earliest decisions as president (in July 1981) was to approve the construction of a seventh missile-launching submarine (put on hold by Giscard d'Estaing) by 1994. Later, at an important meeting of the presidential defense council on October 30, 1981, Mitterrand decided to go ahead with plans to create a mobile land-based IRBM force (the "SX," later postponed indefinitely), to proceed with the development of the Hades tactical nuclear weapon, and, instead of scuttling the Mirage-IV force, to keep fifteen planes in service after 1985 and equip them with advanced air-to-ground medium-range nuclear missiles, enhancing the penetration capability of this dated attack system. The Socialist attention to defense and military security was also reflected in the government's first defense budget, for 1982, which increased defense spending by 17.63 percent over 1981, amounting to a planned 4 percent real increase after accounting for expected inflation. These ambitions were transformed into a long-term (1984–88) military program law for modernizing the armed forces which, however, was a partial victim of Socialist economic mismanagement that forced delays and defense budget cuts, so that during 1985 a major controversy erupted over shortfalls in funding.[16] Whatever their difficulties, the Socialist period of responsibility for France's defense saw a continued augmentation in nuclear capability, including the launching of a sixth nuclear missile-launching submarine, so that with the new warheads France should have the ability to target 480 sites by 1991.

A major dilemma for Socialist defense policy was their reaction to the U.S. Strategic Defense Initiative (SDI) and their estimate of its possible effects on American-European security ties and the viability of the French nuclear deterrent. The main fear expressed in France was that an intensified Soviet-American competition for space-based missile defense systems would degrade the penetration capabilities of the relatively small French strategic force while intensifying the superpower arms race. For this and other reasons, the Socialist government opposed the militarization of space except for intelligence purposes and, along with many others in Europe and the United States, questioned the viability of the Reagan program and worried about its implications for European security. Specifically, Defense Minister Quilès claimed that the deployment of such a system might be extremely destabilizing in its transitional stages and, in any case, Western Europe would be left vulnerable to IRBMs.[17] Despite this position, the Socialists allowed French firms to compete for SDI contracts while Paris attempted to launch its own, smaller-scale European project—labeled "Eureka"—to encourage the development of advanced European technologies similar to those pursued under SDI. The Socialists also initiated a program to develop miniaturized warheads with enhanced penetration capabilities designed to foil missile defense systems. Finally, they began studies focused on the technological capabilities involved in space-based missile defense systems, to learn how to counteract them and perhaps how to develop a viable defense system for France and Europe.

In terms of defense and deterrence strategy, the Socialists inherited the doctrines from the Gaullist era that stressed the proportional deterrent value of a national nuclear force independent of superpower forces but linked to them through a political alliance system. A major point of ambivalence in French strategy has been whether to consider contiguous territory, i.e, West Germany, merely an approach to the "national sanctuary" and therefore a zone of limited "first battle" engagement of French forces, or more of an "extended sanctuary" directly linked to France with a potentially major commitment of conventional and tactical nucear forces in defense of Germany.[18] Under Giscard d'Estaing, the French appeared to favor the latter approach, foreseeing early and extended participation by French forces on West German soil, prior to an attack on French soil that would trigger the strategic deterrent itself. This development raised issues concerning possible French collaboration with NATO, which has retained responsibility for defense on the German front, and was therefore controversial in France.

After they took office, the Socialists responded to the debate by returning to fairly narrow, sanctuary-oriented strategic concepts that seemed to circumscribe possible military collaboration with NATO along American flexible response guidelines. Reasserting France's autonomy of decision as the key to military policy, Chief of Staff Jeannou Lacaze said in September 1981, "The first goal [is], in all circumstances, our complete freedom of decision and assessment so that our country cannot be automatically engaged in a conflict in which we would not feel involved."[19] Although most observers have felt that informal French-NATO cooperation and joint planning actually expanded under the Socialists, public French comments limited this to the nonnuclear forces, while strategic announcements insisted that the Pluton tactical nuclear weapon had reverted to a strictly prestrategic "warning strike" status excluding the flexible response war plans favored by NATO and the United States. This was also the rationale given for the Socialist decision to develop and apparently produce a neutron bomb, which Mitterrand indicated would not draw France into a "forward battle," or flexible response philosophy, but rather would serve to keep it in the forefront of military technology and help counter the Soviet arms advantage in Europe.[20]

These pronouncements stressing the Fifth Republic's traditional military and strategic independence were, however, contradicted by other developments that appeared to indicate a growing French interest in guaranteeing the security of West Germany and the central front.[21] The Socialist innovation of clearly designating the Soviet Union as the primary military threat to France and the object of French deterrence was one step in this direction. Another was the creation of a Rapid Action Force (*Force d'Action Rapide*, FAR), a mobile, 47,000-man organization capable of deployment outside of Europe or placement on the German forward line during a European crisis or conflict. Finally, along with generally better relations with the United States and in the context of Atlantic Alliance affairs, the intensification of French–West German military discussions and commitments to consult during a crisis involving the possible use of French tactical nuclear forces confirmed an evolution away from a stress on independent defense toward a more overtly "European" concept of national security. This was not really in contradiction with Gaullist ideals, since the strategic military autonomy stressed in previous years had been a function of limited means and directed mostly against U.S. domination of NATO. Gaullist France had always claimed a West European vocation for her nuclear-centered defense and by the 1980s appeared to be moving closer to implementing this design.

The period of Socialist rule might turn out to be one of transition in which one set of narrow strategic guidelines slowly yielded to a more expansive conception of nuclear security and deterrence. An open French debate on this issue surfaced between 1983 and 1985, when some observers detected a possible breakdown in Gaullist doctrines to the point where France might somehow include West Germany within its zone of vital national interests subject to nuclear deterrence, and perhaps commit itself to a flexible conventional-nuclear defense of Germany coordinated with NATO.[22] This overstated the pace of developments, which are bound to proceed slowly and face many obstacles, such as the need to maintain the integrity of France's military forces and decision-making from NATO. Nevertheless, during the 1986 Assembly election campaign, virtually all parties (except the PCF) were considering, suggesting or advocating various kinds of new French conventional and nuclear commitments to West Germany. It seemed likely, then, that the Socialists had launched a process of restructuring national security commitments and capabilities in a way that enhances West European defense cooperation without damaging an Atlantic framework that was also valued by the French. This "Europeanization" of France's security policy had acquired such a compelling logic by 1986 that the trend seemed likely to continue its cautious progress under any future French regime. Thus, although the Socialist legacy in foreign and security policy includes some outright failures and many ambivalent accomplishments, they did appear to have managed the difficult feat of reconciling a form of restrained Atlanticism with the Gaullist heritage of national independence and European aspiration in a way that may allow for new, creative innovations in European and Atlantic security that can benefit all of the West.

NOTES

1. See Michael M. Harrison, *The Reluctant Ally: France and Atlantic Security* (Baltimore: Johns Hopkins University Press, 1981); and Harrison, "Mitterrand's France in the Atlantic System," *Political Science Quarterly* 99, No. 2 (Summer 1984): 219–46 (sections of this 1984 article are incorporated in the chapter presented here).

2. For background, see Elce and Hesse, "La France et la crise du Tchad d'Août 1983: un rendez-vous manqué avec l'Afrique," *Politique Etrangère* 50, No. 2 (Summer 1985): 411–418.

3. The French press was full of reports about this incident. See, for example, *Le Point*, September 30, 1985, and *Le Monde*, September 27, 1985.

4. Quoted in *Le Monde*, January 10, 1978.

5. *Le Monde*, July 2, 1981.

6. François Mitterrand, *Ici et maintenant* (Paris: Fayard, 1980), pp. 241–42.

7. *Le Monde*, March 15, 1982.

8. See the discussion by Denis Delbourg, "Est-Ouest: contre vents et marées," *Politique Etrangère* 50, No. 2 (Summer 1985): 321–38.

9. *Le Monde*, October 21, 1981. As a measure of the varied economic stakes in East–West trade, in 1980 it amounted to $23.8 billion for West Germany, $10.21 billion for France and $5.28 billion for the United States. As a percentage of foreign trade, this

amounted to 6.2 percent, 4.2 percent and 1.12 percent, respectively (OECD Main Economic Indicators).

10. By comparison, West Germany planned to take 10.5 billion cubic meters a year, and its natural gas dependence on Soviet sources would rise from 17 percent in 1981 to 25 to 30 percent by 1984. *Le Monde*, January 25, 1982.

11. Agence France-Presse dispatch, June 29, 1982.

12. Jacques Delors, quoted in *Le Monde*, June 26, 1982.

13. The quote is from an unpublished essay by Alfred Grosser.

14. See reports in *Le Monde* for the period around October 22, 1982, and in the *Washington Post*, October 22–23, 1982.

15. See Robbin F. Laird, "French Nuclear Forces in the 1980s and the 1990s," *Comparative Strategy* 4, No. 4 (1984): 387–412.

16. The retiring head of the general staff, General Jeannou Lacaze, claimed in mid–1985 that an additional 35 billion francs would be required to meet the needs of various programs due to an underestimation of costs by the staff of the minister of defense. (*Le Point*, July 1, 1985).

17. *Le Monde*, November 13, 1985.

18. See the discussion in Harrison, *The Reluctant Ally*; and David S. Yost, *France's Deterrent Posture and Security in Europe. Part I: Capabilities and Doctrine. Part II: Strategic and Arms Control Implications* (London: I.I.S.S. Adelphi Papers Nos. 194 and 195, 1984–1985).

19. "La Politique militaire," *Défense Nationale* 37 (November 1981): 9.

20. See Mitterrand's press conference of June 9, 1982, in *Le Monde*, June 11, 1982.

21. See the informed discussion by François Heisbourg, a former aide to Hernu: "Défense et sécurité extérieure: le changement dans la continuité," *Politique Etrangère* 50, No. 2 (Summer 1985): 377–88.

22. The debate was launched by experts such as Pierre Lallouche but soon got bogged down. See Lallouche, "La France dans 'l'après-Pershing,' " *Politique Etrangère* 48, No. 4 (Winter 1983): 859–78.

4

Education: Cultural Persistence and Institutional Change

MICHALINA VAUGHAN

THE WEIGHT OF THE PAST

The educational problems arising in contemporary France and the elaborate but largely unsuccessful governmental attempts to solve them are only understandable in their historical context. The existence of a centralized state system, introduced at secondary and higher levels by Napoleon, and supplemented by the provision of primary schooling under the Third Republic, has necessarily entailed a degree of rigidity. Adaptation to the pressures of expansion and the exigencies of modernization (with its somewhat contradictory aspects of lessening inequalities and broadening vocationalism) has therefore been a protracted and painful process. It has been delayed by the political risks of carrying out reforms which affronted vested interests, both those of families whose children benefited from the existing system and particularly those of a teaching profession whose hierarchical structure has been persistently defended by powerful unions. The preservation of the status quo was legitimated by a concern for the defense of French culture. The pursuit of excellence in a meritocratic system was held to be inseparable from the provision of academic secondary schooling for an elite, as a preliminary to higher education. This legacy of the Napoleonic system was epitomized by the role of the *baccalauréat* (secondary leaving certificate) as a passport to university enrollment.

The need for reform was widely understood in the interwar period and became imperative after the Liberation, as secondary enrollment grew and the country industrialized rapidly. It was only under the Fifth Republic, however, that the political will emerged to bridge the gap between types of schooling dispensed in the middle years.[1] Gradualist policies designed to undermine the prestige of the *baccalauréat* through the provision of alternative terminal qualifications (technological rather than academic) were implemented in the mid–1960s. By then the pressure of numbers was such, however, that the universities could not cope, and overcrowding triggered the "events" of 1968.[2]

The Faure law (*loi d'orientation de l'enseignement supérieur*) of November 1968, which dismantled the Napoleonic university, could be described as a Machiavellian compromise since it did not tackle the crucial issue of selection.[3] The privilege of the *bacheliers* was left intact, as was the prerogative of *grandes écoles*[4] to impose their own devices for selecting elite entrants by ruthless meritocratic competition. To prevent the *baccalauréat* from entailing an automatic right of access to university education would have involved a parallel *loi d'orientation de l'enseignement secondaire*, which de Gaulle held to be too dangerous to propose in the political climate of the time.[5] Only gradual change appeared expedient.

Adopted by parliament in July 1975,[6] the Haby reform was designed to reduce the distance between streams in the middle school and ultimately to reform the *baccalauréat* after parity of esteem had been secured for the vocational ones. It was to be introduced gradually from kindergarten (*école maternelle*) upwards, as the cohort progressed to primary and middle school. Each pupil's ascent was to be regulated by mental age—an emphasis on "self-selection" which was clearly liberal (i.e., child-centered rather than directive) but no less obviously inegalitarian. To the extent that children's intellectual development is affected by sociocultural background, a process of selection by reference to "purely individual" criteria actually confirms and perpetuates the hierarchies of stratification in the wider society. Since education is better able to reflect than to correct inequalities of life chances, the failure of Haby's single middle school was perhaps unavoidable. The law's assumption that a "minimum common knowledge" would be dispensed to all (a parallel, at secondary level, of the Third Republic's legislation on primary schooling) could not be enforced in practice. Not only did approximately one-third of the cohort entering the *collèges d'enseignement secondaire* fail to complete the course, up to 18 percent of children could not gain access to it at all.[7] Officials acknowledged and the teaching profession attacked the inability of the school to become an agency for social promotion.

The most controversial aspect of the Haby reform, redefining the role of the *baccalauréat*, was shelved by Haby's successor at the Ministry of Education, Christien Beullac, in 1979, two years before the date foreseen for its implementation in the *lycée* (i.e., the three terminal forms of the secondary cycle).[8] If politics is the art of the possible, the demotion of the *baccalauréat* from its mythical position as a bourgeois rite of passage was not a policy any government of the center-right could pursue without antagonizing its main supporters. Meanwhile the parties of the left would not advocate it, since they opposed the restriction of educational opportunities as antidemocratic. It could thus be argued that this second failure was as unavoidable on sociopolitical grounds as the first had been on socioeconomic ones.

THE ALIENATION OF THE TEACHING PROFESSION

Although Haby had been an educationalist prior to becoming minister of education and emphasized pedagogic rather than economic considerations throughout his tenure of office (1974–78), he did not gain the trust of the teachers' unions. They accused him of being more concerned with administrative efficiency than with the restructuring of educational opportunities, of being "a manager and an expert" rather than "a prophet and a visionary."[9] In particular they denounced the "revaluation of manual labor" as a disguised restoration of tracking in the middle school. Under cover of fitting the subjects taught to the mental aptitude of pupils, inequalities could be perpetuated, as the distinction between educational maladjustment and an underprivileged home background became blurred.

Ultimately the fate of any educational reform depends on the commitment of teachers to its objectives and its methods. The lack of this support proved very damaging. "Even in a country with a strong Jacobin tradition, a minister of education cannot, by waving his wand, impose a reform. . . . Headmasters . . . do not seem embarrassed, if [it] is not applied or is imperfectly implemented." Thus the most active unionists retained ability grouping, contrary to the provisions of the law, because "their conception of equality differed from that of the minister."[10] Similarly, a wide range of variations emerged in the additional tuition intended to help underachievers (*enseignement de soutien*). Its quality depended on whether teachers viewed it as a form of segregation or as truly remedial.

Even within a centralized educational system, governmental determination to bridge the gap between school and society could be undermined by the reluctance of the teaching profession to accept vocationalism as a worthwhile educational goal. Uninclined to back innovation and profoundly attached to traditional schooling, i.e., to the dissemination of general culture, the unions were bound to be suspicious of a right-wing government's "real" intentions. Individual teachers, even when they did not hold strong political views, did not favor the adaptation of the school to the requirements of a modern industrial society.

This somewhat conservative stance has often been blamed on the increasing employment of women.[11] In 1977–1978 two-thirds of the half-million teachers at work were female (280,000 of them at the primary level and the remainder at the secondary level). Since women entering the teaching profession tend to be of middle-class background and apolitical, they are inclined to interpret inequalities between pupils as natural rather than socially induced. They often lack the commitment of the "black hussars" (as the primary teachers of the Third Republic used to be called) and treat their career less as a social mission than as a job relatively easy to reconcile with the care of family and home.

However, this antifeminist point should not be labored. To the traditional male teacher, faithful to the republican tradition of social promotion through educational channels, the pupil sent to a CET (*collège d'enseignement technique*) to pursue the "short" technical secondary course has failed to derive full advantage of the school. A successful educational performance is one which turns a manual worker's son into a white-collar worker, so that he can leave his class of origin and, it is hoped, turn his children into professionals. Politically committed to social change, the majority of teachers are convinced that the progressive ped-agogical methods advocated by Haby do not serve either the cause of culture or the well-understood interests of able pupils from underprivileged homes. While they are more left-wing and more unionized than the majority of the French population, they retain a strong attachment to traditional methods of tuition, including early streaming and strong discipline.[12] A somewhat paradoxical blend of political radicalism and educational conservatism appears to prevail in a disunited teaching profession.

Disunity is the product of hierarchical divisions and of disparities in qualifi-cations, which increased during the 1950s and 1960s—a period of massive and occasionally hasty recruitment. The "education explosion"—related both to demographic growth and to rising aspirations—created an urgent demand for teaching staff. Between 1958 and 1974, an average of 14,000 secondary teachers were appointed each year. Thus the teaching profession is young: only 5 percent of secondary teachers were over fifty-five in 1975, while 33.5 percent of *agrégés* were under thirty[13] and one primary teacher in two was under thirty.[14] This age distribution made it feasible to bring teachers trained to *baccalauréat* level up to the standard of the *licence* (first degree) through the provision of in-service training. Yet, despite official awareness that such streamlining of the teaching profession was a crucial variable, the Haby reform did not refer to it. Ministerial commitment to it remained purely verbal. Procrastination may be understandable since the cost of upgrading the qualifications of all teachers from nursery school up to *lycée* (excluded) would have been about 3.63 percent of the yearly budget for education, not to mention that it would have affronted the powerful SNES (*Syndicat national des enseignants du second degré*). Parsimony in funding the in-service training that would have upgraded the qualifications of all secondary staff was accompanied by a decrease in the number of new teaching posts created by successive annual budgets. These state economies were officially justified by a decrease in birth rate from 1974 onwards (affecting school intakes as from 1977).

In the 1981 budget the saving on state schools was matched by an increase of 22 percent in the subsidies allocated by the ministry to private (i.e., predom-inantly Catholic) establishments. Not only did the teachers' unions argue that education was the Cinderella of state financing under right-wing governments, they actually denounced a conspiracy to restore clerical control. This issue, which had been a test of republicanism in the early twentieth century and had remained emotional throughout its first half, had been effectively defused under de Gaulle. Although it was included in the Socialist program and retained some mobilizing potency, especially among state school teachers, its importance within the armory of the left should be kept in perspective. It was mainly a part of a historical legacy rather than a blueprint for action. Though the reference to secularism helped rally more teachers to the Socialist opposition, the profession as a group had become alienated from the ruling majority over a long period of frustration in their professional activities. Furthermore, their political stance was indicative of the values and attitudes adopted by the age group and the educational category to which they belonged.[15] Yet the analogy with the Third Republic, flawed with regard to the impact of secularism on Socialist policies, was accurate insofar as it emphasized the role of the teaching profession in the new majority elected in the aftermath of Mitterrand's victory.

THE TEACHERS' REPUBLIC

The Third Republic had been sarcastically described as *"la République des Professeurs,"*[16] because of the increasing number of parliamentary seats held by *lycée*[17] and university teachers in the 1920s. By the same token, the Socialist victory in the legislative elections which followed Mitterrand's ascent to the presidency produced a *République des Enseignants*. One M.P. out of three had been either a primary school teacher (*instituteur*), or taught at secondary level or in a higher educational establishment. There were 160 *enseignants*, i.e., teachers at one of the three levels, elected in June 1981. Within the PS-MRG group (i.e., Socialists and Radicals) the proportion was 58 percent, illustrating the gradual takeover of the Socialist Party by the teaching profession.[18] This was a relatively new phenomenon since, until 1973, *instituteurs* tended to be more common within the Communist parliamentary group and university professors on the right of the political spectrum, while the former SFIO attracted secondary teachers. Under Giscard, the symbiosis between the teaching profession and Socialist politics grew steadily. Aided by the Socialist Party's move toward the center of the political spectrum, this trend highlighted both the willingness of educators to leave the school for the tribune and their ability to gain votes. It has been argued that professional discontent and loss of status encourage teachers and academics to opt out of education. Security of tenure—as civil servants— cushions them against the risk of electoral defeat, while their skills in public speaking and group leadership help them first during electoral campaigns, and later in parliamentary debates. Even the structure of the school year, with rel- atively long periods of leisure, provides an additional advantage for a political career.

In a sense, this inflow of educators into the ruling elite represents a departure from their former corporatism. Indeed, the defense of vested interests, coupled with academic traditionalism, turned the teachers' unions into natural adversaries of governmental modernizing reforms. Margaret Archer has argued convincingly that such resistance derived from the very nature of a centralized educational system in which "the only influence the professional interest group can exert is to block or obstruct governmental policy."[19] The corollary of this stance was a steady input of contributions to the program of the left while it was in opposition. Thus the Socialist plan for national education in 1978 and the related project put forward by Mitterrand during the electoral campaign in 1981 relied largely on proposals formulated by the various teachers' unions. Since these were not unanimous in their views on the way the cycles of education should fit together as a coherent system, they did not provide the new majority with a clear brief. It was obvious, however, that the philosophy implicit in the Haby reform, endorsed under Giscard on individualist and liberal grounds, was not acceptable to the teaching profession. Self-selection was denounced as an insidious version of inegalitarian policies, and child-centeredness as a disguise for the confirmation of privilege.[20] The FEN (*Fédération de l'education nationale*), which groups approximately half of teachers at all levels,[21] opted for a single teaching corps and for the abolition of all cleavages within a continuous educational process. In other words, there was to be no more segregation as an outcome of selection. The second strongest union, the SGEN (*Syndicat général de l'éducation nationale*), linked with the CFDT, claimed that priority should be given to nursery education for children under six, to compensate for the deficiencies of the home. Children were then to move on to a basic school and, at eleven, to a middle school, without any interruption until *lycée* entry age. There was to be a single teaching corps, and a systematic attempt at positive discrimination was to be made in favor of the disadvantaged at all levels, through setting up educational priority areas. Plans for the terminal forms and the *baccalauréat* remained rather vague. Politically progressive and academically conservative views, widespread within the teaching profession, have long been in conflict. As they remain difficult to reconcile, the new majority was not presented with a cohesive reform program. However, a series of initial decisions gave satisfaction to the unions, particularly during the "honeymoon" period.

Yet the issue of structural reforms, although the need for them was a central part of the Socialist program, was to prove controversial and downright disruptive. The relationship between the government, on the one hand, and the parliamentary majority and the teachers' unions, on the other, was irretrievably damaged in the debate prior to the Savary reform of higher education. Thus by the end of 1983, the honeymoon was over. An attempt to regain the support of the teaching profession was then made and yielded even worse results. The electoral pledge to restore the position of secular state schools, undermined by the growth of secondary denominational education under the Fifth Republic, could not be redeemed without risking an escalation of protest. As public opinion was mobilized by the right-wing opposition with the aid of the Catholic Church, President Mitterrand felt bound to withdraw a bill that had already been adopted by the National Assembly. At that stage, in June 1984, the new teachers' republic was defeated on an ideological issue whose importance was rooted in the history of the Third Republic. However, a number of innovations initiated under Savary were actually continued or implemented by his successor, Jean-Pierre Chevènement. Perhaps the greatest penalty attached to the reopening of the *école libre* versus secularism debate was that it overshadowed the real achievements of the Socialist administration in education.

THE SAVARY REFORM OF HIGHER EDUCATION

University reform has been inextricably bound, since before 1968, with the existence of selection by tested merit for entry into prestigious establishments and hence for elite membership. The *grandes écoles*, Napoleonic in origin,[22] owe their prestige to several factors. First is the level of knowledge required for passing the *concours d'entrée*, after two to three years of preliminary study in special terminal forms (mainly in the best Paris *lycées*) which bring entrants to the level of students who have completed the first cycle at university. Then the successful candidates, who receive the status of civil servants and are therefore remunerated by the state, are given the highest quality tuition available, with a vocational bias, but without any narrow specialization. Finally, they are graded at the *concours de sortie* (a competitive examination parallel to that which gives access to the school) and secure posts in the higher civil service according to their ranking. They retain the title of *ancien élève* (*de l'Ecole Polytechnique* or *de l'Ecole Normale Supérieure*) for the rest of their life, since it is more highly regarded than any degree. Not only do they gain the most desirable social and material rewards as members of a highly cohesive administrative elite, their *esprit de corps* and the prestige of their qualifications enable them to "spill over into the private sector"[23] by accepting directorships after resigning from the civil service (a practice known as *pantouflage*).

Acceptable in a democracy to the extent that they reward manifest ability, the *grandes écoles* have made intellectual elitism a feature of French vocational training. By an apparent contradiction, it was this pattern that was adopted in 1945 when the *Ecole Nationale d'Administration* was created to democratize recruitment into the higher administration.[24] It has also been widely imitated in organizing training establishments (some of them privately owned and fee paying) for an ever increasing range of technical and business management careers.[25] Reliance on selection and grading has been a source of popularity with future employers and, therefore, with applicants—at least with those whose families can afford the cost of preparation for entry and, in the minor schools, that of tuition. Therefore this network of establishments is also selective in its recruitment insofar as it discriminates against the less affluent. No reduction of social inequalities in the acquisition of "valuable" qualifications (i.e., of diplomas conducive to careers rather than to graduate unemployment) can occur without a reform of this sector, left outside the ambit of the Faure law.

The need for this reform was clearly perceived by the Socialist Party in opposition and spelt out in its 1977 educational plan. By contrast, the government, and in particular Alice Saunier-Seïté as minister for the universities, were favorable to a two-tier system. In fact, the scope of selection was widened to cover medical studies and entry to the IUTs (*Instituts Universitaires de Tech-*

nologie).[26] The whole policy of differentiation between centers of excellence and the so-called *universités-parkings* seemed calculated to restore selectiveness gradually by restricting the number of graduate courses available to the former category. Mass education at the higher level could only be tolerated within the first cycle of university studies. In addition, the Giscardian establishment, less respectful of the Napoleonic tradition than the Gaullists and more influenced by the American pattern, encouraged competition among the universities. Although the "batting order" was alleged to depend on academic criteria, it was no secret that when the senior staff was politically dependable, official support (i.e., credit allowances and recognition granted to graduate courses) would be more readily forthcoming. As a result, more able students would be attracted and a self-fulfilling prophecy would operate and would justify further privileges.

On becoming minister of education, Savary changed the style of relationships with the universities. Henceforth recognition for second and third cycle (i.e., master and doctoral) courses (*habilitation*) was no longer a one-sided imperative decision. From July 1981 onwards, an appeal could be made against negative ministerial decisions. Another immediate provision was the replacement of thirteen rectors (nearly all appointed during Giscard's presidency) and of the vice-chancellor of Paris, a former member of Saunier-Seïté's cabinet. Although these administrative decisions were denounced by the new opposition as a witch-hunt, they were in fact the reversal of earlier decisions inspired by political considerations. So it could not be argued that this was a vendetta, but rather the predictable consequence of a politicization systematically introduced by the former minister for the universities. Other significant but relatively small-scale reversals of policy included a repeal of the Savage law of 1980 on the composition of university councils, which had favored tenured professors and imposed a quorum on student representation.[27] An increase in junior staff and student participation in university governance would reverse the bias toward the professoriate, as would the overhaul of academic career patterns initiated by four decrees on recruitment and promotion passed in August 1982.

These relatively minor changes were intended merely to rectify imbalances among staff, as a preliminary to a longer-term and wider-reaching reform. Given the majority party's close connection with the educational unions concerned (kept in the dark about ministerial plans under the previous regime), it was only to be expected that extensive consultations would precede the tabling of a bill. According to Savary, his project was based on the longest consultative process[28] ever connected with a reform of higher education. Indeed, the Faure law had been rushed through in an emergency situation, and other ministers of education had not enjoyed the trust of the unions or welcomed their cooperation. Yet this prolonged period of planning might have been detrimental on at least two scores. First, pressures were made at the highest levels of the state hierarchy to save the *grandes écoles*, and public opinion was mobilized by a number of articles signed by eminent spokesmen for this tradition. As a result of a short and sharp campaign, they were exempted from the scope of the Savary reform. Predictably, it took a little longer to gain an exemption for the IUTs, since their supporters were a good deal less influential and less widely known. Still, this was eventually secured too. Consequently no uniformity with respect to selection could be expected, contrary to the initial postulate of the 1976 plan. Second, negotiations with unions focused to a great extent on the respective rights and duties of various categories within the teaching profession. This may have been understandable, due to vested interests and to the favors granted by the previous regime to tenured professors. Still, it had the disadvantage of reducing the great educational debate envisaged by Savary to a corporatist squabble. Perhaps the most disturbing feature was the lack of involvement of either students or other interested sections of society, such as parents and employers. This "worrying silence"[29] gave way to howls of protest when the Savary reform became somewhat unfairly identified with the widening of selection at university level.

In the spring of 1983, student strikes and demonstrations started in order to oppose selection after the first two years of university study. This was obviously comparable in some respects to the precedent of May 1968. However, the economic situation having changed completely in the meantime, the optimistic and utopian climate of the late 1960s has given way to widespread anxiety about employment prospects. While their predecessors wanted to "change life," today's students are more concerned with their own chances of making a living. The likelihood of failing to get a job is increased by the risk of being unable to secure any qualification. This is particularly threatening for entrants of the university first cycle courses in the arts and the social sciences, whose rate of success is approximately between 35 percent and 27 percent, as against 76 percent for IUTs and 60 percent to 63 percent for the preparatory forms to *grandes écoles*.[30] In the absence of screening mechanisms, students were eventually eliminated by their own failure. In the mid–1960s Minister Christien Fouchet had called this process "selection by shipwreck." Understandably, Savary decided that to retain existing quotas for technical, medical and pharmaceutical courses of study was to plump for the lesser evil. However, the proposed introduction of quotas for the second cycle, while defensible on vocational grounds, seemed hard to reconcile with the policy of unrestricted access to the first cycle.

This contradiction was inherent in pursuing two distinct and barely compatible objectives, i.e., the integration of university education with the economy,[31] and the democratization of student recruitment.[32] As a result, the reform elicited two sets of major criticisms from different quarters. Socialist sympathizers blamed it for perpetuating the narrow vocationalism of the Giscard administration, formerly accused by the left of devaluing culture and subordinating universities to the *patronat* (prospective employers). The opposition, on the other hand, claimed that a reform of the *baccalauréat* was overdue and that first cycle intakes should be cut down by implementing student guidance (*orientation*). Admittedly the argument that open access to the universities results in overproducing unemployable graduates could be countered by invoking the low French ration of full-time students (25 percent of the age group between twenty and twenty-four, as against 26.5 percent in the Federal Republic Germany, 30 percent in Japan and 55 percent in the United States).[33] However, the failure rate at the end of the first year at university (recently assessed at 45 percent in law, 50 percent in arts and 35 percent in science courses) makes it doubtful whether entry into higher education as a right is in fact a genuine privilege. As the Savary bill appeared to extend this right of access not only to *bacheliers*, but to all those with equivalent qualifications or experience, it could be described as devaluing the first cycle even further. Thus, student attacks were two-pronged, some focusing on excessive laxity at entry into higher education, others (law students in particular) on the relative rigors of selection at other stages. Furthermore, particular categories of students challenged the sections of the bill they held to be detrimental to their interests. In the case of the provision referring to teaching hospitals, the threat of strikes by medical staff sympathetic to the protesters actually sufficed to make the government amend its proposals[34] in late May 1983.

While students often secured the support of teaching staff within their specialty (as was generally the case in law and medicine), there were divisions between the professoriate and other university teachers about the issue of representation in university councils. The government's long-term intention was to unify the different categories of academics whose qualifications and terms of tenure are unidentical. Hence the provision whereby elections to the administrative councils of universities would be held within a single "electoral college" (article 37 of the Savary bill). Since professors are bound to be in a minority, they would no longer be represented by their peers. In fact, the unions would virtually control access to the councils—a form of politicization deplored not only by the right in opposition, but by academics as sympathetic to the government as Maurice Duverger.[35] By 1986 nearly half of French universities had, perhaps predictably, refused to adopt the statutes outlined in the law of 1983.[36]

The focus of the parliamentary debate on the Savary reform was both on its actual provisions and on the spirit in which it had been drawn up. Thus Faure deplored that fifteen years after his own *loi d'orientation* a "centralizing, bureaucratic and, in short, a Napoleonic law"[37] should have been put forward by a government allegedly intent on furthering regional autonomy. It would be tedious to summarize the 2,000 amendments tabled during a particularly prolonged and acrimonious series of discussions in the National Assembly over a period of three weeks in May–June 1983. The bill was ultimately adopted, but the opposition could claim that many concessions had been secured—either by group pressure, by threats of violence or, less frequently, by rhetoric alone. There is to be very little selection (if any) in the universities. Students will remain largely free to register where they please and will be subject to guidance only with their own agreement. The financial and educational autonomy of the medical schools will endure. And, of course, the *grandes écoles* survive. The issue of selection remains unsolved.

THE ELUSIVENESS OF THE SINGLE SCHOOL

The concept of a single school is inseparable from a reliance on education as the process through which common norms and values are inculcated to a whole age group. It implies a measure of consensus which may be desirable as a goal—a point Durkheimian sociology makes very clear—but which is not easily attainable when ideological discussions are rooted in a long history. Thus, as well as the socioeconomic obstacles to the provision of common schooling at post-primary level, there are religious and philosophical divides within the population. As a result, the difficulties of devising a syllabus for the middle school which would not be socially discriminatory are supplemented by the lack of unanimity about the distinction between education and indoctrination. This is not a theoretical issue of pedagogy, but a recurrent theme in French political life since the Revolution. To republicans, the duty of the state school was to disseminate enlightenment by providing secular instruction. Catholic establishments were perceived as inculcating beliefs contrary to the findings of modern science and as encouraging reactionary political practices. The confrontation—at the grass-roots level—between the primary school teacher and the village priest epitomized this ideological division. The status and financing of Catholic schools became crucial to parliamentary politics in the late nineteenth and twentieth centuries. Debates between secularists were fatal to numerous cabinets before World War II and remained sufficiently lively under the Fourth Republic to disrupt parliamentary majorities.

It was a central tenet of Gaullist policy to achieve national unity by defusing this source of conflict, i.e., by giving formal acknowledgment to both educational networks. The Debré law of 1959 provided state financing for denominational schools to cover staff salaries and basic operational expenses. A right of control commensurate with the assistance given was assured. However, the traditional commitment of the republican state to the provision of secular instruction was not fully upheld. Its responsibility for universal schooling no longer needed to be fulfilled within a framework of *service public*, implying full administrative control and official funding, as well as civil service career patterns for teachers. Instead, a collaboration with private schools, predominantly Catholic, entailed their partial integration into the state system but enabled them to retain their specific character. In practice this meant the provision of religiously oriented tuition and, to this end, the right of assent (or dissent) to ministerial proposals of candidates for appointment to vacant teaching posts. The latter point is important to the extent that the teaching profession was not unified, while the education given was not uniform.

To the electorate this issue of denominational schools did not appear to be highly contentious anymore. The depopulation of rural areas and the attendant decrease in polarization between church and school was one contributory factor. The liberalization of Catholic attitudes to modern scientific knowledge and a lessening of rigid traditionalism among the clergy helped defuse anticlerical responses. A wider awareness of social responsibilities on the part of the Church entailed a shift away from formerly conservative political allegiances. There could no longer be an automatic equation between religious practice and right-wing ideology or between republicanism and secularism. Increasingly the acceptance of ideological diversity was seen as entailing a duty for the state to be tolerant and to acknowledge the parents' right to choose their children's school. This more relaxed approach was facilitated by the steady decline in religious practice, which meant that private schools catered for a dwindling minority, especially as the birthrate declined in the 1970s. Yet one pressure group remained identified with militant secularism, namely, the teachers' unions, particularly the SNI (*Syndicate National des Instituteurs*), grouping primary school and *collège* (middle school) staff members, affiliated mainly to the Socialist and—in lesser numbers—to the Communist Party.

Arguments abound to explain this secularist stance. They range from a traditional attachment to the organizing myth of the teacher as "republican priest" to vested interest in the existence of a fully state-appointed profession and to ideological entrenchment. The concept of uniform education which it is a state duty to provide may also have been easier to define in secularist than in fully "comprehensive" terms. A nondenominational school could be advocated without infringing on the acquired rights of any category among state school teachers; in fact, it would contribute to an enhancement of their position. The same could not be said of a single school in the sense of an unstreamed one, since its existence would affect both career patterns and attachment to traditional methods of tuition, as well as to curricula. Secularism could be a means of cementing professional solidarity and of rekindling reformist zeal, somewhat dampened by the Fifth Republic educational policies of modernization. There is no need to impute Machiavellian intentions to union leaders to explain their firm opposition to the clerical legislation of 1977. Entrenched in power, the right was flexing its muscles. The Guermeur law, granting to denominational schools both building subsidies and greater control over staffing (through state subsidies for separate training and through the right to propose candidates for appointments), went beyond all earlier provisions in furthering the autonomy of the private sector. This really could be construed as reactionary, since the educational policies of the Third Republic were being systematically reversed. Occasionally embarrassed by their own traditionalism in academic matters and its incompatibility with full comprehensivization, the teachers' unions were eager to denounce retrograde legislation and to display their progressive stance. Yet, even on the political left, the Catholic schools were not exclusively perceived as clerical institutions. They could be considered as pluralist, since lay persons, both as parents and as teachers, participated in their management. Furthermore, they were often less conservative in social and pedagogical matters than state schools.[38] No simple dichotomy made sense.

In 1981 it was not the intention of the new majority to reopen the school war—a point stressed both by President Mitterrand and by Minister Savary. The latter, while acknowledging that the long-term policy would be to construct a single secular educational system (*un service public d' éducation unifié et laïque*)[39] said that this would be achieved over time "by convincing, not by constraining."[40] Gradualism did appear the most rational course, both because of the increasing Catholic support gained by the Socialist Party in the 1981 presidential and parliamentary elections, and because of the continuing "secularization" of the private sector. Indeed, in denominational schools, 50 percent of the teachers and over half of the headmasters are no longer clerics, while pupils need no longer be christened, let alone practicing Catholics. However, the SNI promptly deplored ministerial concessions and demanded the nationalization of all private educational establishments. In so doing, the teaching profession displayed both a somewhat insensitive disregard for the historical background in which the *école libre* is rooted and an understandable fidelity to the deeply entrenched secularist commitment of the old French left. This zeal was rekindled by the centenary of the Ferry legislation on secular primary education, celebrated on the day before the first anniversary of President Mitterrand's election, May 9, 1982. On this occasion, the impatience of the teachers' unions, grouped in the CNAL (*Comité national d'action laïque*), was expressed before an audience of some 250,000, while both Prime Minister Pierre Mauroy, and Savary emphasized the need for caution and patience in the ongoing negotiations about the future of *écoles libres*.[41] The exasperation of secularist militants grew as the laborious process of negotiations proceeded at the pace which the minister of education found necessary to persuade the supporters of denominational schools and the episcopate. This slowness enabled the resistance to the proposed reform to become organized and to gain momentum. By November 1983 the CNAL and other similar groups of unionists, influenced by freemasonry (*Grand Orient de France*), demanded the departure of Savary from the ministry. The trade unions of the FEN (*Fédération de l'éducation nationale*) described him as "public enemy number 1 of French education."[42]

In the increasingly emotional atmosphere that surrounded the drafting of the bill, polarization was inevitable. The debate about *écoles libres* became more and more reminiscent of the controversies that had raged under the Third Republic—the *guerre scolaire* or confrontation about schooling, which Mitterrand was determined to avoid, with Savary's help. The left felt frustrated and the right threatened. Principles were boldly asserted, and facts tended to be either left out or ideologically reinterpreted. It might be useful to mention some of them: in 1981–82 private education catered for 12.9 percent of all kindergarten and 14 percent of primary pupils. The corresponding proportion for secondary was 19.9 percent, hence a total intake corresponding to 16.3 percent of school children (as against only 2.7 percent of students attending private higher educational establishments).[43] The outflow from the state sector remained high, particularly at the crucial stage of entry into the secondary cycle (i.e., the *collège*). Between 1975–76 and 1981–82, the increase in this exodus had actually reached 22 percent. These data show both that the *écoles libres* were prospering and that their attraction was related, at least to a large extent, to the quality of the instruction provided. If the criteria for registration had been strictly or even predominantly religious, the peak at the outset of secondary education would not have been so pronounced. The opposition to Savary's reform was to make much of the parents' freedom of choice, both as a positive right which the state ought not to curtail and as an indictment of the quality of state schools.

In its onslaught on public education, the opposition could draw arguments from a whole array of books published by teachers and academics to expose the defects of the system they served. Though their authors generally define themselves as belonging to the left and actually blame the deterioration in educational provision on the Gaullist-Giscardian regime, they helped reinforce the *école libre* lobby. Not only do they denounce politicization within the state system and an egalitarianism that hinders the progress of gifted pupils without helping the disadvantaged, they also confirm that teachers are demoralized, that new pedagogical methods generate chaos and that essential subject matters, such as French and history, are no longer properly taught. Such attacks on laxity, even while putting much of the blame on the Haby reform, stress that the return of the left to power did not halt the process, and may even have accelerated it. With such allies within the public sector, its external critics have no shortage of ammunition.

In addition to qualitative arguments about the inadequacy of public education, supporters of *écoles libres* also make a quantitative point. In 1982 the intake of these schools amounted to 16.3 percent of all pupils at nursery, primary and secondary levels. Yet state subsidies to the private sector equalled 13.4 percent of the credits allocated to the corresponding cycles. Hence a slight shortfall, which could in fact be explained away since a small fraction of private schools (approximately 0.5 percent of Catholic primary and secondary establishments) operate without any subsidy. Furthermore, some services within the state system (e.g., guidance for pupils) cater also for those who do not belong to it. Anyway, such quibbles, while they illustrate the determination of all parties to use every possible technicality in order to further their case, were not really capable of being resolved by compromise.

This is where Savary went wrong. He clearly underestimated the dogmatism of all participants in the debate. His attempt at "depoliticizing" it was doomed, since the right-wing opposition realized the advantages it could derive from mobilizing mass support against the government. Meanwhile the concentration of teachers in parliament and their amenability to pressures from former colleagues and from unions meant that the bill was subjected to a whole array of amendments in May 1984. Such efforts to protect the state sector against any encroachments reinforced the moral panic in the country. The escalation of protest culminated in a demonstration involving 1 million people on June 24, 1984, in Paris.[44] Echoes of 1968 were too strong not to be heeded. The reform was withdrawn, despite parliamentary endorsement, and within weeks, Savary—condemned by the teachers' unions as "too cautious and too scrupulous"[45]—

was no longer at the ministry. A great opportunity for a "historical compromise" between the Catholic hierarchy and the left had been lost. In retrospect, perhaps it is all too easy to conclude that such a compromise could have been imposed by the new Socialist rules in their early days. Still—judging by results—honesty did not prove to be the best policy.

A CHANGE OF STYLE

The new minister, Chevènement, is a strong personality. As both his parents were primary school teachers, his commitment to secular education was not in doubt, but he had not actually taken part in the recent debate.[46] Much more of a political animal than Savary, he adopted a higher profile. The contrast between his predecessor's commitment to negotiated solutions and to gradualism, and his own bold, programmatic statements could not have been sharper.

Although the work initiated under Savary to involve the teaching profession in modernization and decentralization was continued, the impression conveyed to the public was that a definite change had occurred. The public relations campaign launched to this effect highlighted two main themes: the restoration of the public school's prestige and its adaptation to the requirements of a modern economy. The first was intended to reassure parents concerned about slipping standards and lack of discipline. They were assured that "the party was over"; the aftermath of 1968 would not be tolerated. After a long period of permissiveness, the emphasis would no longer be on the children's right to develop at their own pace. Instead the duty to teach the three Rs—which had been a central aspect of Ferry's legislation and the hallmark of the state system under the Third Republic—was reasserted. A campaign featuring a train with the slogan *Vive l'école* which conveyed publicity material around the country was launched in the spring of 1985.[47] The appeal was clearly to the "ordinary parent"—at the risk of antagonizing the teaching profession. In fact, a group of teachers in Brittany went on record as giving the following assessment to Chevènement: "Nought out of ten in pedagogy, ten out of ten in demagogy."[48] The minister refuted such criticism by arguing that the left ought not to forgo claims to "work, merit and talent."[49] A republican elitism was needed and was in fact the legacy of the Third Republic. The concern for quality implicit in this approach would benefit the children of the underprivileged to the extent that their families are not able to remedy the deficiencies of formal education. Thus it is socially progressive to be pedagogically reactionary. Not surprisingly, Chevènement's statements have been described as *discours rétro*—but in the climate of the mid–1980s this was largely a term of praise.

The second leitmotif of this discourse was to reassure families not only about the inculcation of sound knowledge in this day and age, but also about the adaptation of schooling to the requirements of a changing world. On the one hand, good old-fashioned methods were advocated, and commonsense assertions about the need for exertion rather than play were made. On the other, the concept of modernization was divorced from child-centeredness and interpreted in strictly economic terms. The example of Japan, whose prosperity was inseparable from the vocationalism inherent in its educational provision, was held to be the pattern for success in a competitive world. In fact, it was quoted so often that some teachers nicknamed Chevènement ''Jules Ferry en Kimono'' (a kimono-wearing Ferry).[50] Changes in curricula, new vocational *baccalauréats* and technological universities, and additional training for teachers were explained as attempts to face the recession by mastering new technologies. In fact, some of these arguments belong to the traditional armory of the political right—and proved no less popular for that. The public responded positively: the *grandes écoles* were trusted by 71 percent of respondents and the universities by 63 percent in a SOFRES survey assessing the way in which the French view their institutions.[51] Over a period of three years, the universities had made the greatest progress in rating, although the highest score in 1984 was that of the police (74 percent). As a profession, primary teachers ranked third (80 percent), behind fireman (96 percent) and medical doctors (90 percent), but way ahead of priests (58 percent). The widespread pessimism of the teaching profession about the quality of French state education and about its own image appeared to be at variance with the general perception. To what extent the growing trust of the public in the educational system had been enhanced by Chevènement's campaign remains debatable. What seems clear, however, is that his moralistic approach was in tune with public opinion. If the police scored so highly, it was time for discipline to be restored in schools. Arguably, the reactions showed not only that the minister, as an acute politician, had rightly gauged the climate, but also that the swing to the right was bound to jeopardize the Socialist majority. Thus he may have served the cause of the school without actually gaining any political party advantage. Of course, this is just what he maintained that he had set out to do.

A BALANCE SHEET

Undoubtedly the disarray in which Savary had had to withdraw after the fiasco of the bill on private education looked like a heavy legacy. On the other hand, his successor benefited from the results of extensive and friendly consultations with representatives of the teaching profession (particularly with CFDT sympathizers). The ground for reforms later effected under Chevènement had been carefully prepared. For instance, two committees (André de Peretti's on teacher training and Antoine Prost's on *lycées*) had reported too late for Savary to act on their conclusions, though he had introduced changes in the *collèges* in the light of the Legrand report. He had set up priority areas in 1981 as part of a systematic attempt to reduce underachievement in schools. He had also encouraged the growth of technical education and prepared a computerization program covering all secondary establishments.[52] New curricula were being devised. To the extent that most of these reforms were either continued or actually implemented after Chevènement took over the ministry, the credit may not have gone where it was due. Perhaps more important, the style of the new minister meant that the reforms received much greater publicity than they might otherwise have done. Although they had been agreed on with experts, in the kind of slow process of consultation away from the limelight which Savary favored, they captured the public's imagination when his successor described them in glowing terms as a new deal in education.

Without any further attempt at demarcating the two ministers' contributions, except when their policies differed (which is the exception rather than the rule), an outline of the main Socialist reforms in education would be roughly as follows:

Nursery education has been expanded and, as for the 1986–87 school year, parents who so wish may actually obtain it for children from the age of two.[53] Doubts have been expressed, however, about the actual availability of places in working-class urban and suburban areas, where the demand is greatest.

New programs for primary schools have been introduced in 1985–86. They were announced in characteristically flamboyant terms by Chevènement. "The aim of the school is instruction, not excursion."[54] The activités d'éveil (unscheduled periods in which the pupils were to be stimulated rather than taught, and self-expression encouraged) were to be discontinued. No more excursions! Since this aspect of child-centered pedagogy was an integral part of modernization, as interpreted in 1968, the reform is loaded with symbolic meaning. The curriculum will be centered on seven subject matters, among which French is to be central. All children must learn to read, and the wish to read must be encouraged not only in language classes but in the teaching of other disciplines. These include mathematics, science and technology (at least fifty hours being devoted to computer science), history and geography, and lastly, civics (éducation civique). Along with computer science, the latter is the main departure from the traditional primary curriculum. It is intended to train pupils for life in society by acquainting them with such republican symbols as Marianne, the national flag and anthem (La Marseillaise), and Bastille Day (July 14). As well as learning about French political institutions, they will be given an introduction to social practices, e.g., the system of social security, road safety, the post office, the railway network. Thus civics no longer covers ethics, as was traditionally the case under the Third Republic, when éducation morale et civique was a cornerstone of primary secular schooling.

Therefore a misunderstanding might well have arisen. When 84 percent of respondents to a survey conducted in February 1985 approved of this new subject matter, they appeared to believe that it would cover the inculcation of respect for property, work, discipline and politeness: in other words, the old-fashioned virtues.[55] However, this is not the syllabus introduced by Chevènement. In addition, only half of the sample actually thought that primary teachers were the right people to impart civic and moral education. This response hardly tallies with the high rating given to the teaching profession a few months before and casts some doubt about the real popularity of éducation civique. The most important primary teachers' union, SNI, expressed opposition to the new curricula.

Its objections were mainly addressed to the provisions on the teaching of French (in which no single method was advocated), history and geography (whose scope was slightly reduced, but focused on more factual information),[56] and especially civics. No matter how it was received, the reform was a good deal simpler than some of its forerunners. Its printed version ran to only 62 pages, as against the hundreds (over 500 actually) of pages issued under the Haby programs. Perhaps it was excessively simplistic—setting out targets without specifying how or even whether they can be reached. Neither trained staff nor teaching aids are available in sufficient numbers to make the teaching of science and technology feasible. In fact, the curriculum may well be so broad as to be virtually unteachable. As for the emphasis on French language, again programmatic assertions may not be enough. The need for specialized teacher training and for research on the appropriate methods to overcome widespread illiteracy among pupils deserved rather more careful consideration. This criticism may be reiterated about all the curricula changes introduced in quick succession in 1985.

At the secondary level, the revision of curricula for *collèges* entailed the adjunction of new subject matters (technology, computer science and civics). It also involved the streamlining of other courses—either to keep up with scientific progress (as in biology) or with social change (as in the use of television for the teaching of French). While teachers remain free to use the educational methods of their choice, they are assigned unambiguous goals as to the kind and amount of instruction to be given. The number of literary works to be studied in French[57] and the periods to be covered in history are specified. Pupils are to be grouped according to ability in each subject matter (''setting'' rather than streaming), and individual attention must be given to their needs. The purpose of the reform is both to tighten up academic standards and to turn the *collèges* into anterooms of the *lycées* rather than terminal establishments. The concern for results is in sharp contradistinction to the stress on individual fulfillment which was central to the Haby philosophy and which is still important to the teachers' unions. This change of focus is justified in social terms: out of one hundred pupils entering the secondary cycle, only thirty-four actually reach the terminal (pre-*baccalauréat*) form of the *lycée*. Failure is closely correlated with parental occupation: 85 percent of professionals' and upper managers' children reach the *lycée*, as against 25 percent of working-class pupils. The Socialist objective is for 80 percent of the whole age group to reach the *baccalauréat* level by the year 2000.

To make this leap forward, the secondary pupils must learn how to think logically, how to use written, verbal and visual material, and how to work by themselves. Whether the teaching staff at *collège* level is competent to instill the appropriate values and attitudes, as well as to teach exacting subject matters (e.g., biology) to higher standards, remains unproven. Even if in-service training can bring about some improvements, two serious problems will remain. The *collèges* intakes are increasingly heterogeneous. Whereas in 1950 one-half of the age group entered secondary school, more than nine out of ten did so in 1980 (though some at a later age than others).[58] By the time they leave primary school, a sizeable proportion of the cohort has not fully internalized the basic concepts of French and mathematics. Their predicament is all the more serious since they tend to come from underprivileged families. Both the culture gap between home and school and the recurring experience of rejection by teachers generate a "withdrawal syndrome" which may lead to disruption or apathy. In either case the educational system is ill-equipped to cope and merely rejects the problem pupils. Paradoxically, given the lip-service paid to vocationalism, the "dustbin" to which they have been relegated was often the technical short track. A nearly impossible task has to be undertaken to restore the prestige of technical courses and qualifications within the educational system and in the wider society.

Technical education is to be developed over a period of five years, with a budget of 10.5 billion francs voted in the autumn of 1985. This is to cover the cost of in-service training for teachers, particularly at *lycée* level. The expectation is that intakes will grow and that increasing numbers of pupils will prove capable of completing the long cycle up to the *baccalauréat* level.[59] Earlier attempts at upgrading technical qualifications—most recently under the Barre government— have not been particularly successful. The undervaluing of manual labor in French society has proven persistent, despite unceasing governmental efforts throughout the history of the Fifth Republic.[60] In addition, the technical *lycées* have a reputation for heavy workloads and for lagging behind the latest technological developments in the tertiary sector of the economy. Both the possibility of training a new corps of teachers and the widespread twinning of schools with firms are considered with some reticence by the teachers' unions.

The reform of *lycées* was devised too late to be carried out before the elections of 1986. As from 1987–88, there will be eight options for the terminal forms, three in the arts, one in the social sciences, and the remaining four in mathematical, scientific and technological subjects. The purpose is to reduce the hegemony of mathematics by promoting alternative areas of excellence. The *baccalauréat* is to include a component of continuous assessment, in order to encourage private study and to reduce the bureaucratic burden of examinations. New curricula will have to be introduced, with more stress being placed on the teaching of French in the four "literary" sections. Changes in the approach to history have also been announced, to enhance the sense of national identity. Politicians of the most diverse persuasions, from President Mitterrand to the Gaullist Michel Debré, have deplored that history should have become "denationalized."[61] This theme was frequently taken up by Chevènement in connection with the role of secular education.

A CHANGE OF MAJORITY

The extent to which the Socialist administration occupied a middle-ground position or even—under Chevènement—endorsed nationalist tenets means that there ought to be relatively little substantive change. The new curricula introduced in 1985 and 1986 or scheduled for 1987 are sufficiently biased toward the three

Rs and, at higher levels, toward French and history to satisfy the new majority. The culturally authoritarian stream in the French Socialist Party is close enough to the Gaullist stance to make major changes in the content of instruction highly unlikely. The recent emphasis on decentralization and on the autonomy of secondary establishments might fit in well with the forthcoming reorganization of universities. Some twenty years after 1968 the dismantling of the Napoleonic structure may be proceeding at a faster pace, whichever party is in power, because the political penalities attached to state centralization are becoming increasingly obvious. This is not to say that education—however it is organized and financed—will be less committed to the perpetuation of traditional values and less likely to ensure social persistence, alleviated and justified by some meritocratic promotion. Even under Socialist rule—let alone under a right-wing coalition—the school can only mirror society and certainly cannot change it.

NOTES

1. Under Christien Fouchet's tenure as minister of education (1963 to April 1967), the channeling of pupils to the stream best suited to their ability within a comprehensive system was implemented by decree, i.e., without parliamentary debate (W. R. Fraser, *Education and Society in Modern France* [London: R.K.P., 1963], p. 127).

2. The number of *bacheliers* nearly doubled in 1950–60, nearly trebled in 1960–70, and increased by 30 percent in 1970–80 (i.e., they were 6 percent of the cohort in 1950, 20 percent in 1970, and 25 percent in 1980) (*Le Monde*, October 24, 1980). The intake of higher education was growing by 14 percent a year in 1962–67.

3. R. Aron, *Plaidoyer pour l'Europe décadente* (Paris: Laffont, 1976), p. 414.

4. Cf. The discussion of the Savary reform of higher education below.

5. *Le Monde*, March 30, 1978.

6. Eleven decrees, nineteen *arrêtés* and twenty circulars implemented the Haby law. Many of them were drafted by the minister himself. *Le Monde*, September 8, 1977.

7. *Le Monde*, September 6, 1980.

8. *Le Monde*, September 8, 1977.

9. *Le Monde*, January 15–16, 1978.

10. *Le Monde*, January 14, 1978.

11. I. Berger, *Les Instituteurs d'une génération à l'autre* (Paris: P.U.F., 1979).

12. M. Vaughan et al., *Social Change in France* (Oxford: Martin Robinson, 1980), p. 52.

13. A. Norvez, *Le Corps enseignant et l'évolution démographique* (Paris: I.N.E.D.–P.U.F., 1978).

14. Royer Report to the Finance Committee of the National Assembly, November 13, 1978.

15. M. S. Archer, *Social Origins of Educational Systems* (London: Sage, 1979), p. 358.

16. Title of a book by A. Thibaudet (1927), which pointed out that the victory of the left in 1924 had brought to power three former pupils of *Ecole Normale Supérieure* and former *lycée* teachers, Herriot, Painlevé and Blum. However, the dominant profession in parliament remained the legal (*avocats*), with 10 percent of M.P.s being teachers.

17. In the traditional sense, i.e., academic (nonvocational) secondary schools, as distinct from the Haby reform's meaning.

18. The prime minister, the president of the National Assembly and the head of the Socialist Party were all former teachers too.

19. Archer, *Social Origins of Educational Systems*, p. 323.

20. M. Vaughan, "French Post-primary Education: What Is Left of the Haby Reform," *Comparative Education* 17, No. 1 (March 1981): 5f.

21. The SNI (*Snydicat des instituteurs*), catering for primary school staff, is close to the Socialist Party, and the SNES (*Syndicat national des enseignants du second degré*), catering for secondary schools, to the Communist Party. The two disagreed about the scope and mutual relationship of the primary and secondary cycles (*Le Monde*, May 20, 1981).

22. M. Vaughan, "The *Grandes Ecoles*," in R. Wilkinson, ed., *Governing Elites* (New York: O.U.P., 1969), p. 75.

23. E. N. Suleiman, *Elites in French Society: The Politics of Survival* (Princeton: Princeton University Press, 1978), p. 25.

24. P. Scheriff in Vaughan et al., *Social Change*, p. 71.

25. M. Vaughan, "The *Grandes Ecoles*: Selection, Legitimation, Perpetuation," in J. Howorth and P. Cerny, eds, *Elites in France: Origins, Reproduction, Perpetuation* (London: Pinter, 1981).

26. Established in 1965–66 to provide vocational courses at higher educational levels. Their intake absorbed 21 percent of *bacheliers* in 1978, an increase that still fell short of the target set by the Fifth Development Plan.

27. The Senate threw out the government's proposed reform in October 1981, but in January 1982 the Constitutional Council decided that it was in fact legal.

28. From October 1982 to May 1983. A questionnaire sent to all universities elicited 286 replies, while 110 organizations were received in the ministry.

29. J. M. Croissandeau, "L'Université n'intéresse plus personne," *Monde de l'Education*, April 1983.

30. *Le Monde*, May 25, 1983.

31. A. Grosser, "L'Economie, l'Etat et les universités," *Le Monde*, May 21, 1983: "In France economism triumphs today. . . . The universities bill proves it."

32. Wider recruitment is upheld on grounds of social justice and of wasted ability, since only 24 in 1,000 university students are children of manual workers (M. Schiff, *L'Intelligence gaspillée* [Paris: Seuil, 1982], p. 186).

33. Unesco, *Statistical Yearbook* (Paris: Unesco, 1982).

34. The government had initially proposed that heads of departments be elected by staff, but amended this to have them appointed after nomination by the *medical* staff alone. Departments which were to be set up by 1984 would only begin to be created by that date. Further administrative concessions were also granted (*Le Monde*, May 28, 1983).

35. M. Duverger, "Le Meilleur et le pire," *Le Monde*, May 21, 1983.

36. *Le Monde*, March 13, 1986.

37. *Le Monde*, May 17, 1983. Similarly, Professor Charles Debbash, a former advisor of President Giscard d'Estaing and a leader of protest in the law faculties, pointed out that reform should have been negotiated with the universities in contractual terms rather than imposed by legislation.

38. The French bishops, in their plea for Catholic education, emphasized its appeal

to families whose "cultural, social and religious horizons are diverse" and defined it as pluralistic. *Le Monde*, June 18, 1982.

39. The terms used by Mitterrand as a candidate to the presidential election in May 1981.

40. From Savary's speech on the hundredth anniversary of the Third Republic's secularist legislation. *Le Monde*, May 11, 1982.

41. *Le Monde*, May 11, 1982 (300,000 according to the organizers).

42. *Le Monde*, November 29, 1983.

43. *Le Monde*, November 18, 1982.

44. On the escalation of demonstrations in support of *écoles libres*, see *Le Monde*, August 31, 1984.

45. Interview with the general secretary of FEN, acting president of CNAL. *Le Monde*, July 28, 1984.

46. Interview with J.-P. Chevènement, *Le Monde*, July 31, 1984.

47. At a cost of 9 million francs. *Le Monde*, January 8, 1986.

48. *Le Monde*, May 29, 1985.

49. *Le Monde*, January 30, 1985.

50. *Le Monde*, March 13, 1986.

51. *Le Nouvel Observateur*, December 20, 1984.

52. *Le Monde*, March 13, 1986 (120,000 microcomputers have been provided and 110,000 teachers have been given basic training).

53. Approximately 50 percent of two-year-olds attend nursery school.

54. *Le Monde*, April 24, 1985.

55. *Le Monde*, March 22, 1985.

56. *Le Monde*, April 21, 1984. In history, the teaching of periods and dates and, in geography, that of maps, is reestablished.

57. *Le Monde*, October 10, 1985.

58. *Le Monde*, June 6, 1985.

59. *Le Monde*, February 4, 1983.

60. *Le Monde*, March 13, 1986. Up to 80,000 pupils are expected to be studying for the technical *baccalauréats* by 1990.

61. *Le Monde*, October 15, 1985.

Decentralization: A Revolutionary Reform

VIVIEN A. SCHMIDT

Much to the surprise of most contemporary scholars of French politics and administration, within six months of the election of the Mitterrand government in 1981, the Socialists began a process of governmental decentralization which has to date resulted in no fewer than 500 pages of legislation encompassing over 33 laws and 219 decrees.[1] The long history of piecemeal, failed reforms, combined with the traditional complicity among local politicians and administrators that allowed for a larger measure of local autonomy and power than the law actually permitted or the rhetoric admitted, made any thoroughgoing reform appear highly unlikely.[2] Yet, the Socialists did in fact succeed where others had failed, breaking a long-standing pattern of much talk about decentralization and little action.

The Socialists went ahead with decentralization for a variety of reasons, not the least of which was their conviction that such a reform would revitalize the periphery by breaking up the conservative, rural-dominated complicity of prefects and local political worthies, as well as by opening up local government to the more progressive urban groups traditionally left out of the local political equation. The Socialist conquest of local government through the 1970s, which culminated with the party's capture of national power in 1981, moreover, convinced many on the left that decentralization would further their own particular political interests at the same time that it would promote the public interest. Little did they know that decentralization was in short order to benefit the right. But by the time some members of the left had begun to have second thoughts about the reform, the process of decentralization had already become unstoppable—pushed through by Gaston Defferre, who had been determined to make as much of a mark on the Fifth Republic with decentralization as he had on the Fourth with decolonization. And it is Gaston Defferre who can take much of the credit or blame for the pragmatism which ensured that the reform, although less radical than the party program and electoral campaign had promised, was to be irreversible.

The new conservative government that came into power as a result of the March 1986 elections clearly has no intention of dismantling any major part of the reform—and this despite Prime Minister Jacques Chirac's well-publicized history of opposition to decentralization. It is significant that whereas the new minister of economy is charged by title with privatization, the title of the new minister of interior contains no reference at all to decentralization, itself part of the previous minister's title, let alone to recentralization. Decentralization has already been so extensive and has become so much a part of the new political and administrative landscape that most politicians on the right seem to agree with most of those on the left that not only is there no question of returning to the status quo ante, but also that a job is, for the most part, done.

Decentralization, however, has in truth only just begun. For the structural-institutional changes brought about by Socialist legislation are still in the process of playing themselves out—altering administrative roles, rules and relations at the same time as the local balance of political power. Decentralization, moreover, has not fully lived up to the Socialists' expectations as the *grande affaire du Septennat*, the main event of President Mitterrand's seven-year term, which was to have revitalized the periphery politically and administratively. For the reforms have yet to encourage greater local democracy, although they have certainly politicized the periphery. And while they have in fact set the stage for a more fiscally responsible and efficient local administration, it will not necessarily turn out to be a less expensive or less bureaucratic one.

Be that as it may, decentralization has nevertheless been of great significance. For although decentralization may not have gone far enough fast enough, it has certainly gone infinitely farther a great deal faster than anyone would have imagined before the Socialists took power. It has already produced lasting changes in center-periphery relations as well as in local politics and administration—and over the long term it stands to produce a great many more. Hence, recent scholarly treatments have been a bit unbalanced in their assessment of the reforms, as they have focused primarily on the weaknesses of decentralization. What follows is an attempt to right the intellectual balance by examining not simply the weaknesses but also the very clear strengths of current decentralization efforts.

THE SCOPE AND PURPOSE OF DECENTRALIZATION

With decentralization, the Socialists intended to make local government generally more responsible and responsive to the needs of the local population, more efficient and effective in the delivery of services, as well as less costly. To accomplish this, the Socialists altered the formal roles of all major actors in the periphery, redefined their duties and widened the scope of their activities, transferred state administrative functions and financial resources to the locality, and reformed the territorial civil service. In addition, they turned the region into another regular level of local government with locally elected officials and limited the *cumul des mandats* or number of elective positions a local official can accumulate. In so doing, the Socialists hoped to break the hidden complicity between prefects and *notables* or local political worthies benefiting from the *cumul* which had for so long allowed both groups to avoid taking full responsibility for their actions and had contributed to the unresponsiveness, inefficiency and increasing costliness of local government.

Administrative Reforms

The complicity had its beginnings just over a century ago in the decentralizing legislation of the Third Republic, which gave mayors executive powers in *communes* of all sizes—from rural villages to big cities (except for Paris, which had to wait another century)—and made the general councillors of the *départements* elected officials, but which also gave the prefect executive power in the departments and later in the regions (set up in 1958) as well as a priori control or the *tutelle* over all local administrative and budgetary decisions. Over time, the prefect and "his" notables worked out a rather cosy, interdependent relationship in which the prefects tended to protect the locality from the incursions of the center and to allow local notables much behind-the-scenes influence in exchange for their cooperation. As a result of this relationship, local notables could always take credit for popular decisions while leaving the prefect with the blame for unpopular measures in which the notables themselves might have unofficially had a hand. The prefects, in turn, could always blame the central government for not acceding to their own demands or those of local notables, since all major proposals had to climb the hierarchical ladder to Paris for approval and/or had to conform to nationally established plans and policies.[3]

This mutually beneficial relationship, moreover, made it possible for prefects and notables alike to avoid taking responsibility not only for their administrative actions but also for their budgetary requests. The prefects, who came to see themselves over time more as spokespeople for the periphery than as representatives of the central government, had a tendency to engage in the practice of *saupoudrage*, where they would prepare and/or approve excessively large budgets for their local constituencies, leaving it to the central government to pare them back, if it could. The Paris ministries, it is important to note, were no less guilty of *saupoudrage* when it came to the requests of nationally important notables, generally the mayors of big cities for whom they provided subsidies in exchange for votes.[4]

It is in an effort to break this cosy complicity, then, that the Socialists passed decentralizing legislation. The first step was to alter the roles of the major actors in the periphery by redefining the roles of prefects as the main representatives of the state in the periphery, and by differentiating them from the new roles of regional and departmental presidents as well as the traditional ones of mayors as the main representatives of local governments in the eyes of the state.

The decentralization laws, first of all, transferred from the prefects to the presidents of departments and regions executive powers on a par with those traditionally exercised by the mayors of the communes. Second, they also provided for greater flexibility in the rules governing the meeting and work schedules of departmental and regional assemblies as well as in those related to the delegation of authority from assemblies to their executive councils and from presidents to vice-presidents and territorial civil servants. Third, they allowed regions and departments complete freedom in elaborating the internal organization of their technical services as well as, for the first time in the case of the regions, the ability to recruit their own personnel for their own technical services. And finally, most significantly for the communes but also for regions and departments given their new executive powers, the decentralization laws abolished the prefect's *tutelle* over the administrative and budgetary decisions of all levels of local government.[5]

Nevertheless, the prefects were not left completely without power or authority as a result of decentralization, for the new laws replaced the prefects' former executive powers and a priori control with increased "deconcentrated" or centrally delegated powers over the field services of the state and over many matters of local concern previously handled directly by Paris ministries as well as with an a posteriori legal control over all three levels of local government, enabling them to refer administrative matters to administrative tribunals and budgetary matters to the newly created *Chambres régionales des Comptes* or regional accounting courts.[6]

With this new division of power, the Socialists intended to make all local officials fully accountable to the local population for their decisions and the prefects at the same time more accountable to the state. Moreover, by transferring from the state to the regional, departmental and communal levels of local government different administrative *compétences* or functions and duties along with the necessary financial resources and authority, they sought to place administrative and budgetary responsibility squarely on the shoulders of local officials. Furthermore, they also felt that they had found a way to break the vicious circle of the *Etat-Providence* or welfare state and to ensure that local development would have a "more dynamic base than centralization which produces receivers of assistance and creditors toward a supposedly inexhaustible treasury."[7]

With these reforms the regions now have charge of regional economic planning and policy, industrial development, and also professional education. The departments are responsible for the delivery of health and social services, construction and maintenance of public thoroughfares, and school bus transportation.[8] And the communes have retained their traditional duties with regard to municipal services, while they have gained the freedom to set up their own POS—*plan d' occupation du sol* (land use plan) and to issue building permits (where they have a POS). In addition, every level of local government has the charge to promote local economic development despite the regions' primary responsibility in this area; every level has some authority over some aspect of culture, even though the state has retained major control in these fields; every level including the state has authority over some ports and waterways, although the departments and communes are clearly the main beneficiaries of this aspect of decentralization; and every level has clear responsibility for construction and maintenance of pre-university public education facilities with, in most instances, the regions taking the *lycées* (high schools), the departments the *collèges* (junior high schools) and the communes the *primaires* (elementary schools).[9]

To cover the cost of their new administrative duties along with their ongoing expenses, local governments will receive new financial resources from the state—half in the form of the transfer of regular state taxes to the locality and half in the form of revenue-sharing through a variety of government grants based on different sharing formulas from different national taxes. The taxes over which local authorities will now have total control—in most cases to raise or lower as they see fit—include automobile registration and licensing fees, real estate taxes and the local business tax. The new government grants encompass the DGD (*dotation générale de décentralisation*), a block grant for the costs of decentralization where they exceed those covered by the revenue from local taxes and the DGE (*dotation globale d'equipment*), a block grant for capital investment to replace the categorical grants of the past. In addition, the DGF (*dotation globale de fonctionnement*), a block grant for current operating expenses, created in 1979, has been revised with an eye to responding to the needs of the poorer departments and communes.

Along with the transfer of new administrative duties and financial resources, especially at the departmental and regional levels, has come the temporary transfer of experienced personnel from the national civil service to territorial service, and a civil service reform bill intended to make territorial service as attractive as national service. Prior to decentralization, in effect, territorial civil servants had none of the employment protections and benefits of national civil servants and none of the career opportunities and incentives. On the whole, they were more poorly paid, more poorly trained, and much more poorly treated, with little opportunity for upward or outward mobility—since they would lose any seniority and pension benefits they might have had by moving from one department or municipality to another.

Given this situation, the Socialists were convinced that reform of the territorial civil service was an absolute necessity. Without it, the highly trained and well-qualified members of the national civil service on loan to the departments and regions would not stay; and the decentralization reforms would, in consequence, founder from lack of competent personnel.[10] The Socialists therefore passed a new civil service code which allows for mobility not only between the territorial civil service and the national civil service but also within the territorial service, viz., between different units of local government, without any loss of seniority, pension privileges and other employment protections. Moreover, the new code attempts to provide career opportunities and continuity in employment by establishing *centres de gestion* or administrative centers run by an elected council charged with (1) regrouping civil servants into corps; (2) ensuring the application of consistent standards to civil servants regardless of locality; (3) organizing competitions for the recruitment of territorial civil servants; (4) approving transfers and reclassifications of unemployed civil servants; and (5) overseeing appointments of and sanctions against civil servants generally.[11]

Civil service reform, in brief, was to provide local officials with the personnel necessary to enable them to exercise their new powers, perform their new functions, and distribute their new resources effectively. And with this, administrative decentralization was to be complete.

Political Reforms

The scope and purpose of decentralization, however, are as much political as they were administrative. The Socialists sought to end the complicity between prefect and notables not only because it was costly and inefficient but also because it was a conservative force which tended to favor the least progressive groups in the periphery. Although France was no longer the nation of peasants and shopkeepers of the Third Republic, the complicity of prefects and notables which had begun during that time continued to favor those groups and to act as a brake on industrial development.

De Gaulle himself was one of the first to recognize this and to attempt to break this "conservative complicity." By setting up the regions, de Gaulle sought to promote, first, an economic revival which was to wake up the *forces vives* or socioprofessional groups in the periphery and, second, a political revival which was to have followed from his failed attempt to turn the regions into political units in 1969.[12] Even without de Gaulle's reforms, however, the periphery had itself been reviving politically at the regional level with movements related to cultural regionalism and separatism, as well as at the municipal level with the rise of the associational movements in the big cities and towns.[13] The groups involved in this urban activism were mainly the *salariés* or wage-earners consisting of middle-level managers and workers who live in the rapidly growing urban agglomerations which were essentially left out of the rural-dominated, center-periphery relationship.[14] And the Socialists' decentralizing reforms were meant to respond to the demands of the regionalists as well as to those of the *salariés*.

By regularizing the status of the region, turning it into another level of local government with its officials to be elected for the first time by universal suffrage, as well as by providing special statutes for Corsica and the overseas regions and territories (DOM-TOM), the Socialists intended to respond in some measure to the increasing demands for regional self-determination. By redrawing cantonal lines to reflect more accurately the population distribution for departmental elections as well as by having regional councillors elected on the basis of proportional representation according to departmental party lists, the Socialists sought to give more say to the urban agglomerations in which the *salariés* reside and to break, to some extent, the traditional rural domination of the periphery.

The law limiting the *cumul des mandats*, passed at the end of December 1985, moreover, was part and parcel of the Socialists' attempt to break the conservative complicity of prefects and notables as well as to encourage greater local democracy. The *décumul* limits elected officials to only two major political mandates and sets up incompatibilities between certain positions such as mayor of a big city, departmental president and regional president. For the *cumulards* who hold large numbers of elected positions, the *décumul* will be gradual, with the elected official forced to abandon only one major mandate per election. For those elected officials who do not hold more than two major mandates, the limit is already in effect (although there is some question as to whether for this last election an increase of one mandate is allowable for those *cumulards* with only two).[15]

By limiting the *cumul*, the Socialists sought to increase the size of the political class generally and to open up access to political positions formerly monopolized by a relatively small number of notables.[16] The *décumul* is all the more important because it was the notables who were the first to profit from decentralization when their positions of prestige at the departmental and regional levels were turned overnight into ones of political as well as executive power. The *décumul*, though, was promoted for administrative as well as political reasons. Many Socialists worried that a continued *cumul* would either mean that the *cumulards* would not do a very thorough job in any of their positions or that, by leaving day-to-day decisions up to civil servants, they would promote a kind of recentralization via the bureaucracy.[17]

Originally, the limitation of the *cumul des mandats* was to have been only one of several ways in which the Socialists had intended to encourage local democracy. However, the other reforms they had envisioned, such as tying associational movements to local governments by way of laws encouraging citizen participation, establishing referenda, and so on, never materialized. It is the absence of these other political reforms and the way in which certain administrative changes were implemented that have been the major sources of scholarly criticism of decentralization.

THE LIMITS OF DECENTRALIZATION

What is perhaps most striking about this radical reform is its conservatism. Although decentralization went very far indeed, it did not go nearly as far as the Socialists had originally intended. It was not very innovative in the way it transferred administrative functions or financial resources. And it did not do much to promote local democracy. Pragmatism or the politics of the possible was very much at play here, and understandably so. For the very logic which

made decentralization unstoppable also made it more vulnerable to those organized groups with a vested interest in the new system.

The Limits to Administrative Reform

It was only by moving swiftly that the Socialists were able to pass the *loi-
cadre* or framework law on decentralization of March 2, 1982, before those
satisfied with the system as it was were able to consolidate their opposition to
reform. And it was the timetable contained in that law that made the process of
decentralization, once started, unstoppable. Gaston Defferre calculated that only
by abolishing the prefects' *tutelle* and transferring their executive powers before
even beginning to work out the details of the subsequent transfers of administrative functions and financial resources could he gain the necessary support for
the reform. For only in this way, he felt, would the very officials most likely
to resist change, were the details of decentralization to be worked out in advance
of the passage of any law, become instead its most ardent supporters. Once that
first break or *rupture* with the old system was accomplished, Defferre was
confident that the newly powerful local officials would be certain to press hard
for the quickest transfer of the administrative functions without which their
executive power would be meaningless, and for the financial resources without
which they would be unable to fulfill their obligations.[18] Defferre was right. The
main objection to decentralization from local officials, once the process had
already begun, came from members of the opposition accusing the government
of bad faith because they were not implementing their reforms fast enough.[19]

Only by waiting to work out the details of the reform, then, were the Socialists
able to begin the process of decentralization. But because those details were not
worked out in advance, and because the pressure to work them out fast was
intense, expediency often took the place of innovation. Moreover, as was to be
expected, those areas of reform subject to the most organized or strongest pressure
were the ones addressed first, while those areas subject to little pressure or much
counterpressure were considered last, if at all—in many cases because the politics
of the moment made particular reforms no longer attractive to many erstwhile
reformers.

The order of the day for the director of the local collectivities in the Ministry
of Interior, in any event, was to transfer administrative functions and financial
resources and authority as quickly as possible. The breakneck pace at which the
details of these transfers had to be worked out, however, meant that the sweeping
changes and reorganization of services originally planned were themselves swept
aside. Because the politicians' pressure for quick reform was met by counter-
pressures from the various ministries and *grand corps* or elite corps of civil
servants, the transfer of administrative functions took the form that was likely
to be the easiest to pass as well as to implement.

The transfer of health and social services from the state to the department,
for example, did not reorganize those services as originally planned—with the

recipient of benefits in mind—because such a reorganization would have led to a long, drawn out battle with all the ministries all together. The transfer of functions followed instead the traditional division of services so that the different interests could be fought separately, one at a time. But this pitched set of battles meant that the resulting system ended up being at least as complex, if not more so, than the previous one.[20] It also ensured that the kinds of bureaucratic problems previously found at the national level were simply transferred to the departmental level—if not made worse. Because the state has retained certain functions related to "national solidarity," such as protection of minors, handicapped persons and immigrant populations as well as social security, many individuals now have two levels of government to deal with in addition to the different divisions within each level. In the case of the handicapped, the department pays for their lodging, social security supplies their principal source of income, and the state arranges for their employment.[21] Furthermore, given the new division of services between state and department, two government employees frequently perform the task formerly done by one. Retirement homes, for example, are now visited by departmental housing inspectors and state medical inspectors.[22]

The transfer of administrative functions, then, has brought with it continuing complication and sometimes duplication in the delivery of social services. Moreover, it has not as yet been accompanied by a concomitant significant reduction in the size of Paris ministries. Gaston Defferre once remarked that the reform would be measured by the number of closed offices in the ministries. But those offices are not yet closed (as of March 1985, only 700 jobs had been transferred to the periphery), while many new ones have opened up in the departments and regions.[23] Decentralization cannot have significantly reduced the administrative costs of local government, as had originally been intended.

Decentralization has, in fact, been expensive. As of March 1985, the reforms had already cost a minimum of 1 billion francs counting the expense of new employees and new or refurbished buildings to house the newly powerful local governments. The department of Calvados, for example, with a budget of 1.291 billion francs for 1985, took in 129 prefectoral functionaries and added 31 extra at an estimated cost of 3.9 million francs. The region of Poitou-Charente, with a budget of 500 million francs, took in 25 prefectoral functionaries and added 46 at an estimated cost of 5.8 million francs. The construction costs involved in new or refurbished buildings to house either prefectoral or territorial services, moreover, reached 22.7 million francs in Calvados and 70 million francs in Poitou-Charente by 1985. Even in Gaston Defferre's home region—or perhaps most significantly there—costs went up astronomically. Provence-Alpes-Côte d'Azur, with a 1985 budget of 1.5 billion francs, added approximately 110 new employees at a cost of 13.8 million francs and has spent nearly 60 million francs on construction since 1982. In addition, the regional accounting courts have also raised the price of decentralization. In the Lorraine alone, there are now 87 magistrates, secretaries, and supplementary employees to be housed in a 24 million franc building.[24]

These particular start-up costs of decentralization, interestingly enough, have not caused great consternation among locally elected officials[25]—and understandably so, since the state essentially picked up the tab—but such state largesse will not last. Some elected officials, especially at the departmental level, are already expressing concern about the rising costs of social welfare and the diminishing revenues available to pay for them. In fact, some have gone so far as to insist that decentralization involves not so much the transfer of power as the transfer of unpopularity, because theirs is a no-win situation: in order to meet their obligations, they must either raise taxes or cut services.[26] In reality, what this means, in the words of Jacques Rondin, is that locally elected officials will have to start rationalizing expenditures which the state in the past simply rationed.[27] This, in fact, is already taking place in some local governments, exactly as Gaston Defferre had intended.[28] But Defferre has, nonetheless, made cost containment more difficult even for fiscally responsible officials by following the dictates of politics in transferring administrative functions.

Political considerations have interfered not only with the transfer of administrative functions but also with the transfer of financial resources and civil service reform. The Socialists quickly saw that any major overhaul of local finances would be extremely complicated and politically hazardous. Thus they took the most conservative path available and left intact any number of taxes they had themselves long criticized. In addition, civil service reform was effectively delayed for quite a while because the *statuts d'application* or implementation rules were very slow in coming. Hence, the law on the books was inapplicable, and the numbers of civil servants working for territorial governments were in limbo. The delay itself had two main sources: (1) resistance from the *énarques* (civil servants trained at the Ecole nationale d'administration [ENA]) and other members of the upper-level national civil service fearful of a rival territorial service; and (2) opposition from local politicians fearful that such reform would represent a kind of recentralization by the state which would limit their powers considerably in personnel matters by establishing a nationwide set of standards for the territorial civil service modeled on the national civil service.[29]

The Limits to Political Reform

Political considerations, in addition, even interfered with the timing and extensiveness of regional reform. Because the Socialists began losing election after election in the periphery, they kept putting off the regional elections originally scheduled for 1983 or 1984, thereby leaving the regional president, who had already acquired executive power, in the awkward position of exercising power without the legitimacy gained only through election. Moreover, because the elections took place only at the last possible moment, in conjunction with the national legislative elections, the results themselves tell us very little. For the regionals were overshadowed by the national elections, not only because of their timing and format—i.e., election by proportional representation according to departmental party list—but also because of their newness. The light returns had to do with the fact that voters often did not even know the location of the regional polling place since it was different from the national one.

These problems, needless to say, only added to the frustration of regionalists, who complained right from the start that the government should have made a clear choice between departments and regions.[30] Thus, many were distressed to find that the party lists for regional elections would be drawn up by departments and elected on a departmental basis as opposed to being drawn up by regions and elected on an at-large basis.[31] They were fearful that the potential power and significance of the regions would be reduced if rurally biased departmentalists were to gain control of the regions. This in turn would mean that the regions could not become so clearly the creatures of the urban communes and the wage-earners in the way that the departments had always been the creatures of the rural communes and the peasants and shopkeepers.

Regionalists' complaints about the delay in regional elections and departmental control over party lists, though, were minor compared to their concern over the transfer of important administrative functions and financial resources from the state to the departments. For to them this suggested that the departments were indeed favored over the regions. But this was not so, at least according to Defferre. While the departments received only the administrative functions they already had jurisdiction over through the prefects, the regions were from the beginning given much more power and stand to gain still more over time. To have abolished the departmental level altogether, which was what some region-alists might have wanted, was in any case a political impossibility if the decen-tralizing laws were to be passed at all.[32]

The lack of a clear-cut choice between the regions and the department, in any event, is really not as serious as some critics think.[33] It may in fact be a blessing in disguise. For by giving the departments and the regions different mandates, the central government may promote economic progress through the partnership of regions and urban communes, at least in the more urbanized regions, while they may protect another kind of social existence through the partnership of departments and rural communes.[34] By limiting the *cumul des mandats*, more-over, the differentiation of the various levels of local government can only be helped.

The limitation of the *cumul*, though, is another instance of where political considerations entered into play. For most Socialists, after shelving the law for most of their term in office, ultimately pushed the law through at the eleventh hour only because it appeared to be a good way to limit the power of the conservatives, who were likely to gain a majority in the March 1986 elections. And the conservatives in the Senate, for their part, passed the law because they did not want to look bad, given that they themselves had been blaming the delay in passing the law on the Socialists' selfish political considerations.

There were a number of reasons for the delay that went beyond the narrow political considerations of the moment, however. Many shared the view of scholars such as François Dupuy and Jean-Claude Thoenig that the *cumul* was an effective way of integrating the governmental system and of assuring politicians enough political power to counterbalance the administrative power of the prefect, the field services of the state, and even Paris itself.[35] Some politicians went beyond this to suggest that with decentralization, the *cumul* was all the more important because it would help counterbalance the newly powerful intermediate structures of government. For example, Philippe Séguin (RPR)—deputy, mayor of Epinal, general councillor of the Vosges, regional councillor of the Lorraine and recently named minister of social affairs in Chirac's new government—argued that a *cumul* which allowed him to hold national as well as local office was essential because the department and the region were generally unresponsive to the needs of his constituency, a mid-sized city.[36] Jean-Marie Rausch (UDF)—senator, mayor of Metz, regional president of the Lorraine and president of the Association of the Mayors of Big Cities—was less concerned about the newly powerful intermediate structures (especially since he controls one) than about Paris. Thus he insisted that the political benefits of the *cumul* outweighed its drawbacks, and that he could easily accomplish the tasks attendant upon his *cumul* by spending four to five hours on the region, fifteen on the city and ten going to Paris in any one week.[37]

While political power was one of the most frequently cited reasons for opposing any extensive *décumul*, money was another compelling but mostly unmentioned factor. Although any one position may not pay very well, the accumulation of offices can pay handsomely indeed, depending upon the offices accumulated. A *cumulard* who is a deputy or senator with a base salary in the environs of 33,000 francs a month will receive half of his or her legally set mayor's salary of about 10,100 francs for a city of 80,000 to 100,000 inhabitants or about 1,530 francs for a village of fewer than 500 inhabitants; half of the legally set regional councillor's salary of 560 francs per diem ordinarily for no more than five days per month (although this will be determined by the regions themselves following the March 1986 elections); and all of the departmental councillor's salary, which varies according to department, from a low of 873 francs a month on average for Ariège to 13,340 francs for Val-de-Marne. These figures, of course, do not include the higher salary of the presidents of a region or department; the extra compensation for regional and departmental vice-presidents, heads of parliamentary commissions, presidents of an urban community, a *syndicat intercommunal*, and any of the large number of associations over which locally elected officials ordinarily preside; or the reimbursement of expenses for travel, for administrative assistants and for secretarial services—let alone the perks such as chauffeured cars, offices which double as overnight accommodations for parliamentarians, and so on. Jean-Marie Rausch, for example, earns a reported salary of 38,300 francs a month, or about $65,000 a year, for performing his many duties. But he comes nowhere near Jean Lecanuet (UDF) who as senator and president of the Senatorial Commission of Foreign Affairs and Defense, mayor of Rouen, deputy to the European Parliament, departmental president of the Seine-Maritime, and regional councillor of the Haute-Normandie earns an average of 61,500 francs monthly, or about $104,000 a year.[38]

Money, in brief, must explain a portion of politicians' resistance to the *décumul*—and understandably so, since without accumulating a substantial number of positions, elected officials who spend all of their time on their official duties may have a very hard time making ends meet. Among politicians, though, only Jacques Médecin (RPR)—deputy, mayor of Nice, president of the general council of the Alpes-Maritimes—has been completely open about the fact that money was his main reason for becoming a deputy on top of his other offices. On a mayor's salary alone, he explained, he would not even be able to afford his dry-cleaning expenses, which are quite high because his various official functions ordinarily require three changes of clothing during the day in addition to the requisite *smoking* (tuxedo) at night. His account of his pecuniary motivation for serving as a deputy would seem to be accurate since his attendance record at the National Assembly is one of the lowest.[39]

The Socialists' short-term political considerations combined with most politicians' attachment to the *cumul* as a source of political power as well as income to delay passage of the law limiting the *cumul*. This delay led some scholars such as Yves Mény to argue, before the last minute passage of the law, that decentralization itself was really a reform for the notables intended to increase their power and not, as claimed by the Socialists, a reform intended to promote local democracy.[40]

It is not really fair, however, to condemn decentralization as a whole because it has increased the powers of the notables but has not yet encouraged local democracy. Former prime minister Pierre Mauroy himself suggested that although for the moment we may indeed have decentralized Jacobinism, all reform is like good wine—it takes time for it to give its all.[41] In a similar vein, Jean-Pierre Worms, deputy of Saône-et-Loire, commented that, given how long the previous system lasted, one must expect a long apprenticeship, not an overnight change.[42] It is likely to take some time before people, whether individually or as part of associations, even realize that they should go to the *Hôtel du Département* or the *Hôtel de Region* instead of the *Préfecture* for their needs. In the meantime, the notables may very well hold sway, but already those who are benefiting are no longer always the old ones. For although it is true that the old Socialist notables have indeed profited by retaining their seats while the new Socialists of 1981 have been swept out of power, they have been replaced by new notables—if we can call them that—on the right. And this new breed of notables on the right, just as those out of power for the moment on the left, engages in a different kind of politics from the old: one involved in encouraging the participation of associational and socioprofessional groups in decision-making processes, one more focused on managing local government efficiently and effectively, and one more responsive to the needs of the local population. Thus, although it is true that decentralization has for the moment mainly increased the powers of the notables, it has done so for a new breed subject to the law limiting the *cumul*.

Furthermore, despite the fact that decentralization has to date had little impact on the population at large, this is likely to change over time. Such change, contrary to the assumptions of some *autogestionnaires*, would probably not yet have begun even if the laws institutionalizing citizen participation had been passed.[43] For by the time the Socialists had come to power, local political activism of the kind promoted by the *autogestionnaires* had already lost most of its momentum. And those who fault decentralization for not encouraging local democracy therefore are in truth blaming it for not reviving an activism which had all but died. The fact that such activism was moribund, moreover, probably explains better than anything else the failure of the Socialists to pass participatory laws. For without organized pressure for the reform here, given all the other issues demanding immediate attention, it was understandably let go. The lack of such a reform, in any event, does not in any way deny the possibility of participation or increased local democracy in the future.

Thus, even though decentralization has not been the politically revitalizing force many had hoped, it has nevertheless set up the structures which can lend themselves to such revitalization in the future. Similarly, even though the way in which the socialists transferred administrative functions and financial resources does little to set the groundwork for a more efficient local government, let alone a less costly one, decentralization itself has ensured that there is nothing to stop local governments from streamlining their own administrative services, redirecting resources to areas they consider most in need and reducing expenses.

CHANGING ROLES, RULES AND RELATIONS

Despite its limitations, decentralization has had an important impact on local politics and administration. By redefining the role of all major actors in the periphery, it has altered the rules of the game and broken the conservative complicity between prefects and notables. Moreover, at the same time that it has made locally elected officials more accountable to the local population for their actions and the prefects more accountable to the state, it has complicated their political as well as administrative interrelationships. Finally, by turning the heads of every level of local government into powerful, popularly elected officials while limiting the number of offices they can accumulate, it has politicized the periphery generally, increasing the size of the political class, strengthening party politics and introducing national cleavages and concerns at every level of local government.

Administrative Changes

Even though decentralization has altered the administrative roles, rules and relationships of all major actors in the periphery, the actors themselves disagree as to the nature and significance of one another's role changes. Thus, the prefects, renamed *Commissaires de la République*, tend to argue that their new role has brought them different but not diminished powers along with a new, mediative function. They admit, nevertheless, that they have lost some of the trappings of power: although they have retained their uniforms, they generally have fewer chauffeured cars available to them, smaller expense accounts and less plush surroundings. They also agree that whereas before decentralization, they could essentially set the rules of the game of local governmeent, today those rules are determined by the full range of actors in the periphery. And the prefects' demeanor and sense of their role has changed accordingly. For the prefects now see themselves and are seen by others as mediators more than anything else.[44] And although it is true that increasingly through the 1960s and 1970s, the prefect in role sought more to cajole, consult and persuade than to command, the prefect's ability to command remained, to be used wherever necessary.[45] Now, however, the prefects cannot command, and the consultative or mediative posture taken before decentralization has become a major part of the way in which they conceive of their new role.[46]

While the prefects see their role as changed but not diminished in importance, others tend to see the prefect as having gone almost overnight from an authority with tremendous power over all local officials and matters to one with comparatively little. Certainly regional and departmental presidents feel this way; they claim that the main challenge to their authority comes from one another. While regional presidents envy the large budgets of the departments, departmental presidents are jealous of the regions' financial flexibility. For while 90 percent to 95 percent of a region's budget is unencumbered (although this figure is diminishing somewhat as regions hire new personnel and make more investment commitments), 90 percent to 95 percent of the department's budget is already spoken for, to be spent on nationally legislated programs. Moreover, with the regional elections of March 1986, departmental presidents worry that the regions will become a challenge, if not a threat, to their power and to their legitimacy as spokespeople for the periphery, given the department-wide electoral basis of the regional councillor's mandate as opposed to the narrow cantonal basis of the general councillor's mandate.

While regional and departmental presidents worry about one another and see a diminished role for the prefect, big-city mayors worry little about the departmental and regional presidents or the prefects. The big-city mayors' main concern has been the reduction of their financial resources because of the switch to block grants from the myriad subsidies provided by different Paris ministries and the reduction in revenue from the local business tax.[47] And, thus, they recognize that the region has become more important to them as a new source of funding— and a rival. On this score, though, it is the mayors of the mid-sized cities who are most concerned, for they can turn for help neither to the departments—the traditional ally of the rural communes—nor to the regions—the natural ally of the big cities.[48]

Big-city mayors, in any event, are relatively unconcerned about regional and departmental presidents as well as about prefects. Because they had over the years developed an independence based on their own direct Paris access (usually as a result of the *cumul*) and their own technical services, they were little affected by the prefects. And the prefects' new mediative role therefore seems to big-city mayors little changed from their previous role.

The big-city mayors' view of the prefects stands in direct contrast to that of rural mayors, who have always seen the prefect as a powerful intermediary with the state on their behalf. And rural mayors therefore are the ones to have found decentralization most unsettling. In their newfound freedom, the mayors of rural communes can no longer count on the delicate balance or compromise of the past in their relations with the prefect to ensure their tenure in office. Because they now have final signature power (rather than first) over construction permits, for example, they can no longer blame the prefect or the technical field services of the state for unpopular decisions.[49] Old patterns of interaction, nevertheless, die hard. Consequently, the mayors often now claim that the prefects' a posteriori judicial recourse is worse than the a priori *tutelle*, for the threat of court proceedings alone is enough for mayors to capitulate to the prefects' demands. Although they would have to agree that a very small percentage of their decisions actually wind up in the administrative tribunal or regional accounting courts (less than 1 percent), they would insist that this is because they tend to go to the prefects for approval a priori for any matter they feel might be open to question. With the recent revision of the DGE which gives the prefect charge of disbursing investment funds to rural communes on a case by case basis on the advice of a commission of locally elected officials, the rural mayors can claim that recentralization is occurring, minus, however, the benefits of the old system, which made the prefects more dependent on local officials and therefore more willing to consider their needs first.

The new role of the prefect, however, is not the only threat confronting rural mayors. The new powers of the departments, and especially their ability to provide financial and technical assistance to rural communes, mean that they may gain a certain measure of control over the communes even though, legally, no level of local government is to exercise a *tutelle* over any other. But because rural mayors have insufficient resources to make their own decisions about even such things as construction permits, the mayor must go either to the technical field services of the state (for example, the DDE—*Direction départementale d'équipement*, the departmental direction of public works) or to those of the department where they exist (sometimes referred to as the DDE-bis). But either choice involves, to some extent, deciding which *tutelle* is preferable, i.e., that of the newly powerful department or that of the state.[50]

The threat of a departmental *tutelle* over the rural communes has actually led some mayors to pin their hopes on the counter-powers derived from intercommunal charters, the successors of the intercommunal syndicates of assistance. But because these charters or syndicates represent more financial arrangements of convenience than anything else, they are unlikely to challenge the departments' potential control over rural communes. The regions, similarly, could provide some counter to the departments in giving aid to rural communes. But this would be more in the form of industrial development subsidies for small and medium-sized enterprises as opposed to technical services. And it therefore represents less a challenge to a departmental *tutelle* than another kind of *tutelle* in the area of economic development.

The important field services of the state, finally, remain as powerful as they ever were, even though they are formally more under the control of the prefects than before. They remain quite independent of the prefects even though correspondence must pass through the prefecture first.[51] For the level of deconcentration of the technical services such as the DDE is such that the services have agents throughout the department consulting directly with mayors, for example, on the matter of building permits. And thus, while the prefect may be formally in charge of all the field services of the state, those services, especially the technical ones, continue to operate as independently as they always have. The only difference is that they tend to be more responsive to the wishes of rural mayors, partially because they face competitors from the departmental technical services and even private contractors whom the mayors now have the legal right to hire—although they must pay for them themselves.

Decentralization thus is working itself out in different ways at different levels of local government. And this has led some to fear that decentralization will only have promoted administrative confusions, time delays and inefficient public management generally.[52] However, these fears are nothing compared to those concerned with the politicization of the periphery generally.

Political Changes

There are many, in effect, who feel that the politicization of the periphery, combined with the new roles, rules and relationships of local politicians and administrators, may prove to be more of a divisive than a dynamizing and reintegrating force. Although some such as Michel Crozier even before the new decentralization encouraged the introduction of party politics at the local level in order to diminish the power of local elites,[53] others more recently have seen the politicization as promoting only local conflict and the patronage which often goes along with partisan politics.[54] Thus, some argue that the politicization alone will interfere with fair governmental administration, since presidents of regional and departmental councils will be tempted to follow the lead of the big-city mayor in exchanging favors for partisan loyalty. Others fear that having political actors at all four levels of local government (including the prefect, now) will lead to great administrative confusions, and perhaps even the stalemates of the past if rival parties control different levels.[55] It is still too early to tell which, if any, of these dire predictions will come to pass. But what is clear is that politics in the periphery is here to stay, and that it has affected every level of local government, including the prefectoral.

The main question for the prefects is whether they are to be neutral mediators—as they themselves would claim[56]—or political agents of the state—as others, mainly in opposition[57]—insist that they have become. And this depends for an answer primarily on the politics as well as on the personalities of the prefects and the locally elected officials of the particular region, department or commune. In Calvados, for example, where the department was to pay the prefect's expenses through 1986, the president, Michel d'Ornano (UDF), who is also a deputy and president of the region of Basse-Normandie, decided to allow the prefect only the expenses he felt necessary for him to represent the state appropriately—viz., no more meetings with mayors, ribbon-cutting ceremonies or anything else which could conceivably be of political benefit to the Socialists in power at the time.[58] In the Meuse, moreover, a department with only five left-wing deputies out of a total of thirty-two at the time, the political uproar was extreme when a Communist was named prefect in January 1982.[59] In Provence-Alpes-Côte d'Azur, by contrast, the regional prefect appointed by Defferre (then minister of the interior) had been prefect of the Bouches-du-Rhône under Giscard d'Estaing (and thus Defferre's prefect) before becoming prefect of police in Paris while Jacques Chirac was mayor.[60]

Clearly, then, personality and personal ties can overcome political affiliations, at least where they are not extremely pronounced. Where they are, as in the case of Pierre Costa, prefect in the Calvados before the Communist prefect, the outcome was a move into territorial service, as general director of departmental services for Jacques Médecin in the Alpes-Maritimes. Costa, moreover, was only the first of seven prefects and forty-five sub-prefects to move into territorial service. And this is a trend likely to continue, with *l'alternance* in politics reproducing itself in the upper levels of the civil service for those more clearly politically identified members of the prefectoral corps.

The politicization at the level of the state's representation in the periphery, in any event, comes nowhere near the politicization at the other levels of local government. Some of this results, quite naturally, from the fact that decentralization, as Michel d'Ornano put it, has *responsabilisé et personalisé* the roles of locally elected officials by making them more personally responsible to the electorate for their actions.[61] The very fact that locally elected officials complain that decentralization may lead to their unpopularity, given current fiscal constraints, certainly demonstrates their keen awareness of the political dimensions of their newly powerful roles. And this awareness has translated itself into a politicization which has brought national political divisions increasingly into play on the local level.

National political cleavages are especially apparent at the regional and departmental levels. The most obvious indication of this is that the regional councils and the general councils of the departments have become forums for national debate. For example, antigovernment speeches by Olivier Guichard, regional president of the Pays de la Loire when the Socialists were in power, had become so commonplace that the prefect no longer responded to them, let alone left the room as in the past.[62] In the Alpes-Maritimes, where in 1985 there were five Communists, only one Socialist, and fifty-one opposition members, Jacques Médecin found himself reduced to attacking the Communists as the former collaborators of the Socialist government.[63] National influence on local politics, however, does not limit itself to pro- or antigovernment positions. In the Lorraine, the debates have been just as intense among members of the different conservative factions.

Partisan politics thus has already entered the regional and departmental arenas. But because the electoral bases of the two arenas differ, it is possible that partisans of different parties or at least policies (e.g., rural versus urban) will be elected to the different levels. It is here that the limitation of the *cumul des mandats* may have its greatest impact. For by setting up legal incompatibilities between mayors of big cities, presidents of departments and presidents of regions, different people will have to head these different levels of government. Hence, they will therefore be less likely to experience conflicts in role and more likely to develop policies which are most appropriate to their particular constituency. At the same time, the *décumul* is most likely to reinforce party politics at the local level, since locally elected officials will have to begin to put more faith in their fellow party members. This will be the case even if the new conservative government manages to eliminate the present electoral system of the regions, which is currently a boon to party politics; for regardless of the electoral system, parties will continue to be more involved in determining who should run for which offices. In addition, parties will benefit from the increase in the size of the political class. The Socialists have already benefited from this because without the *décumul*, their numbers in office, which had already dwindled appreciably, would have dropped even more sharply. The *décumul*, though, will certainly also benefit the right, since the tendency to accumulate office has been as marked on the right as on the left.

Partisan politics, then, is likely only to increase and, along with it, decisions responding to national political pressures based along party lines. Therefore, instead of having a prefect as the executive power who seeks to accommodate everyone in the process of *saupoudrage*, the departments and the regions are likely to have presidents who will seek to accommodate primarily their own local political constituency. Although this politicization could translate itself into continued *saupoudrage* where the president does not have a firm majority in the council, it is more likely to become the reason for partisan political decisions about who gets what, when, how and where. This is especially the case where regional and departmental presidents use political cabinets which reflect only the views of the majority of the council to direct the affairs of the region or department.

There are, nevertheless, limits as to how much partisan politics can interfere with the equitable distribution of resources. For example, because municipal, departmental and regional levels all have responsibility for local economic development, the extent to which one level or another can exercise political tyranny may be limited, for tyranny at one level may be offset by help at another. Good politics, moreover, is not always partisan politics. Thus, in the future just as in the past, locally elected officials are as likely as not to do the right thing by a political rival if only to avoid the appearance of prejudice or partisanship or, better yet, simply to follow sound economic policy.[64]

CONCLUSION

Decentralization thus has contributed to the politicization of the periphery, although not yet to its democratic revitalization. It has produced important changes in the roles of major actors in the periphery, and this has in turn altered the rules by which they play the games of local politics and administration. Decentralization on the whole is not quite as revolutionary as it might have been because of the pragmatic way in which the Socialists proceeded with the reform. Nevertheless, had the Socialists not been so pragmatic, the reform itself would probably have suffered the ill fate of all such previous attempts. The Socialists have been as successful as they possibly could have been.

NOTES

1. For a short list of scholars who failed to see any possibility for reform, see Mark Kesselman, "The Tranquil Revolution at Clochemerle: Socialist Decentralization in France," in P. Cerny and M. Schain, eds., *Socialism, the State, and Public Policy in France* (London: Frances Pinter, 1985), pp. 165–66.

2. For a brief discussion of the failed reforms, see Yves Mény, "Central Control and Local Resistance," in V. Wright, ed., *Continuity and Change in France* (London: George Allen and Unwin, 1984), pp. 203–14.

3. For descriptions of the complicity, see Jean-Pierre Worms, "Le Préfet et ses notables," *Sociologie du Travail* 3 (July–September 1966): 249–75; Jean-Claude Thoenig, "La Relation entre le centre et la périphérie en France: une analyse systématique," *Bulletin de l'Institut International d'Administration Publique* (December 1975): 77–123; Pierre Grémion, *Le Pouvoir périphérique* (Paris: Seuil, 1976).

4. Jack Hayward, *The One and Indivisible French Republic* (New York: Norton, 1973), pp. 20–21.

5. Jean Ravanel, *La Réforme des collectivités locales et des régions* (Paris: Dalloz, 1984).

6. For a full discussion of the change in the role of the prefect, see Paul Bernard, *L'Etat et la décentralisation: du préfet au Commissaire de la République* (Paris: Documentation française, 1983).

7. Jacques Caroux, "The End of Administrative Centralization?" *Telos*, No. 55 (Spring 1983): 113.

8. For an in-depth look at the overall effects of decentralization on the departments, see René Dosière, Jean-Claude Fortier, and Jean Mastias, *Le Nouveau Conseil Général* (Paris: Éditions ouvrières, 1985). For an in-depth look at the overall effects of decen-

tralization on the region, see Dominique Schmitt, ed., *La Région à l'heure de la décentralisation* (Paris: Documentation française, 1985).

9. "Trois ans de décentralisation," *Démocratie Locale*, No. 38 (April 1985).

10. This was the general opinion of informed and interested observers such as Jean-Pierre Worms, deputy from Saône-et-Loire (interviewed in Paris, May 9, 1985), and Philippe de Lara of the Decentralization Observatory in the Ministry of Urbanism, Housing, and Transport (interviewed in Paris, May 17, 1985).

11. *Le Monde*, March 11, 1986.

12. Philip Cerny, "The Political Balance," in P. Cerny and M. Schain, *French Politics and Public Policy* (New York: St. Martin's Press, 1980), pp. 8–9. For an extended discussion of the problems with regional reform, see Grémion, *Pouvoir*.

13. Sidney Tarrow, *Between Center and Periphery* (New Haven: Yale University Press, 1977), pp. 131–32.

14. Marc Abélès, "Les Chemins de la décentralisation," *Les Temps Modernes*, No. 463 (February 1985): 1402.

15. *Le Monde*, December 26, 1985.

16. Pierre Birnbaum, Francis Hamon, and Michel Troper, *Réinventer le parlement* (Paris: Flammarion, 1977), p. 42.

17. Worms interview, May 9, 1985.

18. Interview with Gaston Defferre, former minister of the interior and decentralization, Paris, May 23, 1985. For a discussion of Defferre's strategy, see Philippe de Lara, "De nouvelles règles du jeu pour la democratie," *Intervention*, No. 3 (March-April 1983): 9; Jacques Rondin, *Le Sacre des notables* (Paris: Fayard, 1985), pp. 29–69; Jean-Pierre Worms, "La Décentralisation: un processus, une chance a saisir," *Echange & Projets*, No. 39 (September 1984): pp. 30–31.

19. *Le Monde*, December 15, 1985; *Le Figaro*, December 22, 1985.

20. Rondin, pp. 144–47.

21. Ibid.

22. *L'Express*, March 8–14, 1985.

23. Ibid.

24. Ibid.

25. Philippe Séguin, current minister of social affairs for Jacques Chirac but at the time of the interview deputy, mayor of Epinal, regional councillor of the Lorraine and general councillor of the Vosges, expressed a great deal of concern at the expense incurred for the new walls of the departmental headquarters (approximately 60 million francs) and the refurbishing of the regional headquarters (an eighteenth-century *Hôtel particulier* and former school); he did not mention the cost of his own tastefully modernized and refurbished town hall, though (interviewed in Epinal, June 18, 1985).

26. This was an oft-repeated view of members of the opposition, especially in the first two years of decentralization. It was communicated to me by Jacques Médecin, deputy, mayor of Nice and president of the department of the Alpes-Maritime (interviewed in Nice, June 7, 1985).

27. Rondin, *Sacre*, p. 156.

28. Defferre interview, May 23, 1985.

29. When questioned about this, Eric Giuily, director of local collectivities of the Ministry of the Interior and Decentralization, agreed that these were two oft-cited reasons for the delay in the reform, but went on to argue that the main reason for delay had to

do with the complexity of the task at hand (interviewed in Paris, May 21, 1985, and June 26, 1985).

30. Michel Crozier, for one, sees the powers of the department increased but insists that it is the region which should have been clearly favored (in "Clochemerle ou la région, il faut choisir," *Projet*, No. 185–186 (May–June 1984). Others who note the unwillingness of the government to choose between region and department are Yves Mény, "Decentralization in Socialist France: The Politics of Pragmatism," *West European Politics* 7, No. 1 (January 1984): 69; Jacques Chevallier, "La Réforme régionale," in J. Chevallier, F. Rangeon, and M. Sellier, *Le Pouvoir régional* (Paris: Presses universitaires de France, 1982), p. 175.

31. For reactions to the change in the regional electoral process, see *Le Monde*, February 2, 1985.

32. Defferre interview, May 23, 1985.

33. Mark Kesselman (in "Tranquil Revolution," p. 178) is actually one of the few scholars to point this out, suggesting that the lack of a choice between region and department may very well reflect the Socialist interest in a "pluralist vitality."

34. To keep the rural communes rural represents a response to the demands of environmentalists and of those taken with the "small is beautiful" formula as well as with the demands of tourism and of the urban professionals who increasingly want their houses in the country.

35. François Dupuy and Jean-Claude Thoenig, *L'Administration en miettes* (Paris: Fayard, 1985), pp. 128–47.

36. Séguin interview, June 18, 1985.

37. Interview with Jean-Marie Rausch, deputy, regional president of the Lorraine, as well as mayor of Metz (Metz, June 18, 1985).

38. *Le Nouvel Observateur*, October 25–31, 1985; *Le Monde*, November 7, 1985.

39. Médecin interview, June 7, 1985.

40. Mény, "Decentralization," p. 66.

41. Quoted in Antonio Martins, "Pluie et bourrasque pour un ex-Premier," *L'Alsace*, June 15, 1985.

42. Worms, "Décentralisation," p. 30.

43. For a current approach, see Georges Gontcharoff, "La Décentralisation peut-elle atteindre le citoyen de base?" *Echange & Projets*, No. 39 (September 1984).

44. In interviews, most local politicians and civil servants remarked on this change, including Giuily, Rausch, Worms and Séguin.

45. Hayward, *Republic*, pp. 23–24.

46. The mediator's posture is essentially the mystification Jacques Chevallier described as part of the "participative state" (in "L'Intérêt général dans l'administration française," *Revue Internationale des Sciences Administratives* 41, No. 4 (1975).

47. Interview with Christian Lalue, director of the Association of Big-City Mayors, Paris, May 22, 1985.

48. Séguin interview, June 18, 1985.

49. Charles Vial, "Haute-Loire: la fin du préfet alibi," *Le Monde*, May 15, 1985.

50. See, for example, Abélès, "Chemins," pp. 1414–15, 1419; Jean-Claude Thoenig, "Le Grand Horloger et les effets de Système: de la décentralisation en France," *Revue Politiques et Management Public* (forthcoming); Irene Wilson, "Decentralizing or Recentralizing the State? Urban Planning and Centre-Periphery Relations," in Cerny and Schain, *Socialism*.

51. Rondin, *Sacre*, pp. 265–72.

52. Caroux, "Centralisation," p. 114; Jean-Emile Vié, "Lacunes et écueils de la décentralisation," in *Décentralisation et Politiques Sociales: Actes du Colloque de Grenoble, January 18–20, 1983* (Paris: Futuribles/C.E.P.E.S., 1983).

53. Michel Crozier, *On ne change pas la société par décret* (Paris: Grasset, 1979).

54. Vié, "Lacunes."

55. Thoenig, "Grand Horloger"; Jean-Michel Bellorgey, "De certains aspects du discours," *Echange & Projets*, No. 39 (September 1984): 21–23.

56. Interview with Michel Cotten, formerly director of local collectivities in the Ministry of Interior (Paris, May 20, 1985); and with Michel Besse, secretary general of the préfecture of the department of the Bouches-du-Rhône (Marseilles, June 5, 1985).

57. Interview with Pierre Costa, director general of departmental services of the Alpes-Maritimes, but formerly a prefect (Nice, June 7, 1985).

58. *L'Express*, March 8–14, 1985.

59. *Le Monde*, February 23, 1983.

60. Besse interview, June 5, 1985.

61. *L'Express*, March 8–14, 1985.

62. Ibid.

63. This was at least the case at the meeting of the general council of the Alpes-Maritimes in Nice, June 6, 1985. And I was informed that ever since decentralization, it had been the rule.

64. Even Jacques Médecin claims to have been so motivated when he provided economic aid to the constituency of the lone Socialist on the general council (Médecin interview, June 7, 1985).

Labor and the Left in Power: Commissions, Omissions and Unintended Consequences

GEORGE ROSS

The left everywhere has traditionally made improving the lot of workers and strengthening unions one of its most cherished goals. The French left shared this goal. What it would actually accomplish after 1981 in this realm was therefore a litmus test of its seriousness of purpose. The test was to be complicated, however, by the fact that Mitterrand and his governments between 1981 and 1986 faced a major economic crisis severely constraining their freedom of action. Connected with this, French unions were weaker, more demoralized and more divided in 1981 than they had been in decades. The results of left rule for labor were thus destined to be much less positive than anyone could have imagined prior to 1981. This chapter will examine the implications for labor of the French left experiment, looking first at unions' postures and their context prior to 1981, then reviewing the "state of grace" and rigor periods between 1981 and 1984 and finally examining the left's turn to industrial "modernization" from later 1983 through March 1986, when the left lost power.

FRENCH UNIONISM IN THE 1970s: PLURALISM, POLITICS AND ECONOMIC CRISIS

In the left's programs prior to 1981 there was agreement to redistribute power and income, bring workers and their unions more into processes of decision-making and redress the balance in the workplace in their favor. Such pledges had most often come in dramatically radical packages calling for "rupture with capitalism" and the like. Whether or not this radical tone could be carried over into left governmental practice, the situation of workers and unions after twenty-three years of rule by the right left plenty of space for meaningful reform.

France had had her postwar economic boom, the famous *trente glorieuses*, which removed French society from nineteenth-century habits and brought it close to the twenty-first century.[1] The postwar social compromise underlying this boom was somewhat different from those elsewhere, however, because the French industrial relations system was never fully regularized and institutionalized. There was no Wagner Act in France, no social democratic live-and-let-live "deal" between capital and labor.[2] Instead constant struggle prevailed, and what went on between capital and labor remained anchored in an earlier era. Employers maintained authoritarian perspectives toward workers. In turn, many workers and much of organized labor regarded employers as exploiters to be dispensed with at the earliest possible opportunity.

The ordinary collective bargaining which was routine elsewhere was thus painfully difficult to generate in France. Contracts, on those relatively rare occasions when they were reached, were not seen as binding, but as truces in an ongoing war to be disregarded when the balance of power changed. Because of this, and because France was France, labor market issues were often passed on to the state for solution, such that politics, legislation and labor inspectors tended to do what decentralized bargaining settled in other places. In consequence, labor market issues were constantly politicized, and both capital and labor were unusually "ideological" in their approaches.[3]

The programmatic solutions advanced by the left to deal with this situation—from the 1972 Common Program[4] to Mitterrand's 1981 election manifesto[5]—were unusually radical. The left claimed to want a transition to something different, a new "New Deal" in France involving vastly increased working-class political and industrial power which would go much further than the older, more social democratic New Deals existing elsewhere. But these older New Deals had flourished in the postwar boom, when it had been relatively easy to transform deadlocked industrial relationships into positive-sum games. The left was to come to power, however, in much less auspicious economic circumstances. Stable, predictable economic expansion in France ended in the mid–1970s in ways that were fundamental for the left's policies after 1981.[6]

The coming of economic crisis in the 1970s was also a pivotal moment for French unions during which they established the positions which French unions held when the left came to power in 1981.[7] In the period following the 1974 presidential elections, the CFDT and the CGT—France's "left" unions—had collaborated with one another in a "unity in action" arrangement (which had existed on and off since 1966). And since the CGT was larger in terms of membership, more centralized and more effective organizationally than the CFDT (the CGT at that point was roughly as strong as the CFDT and FO combined), the CGT increasingly dominated joint CGT-CFDT actions, promoting labor action which would indirectly produce political support for *union de la gauche*. As a result, by 1975–76 the always delicate balance between trade union action and political mobilization struck by French organized labor had shifted well toward the latter. Led by the CGT, the CGT-CFDT alliance rapidly became a support group for left political parties.

The CFDT, increasingly uncomfortable with such developments, changed its strategy after left unity collapsed in 1977–78. Its new approach, *recentrage*— "recentering"—retreated from the overpoliticization of 1974–77 back toward shop floor unionism. The CFDT was newly concerned with the ways in which economic crisis was breaking down social solidarities and creating a "disintegrated working class." To counter such tendencies unions had to constitute themselves as "economic actors" and influence the direction of the fundamental economic decisions which the crisis made inevitable, in the process "recomposing" the working class by creating "new solidarities" and a more democratic "new type of development." Perhaps most important, CFDT *recentrage* was profoundly skeptical about existing left politics and politicians, both mired in statist nostrums, the CFDT thought. Real change could only proceed outside of traditional political channels, from mobilization at the firm and community level. Beyond this, the CFDT did not believe that the left had any prospect of coming to power in the near future.[8]

The CGT also revised its strategy after 1977, but in very different ways, gravitating toward an exaggerated new "transmission belt" posture to further Communist political objectives. After the 1978 elections the Communist Party decided to "reequilibrate the left" by attempting to undercut the growing strength of the PS. The CGT's task in this was to promote hyper-militant "struggle" in the labor market to inculcate the lesson that "crisis was not inevitable." In this new optic, CGT-CFDT unity-in-action was doomed (it ended officially in June 1980) because the CFDT was included among the "reformists" to be attacked. In its own way the CGT also decided to "return to the base" after the political trauma of 1977–78. But it did so in a radicalizing and sectarian fashion. As the 1981 elections approached, the CGT, along with the PCF, was primarily concerned with ensuring the defeat of François Mitterrand, even if it cost another seven years of right rule. As of early 1981, then, the CGT also expected to live in a political environment dominated by the right for years to come.[9]

Force Ouvrière (FO) was quietly consolidating its own, quite different, strategy through this period.[10] FO's traditional anti-Communism, aversion to collaboration with the CGT, refusal of involvement with political parties and American-style attachment to bargaining persisted unchanged. In addition, in the 1970s FO had very shrewdly capitalized upon certain of the contradictions of the French industrial relations system. The 1950 law that governed collective bargaining allowed branch level agreements to go into effect when signed by any officially "representative" union (a status defined by law), even one which represented only a small minority of the workers. The CGT and CFDT—which, taken together, made up the majority of French organized labor—were usually eager to mobilize and confront employers. Often employer associations responded with proposals which only the least militant and weakest union would be willing to sign, proposals which the CGT and CFDT refused, of course. At this point, FO eagerly stepped in to sign.

In effect, FO had turned its moderate and accommodating nature, earlier viewed by almost everyone as a weakness, into a virtue by claiming credit for deals that had been prepared by militant CGT and CFDT action.[11] FO also "dealt" in other ways. It established itself as a regular caller at the Elysée, Matignon and various ministries and then vaunted the virtues of *concertation*— at a moment when the CGT and CFDT were totally excluded from such contact. It also consistently sought leadership positions in union-state-employer "pari- tary" bodies.[12] By 1981, then, FO had settled into a comfortable strategic position as the right majority's favorite union. It, too, was counting on a long future of right political rule, then.

FROM GRACE TO *RIGUEUR*: UNIONS FACE THE LEFT IN POWER, 1981–83

The policy history of the left's first years has been so well reviewed elsewhere that we can be brief.[13] The government initially believed that it could work major reforms, redistribute income and promote new economic growth in a context of international economic crisis. Despite its relative moderation, however, the left's reformist "Keynesianism in one country" approach rapidly ran aground. The government's response to the failure of this initial package was *rigueur*. The net effect of both installments of *rigueur*—June 1982 and March–April 1983—was to hold down French growth and, more pertinent to unions, the growth of French living standards. Earlier left efforts at income redistribution came to a screeching halt. In the interests of profitability, employers' shares in financing the welfare state were reduced. France's already divided and skeptical unions barely had time to adjust to the hopes of the new political situation before they had been dissipated.

Reacting in Dispersed Order

As FO leader, André Bergeron announced that FO intended to "remain itself," to pursue strategic continuity despite the political changes. Nonetheless, the left in power threatened some of the advantages which FO had worked hard to win in the 1970s, its monopoly of *entrée* to governments, for example (which, if it had had little effect in shaping policies, had given FO a visibility that helped its recruitment position). After 1981 all unions had frequent, open access to the government, with the "radical unions" getting better access than FO. FO also lost its privileged position as contract signer. The new government made a special point of promoting collective bargaining on all manner of questions (wages and hours; unemployment—in the *contrats de solidarité*; public sector investment policies—in the *contrats du plan*; work sharing—the thirty-nine-hour week and, later, the implementation of the Auroux laws to reform industrial relations). In this new context all unions were much more eager to sign contracts.

Predictably, FO went to great lengths to denounce the presence of Communist ministers in the government.[14] It also opposed many of the left government's major reforms, the new nationalizations, for example. FO's strong reservations to the Auroux laws—the government's 1982 package of industrial relations reforms—complained that the 1950 law which set the locus of collective bargaining at industrial branch level had been useful, while new obligations to negotiate at both firm and branch level were likely to give the *patronat* new possibilities for "divide and rule" tactics.[15] FO also opposed those parts of the Auroux legislation designed to expand worker "rights of expression" in the firm, denouncing "potential Soviets" which would confuse roles in the firm to everyone's detriment.[16] In each of these principled oppositions to left reforms FO was also confessing to fear for its organization future. Much of what the left was trying to do aimed at strengthening unions at firm level, and FO's organizing capacities at firm level were vastly weaker than those of the CGT and CFDT.[17]

A priori the CFDT seemed to be much better placed than FO to deal with the left in power. As Jacques Chérèque, assistant secretary-general, noted in June 1981, "We don't have to change bicycles, just gears." The left's victory nonetheless posed problems. At the critical juncture of May–June 1981, advocates of CFDT-like views within the PS (the Rocardians) were totally isolated. Neither the president of the Republic—who claimed that he "never understood" the CFDT leadership—nor Prime Minister Pierre Mauroy felt any particular warmth for the union. The CFDT's initial position, then, was complex. As a "left" union, the confederation supported the new government, but it was far from warmly predisposed toward the government's general policy leanings. Reconciling this contradiction between proximity and distance was the CFDT's problem.

The CFDT's emergence as a *deuxième gauche* followed from this contradiction.[18] In the abstract, becoming the "second left" meant using all available means to publicize CFDT analyses of the unfolding situation with working-class opinion as the primary target. Thus the CFDT, usually in the person of Edmond Maire, turned to the mass media to communicate its messages. The government did not understand the true structures of the contemporary crisis. "Old left" ways of a statist, bureaucratic kind led directly into a cul de sac. Movement along the path to a "new model of development" was premised upon willingness to promote social mobilization "from below," to formulate "new social solidarities." Above all, the CFDT did not believe that France could surmount an international crisis through Keynesianism and public sector industrial policy miracles. Innovative measures to decrease social inequalities—through fiscal reform and a compression of the wage hierarchy—and increase real democracy, especially in the workplace, were needed. There was a heavy dose of social Catholicism in all this, which must have sounded strange coming from the mouths of trade unionists. It would be all right for workers to sacrifice in crisis as long as other groups sacrificed commensurately and everyone, including workers, democratically decided things. Thus Maire and the CFDT began to advocate "rigor" through the creation of "new social solidarities," long before the government's actual policy shift in June 1982.[19]

This "second left" campaign intensified after June 1982. To Maire and the CFDT, austerity, which the government had decreed from the top, could be made tolerable only if it rested upon genuine negotiated solidarity between different social groups. Maire warned of the danger of "left Barrism" in his 1982 *rentrée* speech, for example. The "classic left has demonstrated its limits," he later remarked. The government's economic failures followed from its obsessions with the *"tout politique . . .* absolute confidence in huge structural reforms pushed from [the] top downwards . . . revolution by the law."

In part this petulance was a response to the defeat of a number of CFDT policy hopes. The CFDT had hoped for a major shift in energy policy away from Giscard's "all nuclear" program and did not get it. The defeat of "work-sharing" in 1982 was even more important. The CFDT wanted two concrete forms of "new solidarity" from the left: a reduction in hierarchy of remuneration between occupational classifications by squeezing down the distance between top and bottom, and work-sharing. The government very quickly backed away from the first. Work-sharing, however, was higher on the agenda—hence the fifth week of paid vacation, regulation of part-time work and short-term employment contracts, early retirement plus the *contrats de solidarité*—which prodded firms and unions to negotiate job-preserving agreements and greatly expanded job retraining programs, especially for the young. The centerpiece of the work-sharing program, however, was reducing the working week to thirty-five hours by 1985. When push came to shove, however, the government first chose the CGT's definition of this policy and then, with the coming of rigor in June 1982, forgot about the thirty-five hours altogether.[20]

The Auroux laws, on the other hand, were heavily influenced by the CFDT. The promotion of new rights for workers and unions at firm level had been central to the CFDT's agenda since the 1960s. Thus when the minister of labor, Jean Auroux, asked different groups for suggestions about reforms in this area, the CFDT was prepared to move, all the more so given the importance of CFDTers in the ministry itself. A CFDT memorandum of July 1981 provided the basis for much of the Auroux Report which, in turn, outlined the subsequent four laws. In addition, during the legislative process the confederation lobbied extensively with the ministry and parliament to make sure that the results were suitable. The central propositions of the Auroux laws (which we will examine later) were all congruent with the CFDT's *autogestionnaire* leanings.

The shock of 1981 was greatest for the CGT, which had no desire whatever to see François Mitterrand elected president of France. Nonetheless, when four Communist ministers joined the second Mauroy government the CGT suddenly found itself allied to a junior partner in the government of France. The CGT was, of course, nothing if not disciplined. Thus it quickly became perhaps the *major* "interest group" backer of the left between 1981 and 1984 (when the Communists left the government). The new government was on labor's side, the CGT announced. The task remained, however, of "making change succeed." For the CGT "class struggle" would continue, perhaps in even more acute forms "against the *patronat* and the right." Moreover, timid reformers and people who thought that the left's only real task was to "manage the crisis" had to be prevented from closing off "real change." The CGT had decided to support the government for at least as long as the PCF did. But it was aware of the dangers of becoming a trade union "hostage to a friendly government." The CGT thus had to find ways to square a circle, establishing itself as visibly independent of the government while also supporting it.[21]

The principal path that the CGT initially took was to use its influence over the government, often ostentatiously, to get policies enacted which were part of the CGT's own program of economic nationalism and Keynesian expansionism, hoping thus to gather in some credit with workers for government reforms and successes. In this way the confederation could also indirectly support PCF goals, intervening to increase the resources of Communist ministers in policy conflicts, for example. The CGT consistently tried to assert its identity on issues of macroeconomic policy, supporting a Keynesian strategy of *relance* out of crisis, even after it had failed in 1982. The CGT also opposed the government's austerity plans of June 1982 and March 1983, if more in word than deed, talking about the need to "soak the rich." By the governmental crisis of spring 1983 the CGT had quite logically concluded that if industrial policy and redistributive demand stimulation could not be conciliated with participation in an open international market, then openness would have to be sacrificed (through selective trade protectionism and government efforts at "making it in France").

The CGT was often successful in influencing the definition of the government's major reforms. The confederation was alone among the major unions in actually desiring and having precise notions about extensive nationalizations. The CGT also won over the CFDT on energy policy and the "thirty-nine for forty" work-sharing conflict of early 1982, largely through effective pressure on government. The final Auroux legislation fell short of what the CGT maximally desired, however. It had hoped, for example, to abolish altogether management's right to establish a *règlement intérieur* in the workplace and also wanted much larger new rights of expression—in particular rights of political expression—in the firm. It proposed endowing *comités d'entreprise* with new powers to review and hold up layoffs and firings and lost here as well. The CGT nonetheless was basically in favor of the final product.

First Results: Reequilibration

Despite the new political situation, then, each major union continued to dedicate as much energy to gaining advantage over its union rivals as it did to reconstructing union-government relationships or to helping the left. In consequence, even though it was quite sincerely dedicated to prolabor changes, the left had no choice but to try to make the best of a pluralistic union movement. It turned out not to be very good even at this, however, largely through no fault of its own. While the government considered organized labor as a privileged ally and essential negotiating partner—a situation which had not existed in France since 1947—it also had to be very careful to give all unions equal time. This constraint had great consequences. Structurally compelled to listen to all and favor none, the new government quickly gave unions the general impression of soliciting their wisdom and advice, but not paying much attention thereafter. Partly because of this, and partly because of the political left's own propensities, unions concluded that even those decisions which they approved were being made in statist and technocratic ways. As André Bergeron of FO observed, the government had difficulty learning that *la concertation ne sert pas seulement à bavarder.*

Bavardage notwithstanding, the government had to make policy. And policy-making, as we have already noted, often confirmed one union's positions over another's, leading some unions to feel rewarded and others to feel penalized and critical. In a loaded context of competitive union pluralism, this accentuated the intensity of interunion rivalry. Because the CGT was tied to the PCF, for example, it had privileged links to the government. This situation created additional incentives for the CFDT and FO to distance themselves from the government. To compensate, in turn, the CGT was obliged to make its own stream of rhetorical criticisms of certain government policies.

The government thus faced an impossible tactical situation. Almost no matter what it did, parts of the labor movement were virtually certain to complain. In time the results of this complicated new system of union-government relationships created an impression that the unions, whatever they were actually doing, were constantly carping about governmental actions. Since the unions, or at least the CGT and CFDT, were in fact the government's *gros bataillons* of support, this impression fueled widespread sentiment which developed after the brief 1981 "state of grace" that the left government was not much loved by anyone. If the unions seemed to believe that the government was constantly making mistakes and failing, then who could believe that it was succeeding? For a left whose electoral position was far from secure, such an impression was exceedingly bad news.

After 1981 each major union had carefully assumed a different posture vis-à-vis the left. The CGT had announced "Yes . . . but more, and more quickly," the CFDT "Yes . . . but you should be doing it differently," and FO "It is really none of our business . . . but you're doing it all wrong." By early 1984, after the 1983 social security elections, certain surprising results of this rivalry game had become clear, as table 6.1 shows.

The trends were obvious. The "left" unions, which supported the government, had not profited from such support. The CGT's relative decline from the 1970s continued. The CFDT, which had hoped to displace the CGT as France's most powerful union, fell flat. As one CFDT official said after the 1983 social security elections, "The second left has become the third union in France." In contrast, FO, which had regarded the coming of the left to power with apprehension, had in fact done well from withholding its support. By its consistent nay-saying FO

Table 6.1
Relative Union Strengths

Results in Professional Elections, Percent of Total Votes, All Colleges

	1974	1975	1978	1980	1982	1984
CGT	42.8	38.1	38.6	36.5	32.3	29.3
CFDT	18.7	19.4	20.4	21.3	22.8	21.1
FO	8.3	8.4	10.0	11.0	11.7	13.9

1979 and 1982 Prud'homme Elections (percent)

	1979	1982	Gain/Loss
CGT	42.5	36.8	-5.6
CFDT	23.1	23.5	+0.4
FO	17.4	17.8	+0.4

October 1983 Social Security Elections (percent)

CGT	28.29
FO	25.17
CFDT	18.38
CGC*	15.93

Note: The social security electorate, and to a lesser extent the
        Prud'homme electorate, included large numbers of occupations
        that did not ordinarily vote in professional elections to works'
        committees. In addition, the social security election was
        conducted by a mail ballot--sent to everyone on social security
        rolls--rather than in the workplace.

*The CGC, the Confédération générale des cadres, a union of white-collar
        employees and managers, seems to have become a lightning rod for
        protest voters in 1983.

Source: Circulaire du Ministère du Travail: Les élections profession-
         nelles 1985.

could, and did, *ratisser large*, picking up new support from both disaffected working-class supporters and opponents of the left. In addition, both the organized *patronat* and the political right (the RPR in particular), each with an interest in reducing the strengths of the "Marxist unions," were not averse to lending FO a helping hand. Union support for the left in power would have paid off only if left reformism and economic policy had succeeded. By 1983 it was clear that none of the left's major reforms had done much for workers, while *rigueur* had hurt. As a result popular enthusiasm for left unions and for the left more generally was hard to find.

The story of left-union relationships through 1983 did not end here, however. One of the left's major structural reform goals involved reorganizing France's industrial relations system, a goal that was operationalized in the Auroux laws, which were legislated in 1982 and began to function in 1983. The first Auroux law endowed union sections at firm level, union representatives, *délégués du personnel* and *comités d'entreprise* with increased resources and powers.[22] It also extended the coverage of some of these institutions to firms with less than fifty employees and established new "group committees"—the equivalent of works' committees—to cover an entire industrial complex. Law II provided for obligatory annual firm-level wage bargaining and a clause which allowed majority unions to veto the implementation of minority union-signed contracts, in addition to modifying the 1950 law about branch-level bargaining. Law III amalgamated formerly separated shop committees on health, safety and working conditions and endowed the newly combined larger committee with greater powers. Law IV discussed workers' rights in the firm, defined the permissible legal scope of employer-defined internal work rules (*réglement intérieur*) and established new shop-level "rights of expression." The public sector, in general, benefited from stronger versions of most of these same changes, plus new provisions for the election of workers' representatives to boards of directors.

No one—excepting, perhaps, the CNPF, would have mistaken these measures as steps toward *autogestion* and socialism. But they were a definite attempt to bring France's backward, conflict-ridden industrial relations system up to date. Strong incentives to decentralize collective bargaining from its earlier industrial branch focus to firm level could make capital/labor discussions less global and more workplace-specific. If the legal positions of unions and workers were strengthened at firm level at the same time, employers would have to take them more seriously. In the best of all possible worlds employers and unions would then gradually learn to treat one another with more respect and, in consequence, both would be able to assume more collective responsibility for what happened in the world of work. As this occurred, both the *patronat* and the unions would be less prone to seek redress of grievances from politics and the state. In the longer run the workplace, industrial relations, unions and employers might all become less politicized and volatile. In short, the Auroux laws might turn out to be something of a

Gallic Wagner Act. But what would actually result from the Auroux laws would take time and be as much contingent on the balance of power between capital and labor as on the wording of statutes.

MODERNIZATION: 1984–86

The rigor episode was difficult for unions to swallow. In 1983 it became gradually clear that the left in power was undertaking policies that its right-center predecessors had desired but had been afraid to implement. Public sector incomes policies and guidelines for the rest of the economy were deindexing wage growth from inflation. This, plus new taxation and other measures, had extracted enough buying power from the economy to precipitate a dramatic decline in inflation levels. In the process, however, a slight decline in workers' living standards had started.[23] Still, despite this reversal of the government's initial redistributive intentions, which had its complements in the realm of social policy, the left had continued to honor its pledge to cap unemployment growth, using a panoply of active labor market policies (power over public sector employment policies, administrative control over private sector hiring and firing and resources to keep foundering companies afloat).[24] By later 1983, however, the government began to abandon these employment maintenance policies, and by the time that François Mitterrand himself gave an interview to *Libération* in May 1984 the die of "modernization" had been cast.[25]

Modernization—which the PCF left the government in summer 1984 rather than accept—was a break toward the centrist, technocratic neoliberalism which had become internationally fashionable in the 1980s, involving a sea change in PS political concerns. Bettering the lot of workers and the poor—the core of "old" leftism—had given way to adapting French capitalism to a newly threatening international market. Thus starting in the winter of 1983–84 firms were allowed to lay off workers much more easily. By spring 1984 major cutbacks in the nationalized steel industry were decided, followed by more in coal mining and shipbuilding. In summer 1984 the government allowed the large Creusot-Loire conglomerate to go bankrupt rather than bail it out. In the fall of 1984, after the full magnitude of Renault's losses became clear, a shaken-up Renault administration was charged with cutting losses and jobs, which it proceeded to do. The nationalized industries as a whole were enjoined to return to profitability in 1985 and given unprecedented freedom to lay off workers to do so. The budget was pared back even further while innumerable measures were taken to promote private sector profitability and, hopefully, investment. Among other things the Socialists prompted, and presided over, the greatest boom in the history of the Paris *bourse*.

Modernization worried the unions, of course. A government concerned with rejuvenating French capitalism was unlikely to be a very reliable ally for labor. The pre–1984 left government had tried to maintain employment levels in those areas of the French economy where the left unions were strongest. The rapid loss of tens of thousands of jobs in steel, mining, shipbuilding, automobiles and engineering would therefore strike hardest in the heartlands of CGT and CFDT support and place them in a very difficult tactical situation. It would also create huge regional and individual hardships, with unemployment rising from 9 to 10.5 percent—by several hundred thousand—in little over a year. The government did expand its "social" plans for cushioning these new unemployed—using "conversion leaves" and regional policies in the hardest hit sectors and innovating to create the TUCs (*travaux d'utilité collective*, a sub-minimum wage public works program) for youthful unemployed. Still, the situation abruptly got much worse.

Redeployment into Opposition

The CGT's response to the new context, not surprisingly, paralleled the PCF's. As the shape of modernization became clear, both party and union promoted greater and greater protest, even before the Communist ministers finally retired in July 1984.[26] After July, however, the CGT hesitated before fully defining a new position. Complex intraparty struggle caused the PCF to move back toward a sectarian anti-Socialist line like the one which it had pursued between 1978 and 1981. This kind of line, when translated into CGT strategy, had caused the CGT considerable problems prior to 1981. The CGT had its share of *Socialisant* members and a token number of Socialist leaders for whom directives to attack a Socialist government would not be easy to swallow. Thus for some time after July 1984 there was much more CGT talk than action, reflecting foot-dragging by CGT leaders (Secretary-General Henri Krasucki among others) who were afraid of the consequences of adopting a sectarian course.[27] By spring 1985 things had come to such a pass that the CGT and its secretary-general were taken to task by the PCF Central Committee because of their reluctance to attack *le pouvoir socialiste*. By this point, however, hardliners had taken control.

Even with its politics more clearly defined, however, the CGT still had trouble deciding what to do. Along with the PCF it had adopted modernist *autoges-tionnaire* rhetoric and analyses in the 1980s. It claimed to want to become a "proposition force" for "new criteria of management" at firm level. According to this line, the *patronat* and the right—to which were appended the Socialists in 1985—wanted to continue multinationalizing at expense of France's national economic integrity. Such purposes would prevail in the longer run, against workers' interests, unless workers and their unions mobilized to propose different goals.[28] However, this *autogestionnaire* modernism coexisted with, and was often contradicted by, the classical job-protecting defensiveness which had been the CGT's lifeblood for decades and which was a reflex in the CGT apparatus. When the PCF's "bash the Socialists" political line was superimposed on this internal conflict of purposes—in the midst, of course, of the most threatening economic setting since the 1950s—the CGT teetered organizationally on the edge of confusion.

Thus, despite rhetoric which strived toward new pinnacles of militancy, it proved difficult for the CGT leadership to generate much rank-and-file enthusiasm.[29] Whether the rank and file wanted to act or not, the CGT nonetheless quickly slipped into what the French call "commando" actions, hyper-militant minority movements energized by trusted *cadres*. Such was the confrontation between police and CGT/PCF organizers at the SKF plant in Ivry in spring 1985, for example, when helmeted activists (including a number of employees of the local Communist municipality) tried to prevent a plant closing with missiles—bricks, nuts and bolts, etc.—directed at the Compagnie républicaine de sécuité (CRS). Such were the guerrilla tactics used against Renault's efforts to transport machine tools from Douai to Spain in the following summer. The confederation's campaign against changes in managerial strategy at Renault in 1985 was more than symbolic of the potential costs of all this, however. Proposing "new criteria of management," behaving in an old-fashioned, job-defending way and mobilizing in commando fashion against government policy in *forteresse Renault*, which everyone believed to be its biggest bastion, the CGT failed and in the process lost the de facto power of "codetermination" which it had held at Renault since 1945.

Irony of ironies, the CGT's shift into opposition and militancy brought it much closer to the stated positions of its archenemy, FO. FO, "unmoving and unchanging," had been first into the lists of protesting the decline of living standards and the government's conversion to neoliberalism, even if FO had no intention of promoting strikes of any kind, let alone the CGT's kind. This general *rapprochement* implied no cooperation with the CGT, of course. For the FO leadership had much different strategic goals. Looking beyond March 1986, it was eager to regain the status that it had prior to 1981, that of privileged union interlocutor for the right and the *patronat*.

Between 1981 and 1986, however, water had flowed beneath these particular bridges. Significant parts of the *patronat* and the right had been converted to vehement forms of neoliberalism which allowed little space to unions at all. Thus FO would have its work cut out for it persuading its former counterparts to negotiate at all. Moreover, FO's very successes under the left had created new internal tensions. FO had been slowly penetrated over the years by ultra-left minorities. Under the left in power it had also been "colonized" by rightists—RPR unionists in particular. Serious disagreements over strategy between such widely divergent groups seemed quite possible. In addition, FO's very powerful Secretary-General Bergeron was on the verge of retirement, raising the specter of a difficult succession struggle.

The CFDT also denounced the modernization shift in its typically maverick "second left" way.[30] The CFDT was willing to admit that industrial restructuring in the interests of enhancing France's international competitiveness was a necessity. However, it rejected a definition of modernization which involved "neoliberalism, even with a social face"—a reference to PS ideas. To the CFDT restructuring ought not to be an imposition of managers and/or the state. Rather it should result from negotiations in which unions "proposed rather than submitted." Not far beneath the CFDT surface there was something that looked like advocacy of a Gallicized version of Anglo-Saxon "givebacks." Unions would have to trade certain *acquis* to get new influence over industrial change. The most striking illustration of this came in the 1984–85 negotiations with the CNPF on "flexibility" in the length of the work week in which the confederation took the lead among all unions present in proposing—before anyone had really asked for it—to abandon parts of existing labor law on hiring and firing.[31]

There was more than a hint in CFDT responses to modernization (and to its terrible defeat in the 1983 social security elections) of temptations toward *Force ouvriérisation*. CFDT leaders could easily calculate what FO wanted from the change to government of the right in 1986 since FO was completely predictable. If, however, FO was likely to be divided internally and, given its "pure and simple" unionist outlook, unlikely to warm to the task of codetermining French industrial restructuring, then space might exist for a repositioned CFDT. Perhaps the CFDT could become a more intelligent and less old-fashioned *interlocuteur valable* for the *patronat* and the right than FO. The CFDT's historical trajectory made any firm conversion to this kind of line unlikely, however. The CFDT, after all, had been the trade union carrier of *autogestion* and still contained a strongly radical minority in the mid–1980s. Divisions within the CFDT after March 1986 were quite likely, then.[32]

Union Decline

After 1984 *all three* major unions came to oppose the left in power in different ways, each clearly anticipating the defeat of the left that was to occur in 1986. This in itself spectacularly underlined how ineffective the left experiment had been at changing the basic attitudes of French unions toward politics and toward one another. The CGT remained as devoted to the PCF as it had always been. When it shifted from the "yes . . . but more, and more quickly" posture toward the left in power of 1981–84 to "no . . . to Socialist betrayers," it found itself in more or less the same position as it had been prior to May–June 1981, acting as a para-political force to undermine the PS. The CFDT shifted after 1984 from a "yes . . . but do it differently" position to a "no . . . but we would like to collectively bargain modernization" posture, having profited little from the left in power either. FO, faithful to André Bergeron's 1981 promise to "remain itself," continued with its "it is really none of our business . . . but you're doing it all wrong" position, with modernization leading to more stress on the "doing it wrong." Divisions among the "big three" were as deep in 1986 as they had been in 1981, then. All that had changed were justifications for the animosity.

If the left had hoped to strengthen organized labor, it had failed here as well. The CGT and the CFDT had both been in membership and financial decline since the later 1970s, with the CGT suffering a bit more. If anything, the left

Table 6.2
Trade Union Memberships and Strike Activity

Year	CGT Official	CGT Est.[1]	CFDT Official	CFDT Est.[2]	FO
1974	2.34	1.72	1.01	--	0.87
1976	2.35	1.69	1.15	1.07	0.90
1978	2.19	1.49	1.12	1.07	0.98 (est.)
1980	1.92	1.17	1.03	0.96	1 (est.)
1982	1.72	0.98	1.04	0.96	1 (est.)
1984	1.40	--		0.90 (est.)	1+

Note: In millions; the CGT and CFDT official figures include retired members.

[1] The CGT Est. figures are estimates of CGT membership once retired members and CGT overinflation of numbers have been factored out by Jacques Kergoat; see Le Monde, November 19, 1985. Second guessing the CGT's official figures is risky and Kergoat's figures can only be seen as approximate.

[2] The CFDT Est. column is the CFDT official figure minus retired members. The CFDT has been quite honest about its numbers. FO membership statistics are few and far between (see Alain Bergounioux, Force Ouvrière, Paris: Que sais-je, 1982).

Source: Adapted from biennial congress reports of the three unions.

in power had accelerated these trends (see Tables 6.2 and 6.3). FO had done somewhat better, but doing better here meant maintaining a steady state. The level of unionization in France as a whole was declining. The labor "organization" that had profited most from the left in power was thus the silent front of the nonunionized. In terms of strikes—a good index of the effects of union divisions, economic crisis and the left's policies after 1982—the mid–1980s were the calmest years since the early 1960s.

What Changes for French Industrial Relations?

The Auroux laws were the left's major legacy to the future of French industrial relations. It is extremely difficult to say definitive things about their effects since they had only been in operation for three years at time of writing. What went on during the period of left power after 1984 was much more the tentative establishment of new habits than anything else.[33]

The proposal to institutionalize worker rights of expression on the shop floor was perhaps the most promising aspect of the new reforms. Interestingly enough,

Table 6.3
Number of Days Lost in Strikes, 1962–1984

Year	Days Lost (Millions)
1962	1.9
1964	2.5
1966	2.5
1968	150.0
1970	1.7
1972	3.7
1974	3.4
1976	5.0
1978	2.2
1980	1.7
1981	1.5
1982	2.3
1983	1.5
1984	1.3

Source: INSEE Documentation Francaise, Tableau
de l'économie française 1985, p. 73.

it was the CGT which seemed the most active in pushing for the establishment of rights of expression, with the CFDT a far second and FO, which opposed the new rights, third.[34] Workers themselves had varying reactions to "expression," however, with timidity and skepticism being the most apparent. Problems arose because of the insufficiency of information available to workers. The role of *cadres* in the process bothered everyone. Managers and *cadres* wanted to control "expression" for their own purposes. Unions did not want this (with the *cadre* unions affiliated with workers' unions caught in a crossfire), of course. Workers alternated between confusion and suspicion. There were also difficulties about the excessive formality of the proceedings and disbelief that "expression" would have serious consequences for the firm. The official union bodies in firms—the *Sections Syndicales d'entreprise*—were often perplexed about the relationship between their activities and "expression"—should they let the workers express themselves without union assistance or not?

In all of this uncertainty there was some enthusiasm about the positive effects of "expression" on intrafirm communications and "atmosphere." Workers and *comités d'entreprise* learned more about their workplaces, which they could use to understand where their work fit in the broader scheme of things and what change was called for. This was also advantageous to the firm to the degree that "economic education" was advanced and "realism" engendered. Where more and freer communication opened up, shop floor issues like safety and working conditions were more easily broached and resolved. Sometimes discussions on such matters evoked considerable surprise in all quarters about the problem-solving creativity of the "expression" groups. Productivity was often enhanced.

The first years of the "obligation to negotiate" on firm level saw an increase in bargaining whose meaning was not completely clear. In 1984 66 percent of the firms legally obligated to negotiate actually did so (versus 44 percent). But of these only slightly more than half had concluded a contract. And while this did represent some progress for France, it was not at all clear how good these contracts were, especially on wages. Quite often the contracts were mainly concerned with "flexibility" of working hours. Thus, in general, there was a trend to more bargaining of a decentralized kind, but the law included no obligation to bargain or conclude in good faith.

The final outcomes of reforms like the Auroux laws take years to be clear and depend upon the relative strengths and intentions of labor and capital over the long run. There were nonetheless ironies in the first years of the Auroux reforms. Business organizations like the CNPF initially opposed the laws as a declaration of war on management. But the obligation to bargain with labor at a moment when labor was feeble and when there was little to concede was not onerous and, moreover, coincided with trends among more enlightened managers to negotiate more in a decentralized way. In addition, the introduction of new obligations ("expression") coincided historically with the promotion of new firm-based managerial strategies of the quality circle type. Indeed, "expression" groups and quality circles often came into existence at the same time, giving French workers a plethora of new fora of communication where none whatever had existed a brief moment earlier.[35] Thus *patronal* antagonism to the Auroux reforms, which would have been logical if the laws had really worked to strengthen unions, rapidly turned to benevolent neutrality.

Evidence suggests, then, that unions gained much less from the Auroux reforms than the legislators had intended. Turning on their own toward direct dealing with workers, employers in many cases used the new mechanisms as ways of short-circuiting unions on the shop floor. The laws did seem to begin achieving one of their objectives, to decentralize more capital/labor relationships toward firm level, with a strong helping hand from parts of the *patronat* which wanted to move in such directions for their own reasons. Thus rather than giving unions any new foothold at firm level, the reforms seemed congruent with a new *patronal* armamentarium of deregulation, pressuring unions and workers to assume greater responsibility for firm success. As of 1986, the unintended pro-business consequences of the Auroux reforms were perhaps more surprising than their failure to strengthen the unions. But any global predictions would be premature.

CONCLUSIONS

If we weigh the left's good intentions in 1981 against the outcomes of 1986, it is hard to be very positive. The living standards and job security of workers were threatened by crisis in 1981, and many of the threats were actualized under the left. Despite important changes—early retirement, extended vacations, shorter, more flexible working schedules, protection of the French welfare state—living standards by and large stagnated, while unemployment rose. Steelworkers, shipbuilders, coalminers, autoworkers, young people, inhabitants of Lorraine and the North—the list could be much longer—would therefore balk at any *bilan globalement positif*. Unions were divided and weak in 1981. They were quite as divided and considerably weaker by 1986. The Auroux laws, whose implementation had only just begun by March 1986, were promising, but in ways which the left had not originally anticipated. They did not massively reinforce the power of workers and unions in the workplace and create a more civilized and predictable industrial relations system. Rather they seemed to connect with changing managerial strategies to decentralize capital/labor dealings to capital's advantage, allowing French industry considerably more flexibility in its handling of manpower and the labor process and enhancing efforts to develop a firm-level culture of cooperation. Such changes may well turn out to be positive for French industry, but their impact on French organized labor is likely to be less felicitous.

Of course, the left could not be held completely responsible for all this. The left in power presided over the continuation of deep-seated trends which it was unable to control. It came to power at the worst possible moment to implement its ambitious program, inheriting a legacy of ineffective economic policies and industrial decline; on top of this, it had to face the consequences of the 1981–82 international recession. Moreover, profound union divisions, the "crisis of trade unionism," and the relative decline of "left" unions all had begun before 1981.

Parceling out praise and blame to the left is much less interesting than speculating about the deeper implications for workers and unions of what happened between 1981 and 1986. For it may be that monumental change is in the works, even if such change is far from what the left set out to facilitate. For generations a "certain leftism" was characteristic of the French working class. Anticapitalism, strident radicalism and somewhat manichaean anti-"bourgeois" attitudes lasted longer in France than elsewhere. In very complex ways the combined organizational and "class-forming" efforts of the PCF, CGT and the left segments of French social democracy had played central roles in the perpetuation of such attitudes and postures. Ironically, what may turn out to have been most important to French labor's future about the left's stay in power in the 1980s is that the left presided over the decline of the central agencies perpetuating these attitudes. Only time will tell what will take their place.

NOTES

1. For the origins of the term, and for a good brief introduction to these social and economic transformations, see Jean Fourastié's *Les Trente glorieuses* (Paris: Pluriel, 1981).

2. Peter Lange, George Ross, and Maurizio Vannicelli explore this in *Unions, Change, and Crisis: French and Italian Trade Union Strategies and the Political Economy, 1945–1980* (London: George Allen and Unwin, 1982), Chap. 1, Part 2 for France, Chap. 2, Part 2 for Italy, which is the only other comparable case. For a more detailed view, see George Ross, *Workers and Communists in France* (Berkeley: University of California Press, 1982), Chaps. 2 and 3.

3. To get a good idea of what this all looked like during the *belle epoque* of postwar class conflict, see François Sellier's classic, *Stratégie de la lutte sociale* (Paris: Editions ouvrières, 1961); see also the same author's *La Confrontation sociale en France, 1936–1981* (Paris: P.U.F., 1984).

4. *Programme commun de gouvernement du Parti communiste et du Parti socialiste* (Paris: Editions sociales, 1972), Preamble and Part II.

5. See *Le Manifeste du PS, 24 Janvier 1981*, p. 67 in *Le Monde, Dossiers et Documents: L'Election Présidentielle 26 avril–10 mai 1981* (Paris, May 1981).

6. The best review of all this is to be found in Alain Lipietz, *L'Audace ou l'enlisement* (Paris: La Découverte, 1983). See also the opening chapters in Alain Fonteneau and Pierre-Alain Muet, *La Gauche face à la crise* (Paris: Presses de la Fondation Nationale des Sciences Politiques, 1985).

7. The following general works on French unions are worth consulting, arranged in reverse chronological order of publication: Gérard Adam, *Le Pouvoir syndical* (Paris: Dunod, 1983); René Mouriaux, *Les Syndicats dans la société française* (Paris: FNSP, 1983); Hubert Landier, *Demain, quels syndicats?* (Paris: Pluriel, 1981); Jean-Daniel Reynaud, *Les Syndicats en France*, 2 vols. (Paris: Seuil, 1975).

8. On the CFDT more generally, see Hervé Hamon and Patrick Rotman, *La Deuxième Gauche* (Paris: Ramsay, 1982); and René Mouriaux, "The CFDT: From the Union of Popular Forces to Success of Social Change," in Guy Groux and Mark Kesselman, eds., *The French Working Class: Economic Crisis and Political Change* (London: George Allen and Unwin, 1984); also Martin A. Schain, "Politics and Mass Mobilization: Relations Between the CGT and CFDT," Chap. 11 in *Socialism, the State and Public Policy in France*, ed. Philip Cerny and Martin Schain (New York: Methuen, 1985).

9. On the CGT see René Mouriaux, *La CGT* (Paris: Seuil, 1982); Ross, *Workers and Communists*; and George Ross, "The CGT," in Groux and Kesselman, *French Working Class*.

10. On FO see Alain Bergounioux, *Force ouvrière* (Paris: Que sais-je? 1982).

11. This situation also prevailed in the public sector, where the state, and not branch level employers' associations, was the bargainer. The facts here are eloquent. From 1974

to 1980 the CGT and CFDT refused to sign *any* contracts in the public sector, while FO, in contrast, signed them all, excepting only 1977. Disparity in the private sector was smaller, but still substantial. FO signed in 70 to 80 percent of cases, the CGT ranging from 40 to 55 percent, with the CFDT slightly higher.

12. André Bergeron, FO secretary-general, for example, was president of UNEDIC, the unemployment compensation board, while another FO confederal secretary presided over the health insurance board.

13. In French see Michel Beaud, *Le Mirage de la croissance* (Paris: Syros, 1983); Lipietz, *L'Audace ou l'enlisement*, Part II; and Fonteneau and Muet, *La Gauche*. In English see Peter Hall, "Socialism in One Country . . . ," in Cerny and Schain, *Socialism*; George Ross and Jane Jenson, "Political Pluralism and Economic Policy," in John Ambler, *The French Socialist Experiment* (Philadelphia: ISHI Press, 1985). For an excellent econometrically based evaluation of the first period see Jeff Sachs and Charles Wyplosz, "The Economic Consequences of President Mitterrand," *Economic Policy*, No. 2 (April 1986).

14. Two of these ministers were placed, in fact, in functional areas in which FO had strong vested interests: Anicet Le Pors in the *Fonction Publique* and Jack Ralite in Health. FO harped on the Communist "boring from within" issue perhaps even more than the hard-line right. See *FO Hebdo*, January 20, 1982; *L'Implantation des militants du PCF dans l'appareil d'état et dans les entreprises nationales*, brochure (Paris: FO, 1982).

15. In addition to its opposition to firm-level bargaining, FO also opposed the reforms' provision to allow unions which, taken together, represented more than 50 percent of votes in a firm's most recent professional elections, to veto implementation of a contract, even after it had been signed by another, nationally "representative" union.

16. FO rejected the notions of "workers' control" and *autogestion*, which both the CGT and CFDT promoted and which it correctly saw in reform proposals for *conseils d'atelier*. According to FO the danger was that unions would be co-opted by management and lose their essential character in the process.

17. A particularly good source on different unions' positions on the Auroux laws is the CFDT-BRAEC Dossier #22, October–December 1982, "Les Autres et les droits nouveaux."

18. Cf. Hamon and Rotman, *La Deuxième Gauche*.

19. For various excerpts of Maire see *Le Monde*, August 25 and 26, 1981; *La Croix*, September 18, 1981; *Le Matin*, October 15, 1981; *Témoignage chrétien*. November 2, 1981; *La Vie Française*, May 17, 1982.

20. The first step of work-week reduction was from forty to thirty-nine hours. The CGT and FO argued that this should be accomplished with no reduction in wages— "thirty-nine for forty"—while the CFDT favored reduction. A number of sharp CGT-led strikes plus Communist pressure inside the government led President Mitterrand himself to decide the issue in favor of the CGT. For CFDT evaluations of the generality of left government behavior in this period see CFDT, *L'Année sociale 1982* (Paris: Syros, 1983).

21. For an official statement of the CGT's positions see *Le Peuple*, June 13–July 18, 1982, a report of the 41st CGT Congress. See also CGT, *Rapport sur la situation économique et sociale de la France, Mai-juin 1981–1982* (Paris: CGT, 1984).

22. On the coming of the Auroux laws see Jean Auroux, *Les Droits des travailleurs* (Paris: La Documentation française, 1981); and *Le Monde, Dossiers et Documents: Les Nouveaux Droits des travailleurs*, June 1983. In English see Janine Goetschy, "A New

Future for Industrial Democracy in France?," *Economic and Industrial Democracy* (February 1983); Duncan Gallie, "Les Lois Auroux: The Reform of French Industrial Relations," in Howard Hachin and Vincent Wright, eds., *Economic Policy and Policy-Making under the Mitterrand Presidency, 1981–1984* (New York: St. Martin's, 1985).

23. Here see CGT, *Rapport annuel sur la situation économique et sociale de la France, 1983* (Paris: CGT, 1985), Volume 2, Chaps. 1 and 2.

24. Aude Benoît, *La Politique de l'emploi* (Paris: La Documentation française, 1984), provides a good overview of the left's labor market policies.

25. *Libération*, May 10, 1984.

26. Tension rose beginning in autumn 1983, such that there had to be a PCF-PS "clarification" meeting in December. The Talbot conflict in December and January complicated things further. Here the CGT got involved in the "codetermination" of 1900 layoffs at Talbot by virtue of its privileged connections with PCF minister Jack Ralite and Pierre Mauroy (the company proposed many thousands more and, through CGT and PCF intervention, the number was reduced). Unfortunately, the Talbot CFDT, which had not been a party to such codetermination, did not accept its results, leading to a militant strike. In response the Talbot CGT had to reverse its position and "out-militant" the CFDT. The incident was a bellwether for the CGT, demonstrating to any who had not already seen the logic of events how difficult it would be for the union to "codetermine" modernization. The government's April 1984 decisions to "modernize" the steel industry at the cost of devastating the economy of Lorraine brought the two left parties to the breaking point. In response to the steel plan the CGT called a "March on Paris" from Lorraine, and the PCF very nearly quit the government.

27. Interestingly enough, the key CGT industrial federation affected by modernization, the metalworkers', was the major internal obstacle to PCF sectarianism. Its leader, André Sainjon, facing a situation in which his federation was in dramatic membership and mobilizational decline, leaned more toward "concession bargaining" using government influence than toward confrontation. He, along with Krasucki, was to become a major target of PCF ire.

28. This "modernist" discourse about "new criteria for management" came from the PCF's economic line. See Philippe Herzog's most interesting book, *L'Economie nouvelle à bras le corps* (Paris: Messidor, 1984), and other publications of the PCF Section Economique such as *Economie et Politique*. The CGT economic research unit itself began in 1982 to publish an extremely useful bulletin, *Analyses et Documents Economiques*, which took up this line, and tried very hard to "form" new CGT cadres who would understand and deploy it.

29. The CGT's 42nd Congress in the spring of 1985 was a good place to look for the logic and contradictions of the confederation's new trajectories. In its preparation the pro-PCF leadership had had great difficulty maneuvering a hard-line anti-Socialist Congress document around a small number of Socialist CGT officials. When compromises were suggested, however, the proposers of the compromises were attacked in turn for being "soft on *le pouvoir socialiste*."

30. Edmond Maire's two long articles in *Le Monde*, November 2–3, 1984, provide a good outline of the CFDT's new thinking.

31. See *Le Monde*, January 2, 1985, for a discussion of the CFDT's failure on flexibility. See also "Le CFDT pris au piège de la modernité," in *La Vie Française*, February 17, 1985.

32. Many of the conflictual issues which the flexibility debate raised inside the CFDT

were rehearsed again at the CFDT's 40th Congress in June 1985 along with broader themes relating to the confederation's increased moderation. See CFDT, *Syndicalisme Hebdo*, No. 2071, June 20, 1985. For a particularly interesting and thoughtful CFDT document trying to synthesize various internal points of view, see *CFDT Action économique-emploi*, "Avancer par l'action économique pour l'emploi" (Paris: CFDT, November 1985).

33. Several sociologists followed the implementation of the Auroux laws. Among the works published to this point one ought to consult Anni Borzeix, Danièle Linhart, and Denis Segrestin, *Sur les traces du droit d'expression* (Paris: CNAM, 1985), a series of well-done case studies; Philippe Bernoux et al., *De l'expression à la négociation* (Paris: GLYSI, 1985); ANACT, *L'Expression directe et collective des salaries: un bilan pour demain* (Paris: ANACT, 1985); National Assembly, *Commission des affaires culturelles, familiales, et sociales*, Document No. 2681 (1985) (a *Rapport d'information* on the application of the Auroux laws); Ministère du Travail de l'Emploi et de la Formation Professionel, *Droit d'expression des salariés, deux ans d'application dans les entreprises*, in *Travail Informations* (Paris: April–June 1985). The CFDT also collaborated with a group of CNRS researchers from Aix-Marseilles to create a data bank on "expression," labeled PAROLES; see Alain Chouraqui et al. in *CFDT-Aujourd'hui*, September–October 1985.

34. As measured in terms of contracts signed by Michele Millot and Jean-Pol Roulleau, "Les Relations sociales depuis les lois Auroux," *Projet* (November–December 1985): 32–33.

35. On new *patronal* attitudes see Pierre Morville, *Les Nouvelles Politiques sociales du patronat* (Paris: La Découverte, 1985). On the labor market side of this see Chapter 2 (by Pascal Petit) in Robert Boyer et al., *La Flexibilité du travail en Europe* (Paris: La Découverte, 1986).

7

Racial Politics: The Rise of the National Front

MARTIN A. SCHAIN

INTRODUCTION

Two important changes have altered the terrain of the French party system during the period of Socialist government in France since 1981. The first has been the decline in electoral support for the French Communist Party, and the second has been the rapid rise in electoral support for the far right National Front, led by Jean-Marie Le Pen. Both phenomena are part of a broader trend of voter instability on both the left and the right that has been evident throughout Western Europe since the late 1970s. However, if voters in other major European countries have generally shifted their support toward smaller issue-oriented parties of the center-left, large numbers of voters in France have moved toward a party that speaks the language of the xenophobic, traditional right, the National Front.

Suzanne Berger has argued that established parties in the 1970s failed to forge a connection with "the new political ideas and organizations, the intense and proliferating activity of citizens' groups [that] sprung up around newly perceived political grievances."[1] This failed connection, she argues, "is the great missed opportunity of the last decade and the main cause of the weakness of political will and imagination." If Berger is correct, and support for all established parties throughout Western Europe is waning as a result, the recipient of this support in France focuses our attention on the importance of the *content* of shifting values and interests. While during the 1970s it was frequently presumed that the electoral benefits were being gained by parties addressing postindustrial quality of life issues more or less ignored by the traditional left and right, the French case seems to indicate the emergence of other possibilities. The issues of race and crime, around which the National Front has mobilized large numbers of voters, are the kinds of "quality of life" issues the potential of which has been generally ignored in the literature on postindustrial values.

Nevertheless, it seems simplistic to argue that the emergence of the National Front can be attributed only to the recognition by large numbers of French voters that "Le Pen says what everyone else is thinking," since Le Pen has been saying the same thing for a very long time. Moreover, many of the themes of immigration and security that have been the focus of the Le Pen rhetoric have been co-opted in various ways by leaders of other political parties. Why then have 10 percent of the French electorate chosen to vote for the National Front since 1983 (but not before), rather than for another party of the right (or left) that also advocates similar themes and issues?

The rise of the National Front focuses our attention on the process through which this party has gained access to the political system and has mobilized electoral support. The extreme right, and most specifically the National Front, has attracted electoral support during the period 1983–86 that has been confirmed in four very different kinds of elections: local elections in 1983, with a mixture of local and national stakes; national ("European") elections in 1984, with national symbolic stakes but few real consequences; departmental elections in 1985, with mostly local stakes; and, finally, the legislative elections in March 1986. On each occasion, the National Front has demonstrated its ability to attract between 8 and 11 percent of the vote nationally, with far higher percentages in many constituencies. The initial electoral breakthrough of the National Front occurred despite the fact that all the established parties defined the party led by Le Pen as outside the realm of political acceptability. Thus, not surprisingly, the electoral emergence of Le Pen during the past four years has been seen by many political observers as a measure—in itself—of the legitimation of the major issues for which he has become the leading spokesman.[2]

In this chapter we argue that this electoral shift took place in the context of both crisis and transformation. The crisis that emerged rapidly after the onset of austerity in 1982 was the declining political confidence in the government of the left, as well as the sense of economic crisis encouraged by government policy and rising unemployment. The transformation was the continuing lack of confidence in the parties of the right as an alternative to the government of the left. In this context legitimacy was constructed through three related processes. The first has been through a minimal level of electoral support, a direct measure of some level of positive attraction of the party among the electorate. The second has been the broader acceptance (diminishing rejection) of the party as a carrier of key issues among a broader sector of the electorate that still identifies with other parties. The third has been the acceptance by political elites of the party as a legitimate partner for influence, mobilization and/or decision-making.

LE PEN AND THE GANG OF FOUR

The National Front emerged as a major political force in France after a long period of party stability. During the first twenty-three years of the Fifth Republic, a new party system had emerged that was aided by and contributed to the institutionalization of the presidentialist regime.[3] By 1981 the flaccid politics of what Maurice Duverger had once called the "marais" had given way to a dualistic four-party system, polarized between an organized "presidential" majority and an increasingly well-organized opposition coalition. Although both political competition and policy choices were defined by left-right competition, on one hand, and intracoalition maneuvering, on the other, four-party hegemony appeared to have become well established by 1981. As late as 1983, Frank Wilson confirmed that "minor parties remain isolated on the fringes of French politics."[4]

A large number of political leaders of fringe parties on the left had been integrated into the expanding Socialist Party of the 1970s, and they had brought their votes with them. On the right, the Giscard ascendancy in 1974 had attracted the former center opposition groups into a "majority" coalition with other centrist parties, which four years later regrouped loosely as the UDF. By 1981, then, there was growing evidence that the four now-established national parties exercised considerable control over local and national candidacies and dominated the electoral arena to a degree that had been unknown in France, except (arguably) for the brief tripartite period of 1944–47. Together, they attracted 94 percent of the voting electorate in 1981, up from 89 percent in 1978. Ninety-five percent of the deputies elected in 1978, and 94 percent elected in 1981, were directly affiliated with one of the four major parties. Moreover, disciplined party voting had become a normal aspect of the parliamentary process.[5]

Thus, in the late 1970s, while elite fragmentation, problems of recruitment, and declining public confidence and voter loyalty undermined the more "stable" party systems in Britain, Germany and Italy, the party system of the Fifth Republic was consolidating. If in other countries the major parties seemed incapable of building bridges to a changing society, and integrating the antiparty movements of the late 1960s and early 1970s, the French party system either swallowed them whole (Michel Debatisse, Gérard Nicoud and Michel Rocard) or marginalized them.[6] The domination of the central organization of each of the four major parties seemed to be reinforced with each election. "Without the explicit endorsement of one of these four parties, there was no hope for election. Even in municipal elections, where locally-based parties and personalities once dominated, the four major parties now prevail."[7]

As for the National Front and Jean-Marie Le Pen, their electoral fortunes probably reached a low point in 1981, when Le Pen was not able to find the necessary 500 "sponsors" for his presidential candidacy. In none of the elections prior to 1983 did the National Front attract more than 1 percent of the national vote, and in the legislative elections of 1981, the two parties of the extreme right gained together only one-third of 1 percent of the votes. As a candidate, however, Le Pen proved to be somewhat more popular, with 2 percent of the vote in the local elections of 1977 and 4 percent in the legislative elections in 1978 and 1981. Clearly, prior to 1981, Le Pen was unable to mobilize a significant portion of the electorate, although the themes and issues that he developed through the National Front were generally the same as those he used after 1981.

Finally, interest in politics did not seem to diminish among the electorate. Indeed, there appears to have been a tendency toward greater political activism, with higher percentages of people in 1983 willing to join parties, attend meetings and join street demonstrations organized by their party, compared with 1979.[8]

However, this analysis ignores some accumulating evidence of party "decay," much of which predates the rise in support for the National Front. In general, while interest in politics and willingness to engage in political activity remained as strong as ever, it appears that disillusionment with those who practice politics was growing and attachments to established political parties by the French electorate were diminishing. There was evidence of a growing sense of distance from politicians and from political parties. A majority of electors now feel that politicians are not concerned with what they are thinking, and this sense of distance has been growing since the 1970s.[9]

Even before the *alternance* of 1981, only a small minority of Frenchmen surveyed (22 percent) expressed confidence "in political parties in general," and this support did not increase even during the honeymoon period of the government of the left.[10] When asked about specific parties in 1983, respondents expressed considerably more confidence than they had in the more general survey. However, they expressed a poorer opinion of the opposition parties than of the Socialists, despite the defeat in local elections of the Socialist-led government eight months before the survey, and despite the generally low confidence in the policies of the government of the left expressed during this same period. Indeed, for only two of the parties did a "good opinion" outweigh a "poor opinion"— the Socialists and the RPR—with the positive gap slightly wider for the Socialists.[11]

If positive support for all established parties has diminished, negative rejection of all of the major parties has grown. Rejection (respondents stating that there is a party that they would never vote for under any circumstances) generally increased during the Fifth Republic as the electorate became increasingly polarized, particularly among the electorate of the right rejecting the resurgent parties of the left.[12] However, rejection of parties of the right remained relatively modest in the 1960s (about 27 percent in 1969, according to Campbell). What has changed is the tendency toward increased rejection after 1979 of both parties of the right and the left. (See Table 7.1.) The policy failures of the left have certainly increased hostility toward the Socialists, and the increased hostility toward the Communists probably goes back to the elections of 1978. Nevertheless, it is striking that the established parties of the right have not become more attractive as hostility toward the left has grown.

These patterns of diminishing support and increasing hostility appear to have been translated into declining voter loyalty during the post–1981 period. Between 1981 and 1984 only 40 percent of the electorate voted consistently for a (any) party of the right or the left (another 9.6 percent consistently abstained), compared with 59 percent between 1973 and 1978. However, this voter instability was only of marginal benefit for the established parties of the right, since only 10

Table 7.1
Voters Rejecting Parties of the Right and Left during Two Periods of the Fifth Republic (in percent)

Year	Reject Left	Reject Right		
1958	42	8		
1967	48	33		
1969	63	27		

Year	Reject PCF	Reject PS	Reject UDF	Reject RPR
1979	46	11	18	25
1984	58	18	22	26
1985	63	20	20	27

Sources: 1958-69: Bruce A. Campbell, "On the Prospects of Polarization in the French Electorate," Comparative Politics (January 1976): 283. 1979-85: Gérard Le Gall, "Radiographie de l'image de P.C.F.," Revue Politique et Parlementaire (January-February 1985).

percent of the "unstable" voters shifted their support from left to right between 1981 and 1984. Most of the rest simply abstained.[13]

Granted, the elections for the European parliament in 1984 generally provoked little enthusiasm in France (or in other European countries). However, given the high level of political interest, as well as the widely perceived impression of the 1984 election as a domestic poll, the level of abstention should probably be interpreted as a rebuke to the right as well as the left.

In fact, this impression is supported by the inability of the established parties of the right to increase significantly their electoral support among registered voters in any recent election. (See Table 7.2.) It is also supported by the tendency among voters who were alientated by the policies of the government of the left (who did not abstain) to shift their vote to Le Pen rather than to one of the established parties of the right. A survey in May 1984 indicated that among those voters who supported Mitterrand in the second round of the presidential election of 1981, and intended to vote for the right in the European elections the next month, about 500,000 (over one-third) planned to vote for the list headed by Le Pen, rather than the Simone Veil list.[14] In 1986 an exit poll indicated that

Table 7.2
Major Party Support Among Registered Voters in Elections Before and After
1981 (percent of registered voters for each party)

	Election to the European Parliament	
	1979	1984
PCF	13	6
PS	15	11
UDF	17 ⎫	⎫
RPR	10 ⎭ 27	⎬ 23
Abstention	39	43

	Cantonal Elections	
	1979	1985
PCF	14	8
PS	18	17
UDF	13 ⎫	12 ⎫
RPR	8 ⎭ 21	11 ⎭ 23
Abstention	35	36

	Legislative Elections			
	1973	1978	1981	1986
PCF	17	17	11	7
PS	15	20	26	24
UDF/RPR	38	35	28	31
Abstention	19	17	29	22

Sources: Le Monde, Dossiers et Documents: Les élections
législatives du 16 mars 1968, p. 68 and Le Monde,
March 12, 1985, p. 6.

almost 600,000 of the (2.7 million) National Front voters had supported Mitterrand in 1981.[15]

The electoral breakthrough of June 1984 came during a period of perceived economic and political crisis and was seen more as a "warning" and "sanction" against all established parties than an agreement with the policies and men of the National Front.[16] However, even before the breakthrough, the dynamics of the party system had evolved in a way that made such a change possible. The growing public distrust of the parties that Le Pen has frequently referred to as "the gang of four" had begun in the late 1970s. The reaction against the austerity policies of the government of the left was a key element of this distrust. This, combined with a growing reluctance among voters to place their confidence in the RPR and the UDF, opened a political opportunity to the National Front that had not existed before.

THE CHALLENGE

Still, to understand the vote simply as a manifestation of protest is to ignore the more positive attractions of a party that had little support prior to 1983. There were fourteen lists seeking support in June 1984, only four of which attracted more than 4 percent of the vote. What, then, changed between 1981 and 1984 in the attractiveness of the National Front?

Perhaps the most important change was that the small sect had become more broadly acceptable. Indeed, its level of acceptability exceeded its level of voter support, and a broader spectrum of voters found Le Pen and his followers acceptable than ever voted for them. This appears to be true both about the ideas espoused by the National Front as well as about the party itself.

By May 1984 SOFRES found that 18 percent of those surveyed (and 21 percent of those who responded) "felt a lot or some sympathy for Jean-Marie Le Pen." Among those with a party preference, sympathizers increased to 37 percent of the supporters of the RPR, 24 percent of those of UDF and 9 percent each of the supporters of the Socialists and the Communists. These sympathizers constituted a reservoir of legitimacy for the National Front. Even higher percentages agreed with Le Pen's position on immigrants, law and order (*sécurité*) and "the struggle against communism."[17] Between January and May 1984, the percentage of respondents who wanted to see Le Pen play a more important role in the months to come doubled from 12 to 23 percent.[18]

The electoral support for the National Front in June 1984 further enhanced the acceptability of the party. Six months after the SOFRES survey in May 1984, sympathizers had increased from 18 to 26 percent (31 percent of those who responded), with 46 percent of the RPR, 37 percent of the UDF, 12 percent of the Socialist and 17 percent of the Communist identifiers finding sympathy for Le Pen and his ideas.[19] At the same time, however, voters who identified with the established parties of the right, who had increasingly approved of electoral alliances with the National Front until June 1984, expressed increasing disapproval after the European elections. Nevertheless, in the fall of 1984 almost half the RPR identifiers and 43 percent of the UDF identifiers approved of electoral agreements between their party and the National Front.[20]

Thus, after the 1984 elections, the acceptability of Le Pen and the National Front was reasonably broad on several levels, and had grown over time. His acceptability was substantial if we consider that although fewer than 2 percent of Socialist and Communist identifiers claim to have voted for the National Front in 1984, 9 percent of these same voters claimed sympathy with Le Pen's ideas, and that percentage rose significantly after the election. Similarly, with 7 percent of the votes of the UDF identifiers, and 11 percent of the votes of the RPR identifiers, 37 percent of the former and 24 percent of the latter claimed sympathy with Le Pen before the elections, and these percentages also increased in the fall of 1984.[21]

In 1985 some of the more broad-based support for the National Front began to diminish, and there were signs that the party might suffer a sharp reverse in the legislative elections in March 1986.[22] Le Pen was more broadly perceived as extremist, and less widely accepted "as part of the opposition in the same way as the leaders of the RPR and the UDF." Support among those who identified with RPR and UDF for a coalition agreement with the National Front was less than half what it had been for an electoral agreement in May 1984. Nevertheless, even at these lower levels, support for coalition participation with the National Front remained substantial among those who identified with the parties of the right (over 25 percent).

Moreover, the acceptance of the "ideas" of the party had stabilized and even grown. General agreement with the ideas of Le Pen diminished slightly (from 26 to 23 percent) during 1985, but acceptance of specific positions of Le Pen grew during the same period. While there was a sharp falloff in support for his criticism of other parties (including the Communists, but particularly the RPR and the UDF), approval of his positions on immigrants and law and order increased.[23] Disapproval of these positions also grew, but approval of Le Pen's positions on these important issues seemed to define the political space in which the National Front could harvest electoral support. Finally, the commitment of party loyalists toward the National Front in 1985 seemed strong and substantial. In the cantonal elections in 1985, the National Front voters were more likely than the voters of any other party to have voted "to support the political family to which they feel close," rather than for the personality of a particular candidate.[24]

How, then, can we explain the increased acceptability of the National Front and its leader? Certainly the perceived economic and political crisis is one element, and the increasing distrust of the "gang of four" is another. However, conscious decisions by political elites have helped to move Le Pen's party from potential to the early stages of what Ariel Levite and Sidney Tarrow have called legitimacy and inclusion.[25]

The social issues that define the political space into which the National Front has moved were first defined and legitimized as *political* issues by established party elites. Moreover, the reaction, particularly of political elites of the right, to the increase of electoral support for the National Front helped to further legitimate its issues and helped the organizers of the party to construct a legitimate place in the French party system.

THE OPENING: THE EMERGENCE OF THE RACE ISSUE

What most clearly differentiates those who have voted for the National Front from supporters of *all* other parties is the priority that they have given to the issues of law and order and immigrants.[26] (See Table 7.3.) While most voters have been concerned with a broad range of issues, particularly problems of unemployment and the economy, and many supporters of the Veil list in 1984 were concerned with the problem of private education, National Front voters were overwhelmingly concerned with law and order and immigrants. Although these issues clearly have concerned a great many voters in recent years, for National Front voters they had become a *political priority*. The Le Pen list attracted 11 percent of the vote in 1984, but 22 percent of those were most concerned with law and order, and 48 percent of those most concerned with immigrants. With 9 percent of the electorate in the 1985 cantonal elections, the National Front attracted one-third of the voters most concerned about these issues. In both 1984 and 1985, voters who claimed to have supported the National Front were those least concerned about such issues as unemployment and social inequality (even though those who were unemployed voted in disproportionately large numbers for the National Front—12 percent in 1984 and 14 percent in 1986).[27] (See Table 7.3.)

Although Le Pen has been raising these issues for many years (as well as several others—see below), it was only after they had become important for the major established parties that the legitimate political space was opened up for the National Front. Indeed, it is important to recall that the presence of North African immigrants in France has been a social issue of some importance in France for a long time. (See Table 7.4.) However, it was the Communist Party that first attempted to mobilize voters with the issues of immigrants/race and law and order during the presidential campaign of 1981, although all of the major parties had dealt with these issues in a somewhat more muted way at the local level during the 1970s.[28] The Communist Party later backed down from its strident campaign and claimed that "in a climate of ideological warfare without mercy, certain initiatives that we took have opened us up to the falsification of our real positions and objective by the media." While the party admitted that there were some faults in the way it approached the problem, "our initiative . . . courageously approached problems that everyone must recognize as important today."[29] Virtually the same rhetoric that was used so effectively by the National Front in 1983 was first used by the Communist Party and its representatives in 1980–81.

The PCF campaign was opposed by the national leaders of all the other major parties, but numerous local officials of these same parties supported many of

Table 7.3
Motivations of Voters in 1984 and 1985

Party	Law & Order		Immi-grants	Unemploy-ment		The Economy		Social Inequal.	
	84	85 /\	85 84	84	85	84	85	84	85
PCF	9	12	2	37	71	14	44	33	34
PS	8	15	3	27	61	11	32	24	46
RPR/UDF	17	25	3	20	62	11	49	7	15
FN	30	73	26	17	41	6	36	10	11
Total	15	25	6	24	61	10	42	16	26

Note: Since several responses were possible, the total across may be
more than 100%.

Source: Exit poll, SOFRES/TFI, June 17, 1984; Le Nouvel Observateur,
June 22, 1984; Bull/BVA, March 10, 1985 in Pascal Perrineau,
"Le Front National: un électorat autoritaire," Revue
Politique et Parlementaire (July–August 1985): 27.

the Communist arguments.[30] The PCF initiative succeeded in defining the terms
of the national debate in 1981, and it is striking that almost every side of the
debate accepted the Communist definition of the issue: that immigrants from
North Africa were too numerous; posed problems of racial/ethnic conflict; and
their presence was related to problems of law and order.

However, it was not until 1983—after the first full year of Socialist austerity
and growing unemployment—that it became evident that the racist cat was truly
out of the political bag. Le Pen ran for the city council in the Twentieth Arrondissement of Paris. His open racism was certainly exceptional in the winter
campaign, but the more general themes that he raised were quite widespread.
In the bitter contest in Marseilles (where in 1984 the National Front would
outpoll the Communists with 21 percent of the vote, and in 1986 would come
in just behind the Socialists with over 24 percent of the vote) the minister of the
interior and his (UDF) opponent clashed on who was and who would be more
effective in enforcing security and suppressing immigration. Gaston Defferre
argued that he would be more effective in controlling the Arab population of
Marseilles, and Jean-Claude Gaudin retorted that he would demolish the Arab
ghetto in the center of the city. Both candidates played on the worst fears and
prejudices of the electorate.[31]

Table 7.4
Percentage of People Finding Categories of Immigrants "Too Numerous in France"

	1968	1977	1984
North Africans	62	63	66
Black Africans	18	25	41
Asians			31
Spanish	27	27	19
Jews	13	17	12
Foreigners in general	51	61	61

Source: SOFRES, "Les Attitudes des sympathisants de
l'extrême-droite," results of a survey conducted
for LICRA, November 1984, p. 17.

The widespread tendency by the established opposition parties to link immigrants to problems of law and order and growing unemployment fed into the preconceived notions of a majority of the electorate and put local governments of the left on the defensive.[32] Probably the worst confrontation on the immigrant issue occurred in Dreux, where the Socialist mayor, Françoise Gaspard, had been particularly outspoken on behalf of the rights of immigrants. The left won in March by eight votes in a campaign dominated by anti-immigrant themes fueled by an alliance between the RPR/UDF opposition and the National Front.[33] Voting irregularities, however, forced a "third round" in September, which in many ways proved to be a watershed for the acceptance of the National Front, since by then the local election in Dreux had become a test for the national parties.

This was most unfortunate, because the National Front had been well established in Dreux for some time. Its secretary-general, Jean-Pierre Stirbois, had scored reasonably well (by pre–1983 standards) in the 1978 legislative elections, with just over 2 percent of the vote, and in one of the cantons of Dreux had gained 12.6 percent of the vote in the cantonal elections of 1982. Both the government and the opposition attempted to cool down the political environment. Gaspard withdrew from the race and ceded her place as head of the list to a lesser known, "earthier" man, and Prime Minister Mauroy urged the voters of Dreux to rally behind the policies of Justice Minister Robert Badinter. Under pressure from the national parties, the opposition list refused to cede places this time to the National Front.

Nevertheless, the Stirbois list received almost 17 percent of the vote in the first round of the September election, and, as a result, four candidates from the National Front were integrated into the United Opposition list that was victorious in the second round. In return for their collaboration in this significant victory, three of the four National Front candidates were named assistant mayors (including Stirbois). However, far more important than the local posts was the decision by national opposition leaders to bless both the electoral and governmental collaboration with the National Front. Thus, what Jacques Chirac had denounced as an alliance "against nature" in March had become "completely natural in Dreux" for victory in the second round in September.[34] A week after the Dreux election, Chirac noted that he "would not be bothered at all about voting for the opposition list in the second round."[35] Indeed, he argued that more common lists should be concluded, if necessary, to defeat the left.

At this time, among the major opposition leaders, only Simone Veil strongly opposed collaboration with the National Front. However, she was quickly isolated by Chirac, Raymond Barre and Giscard d'Estaing, who explained her position as "moral" and linked to personal problems (certainly a reference to the fact that she is Jewish and was deported during World War II). For his part, said Giscard, he "approve[s] of the vote of the Dreux voters," and he argued that "we must deal with the problem which is at the origin of the rise of the extreme right: immigration."[36]

Two other elections in 1983 added luster to the political attraction of the National Front. In November the Communist "bastion" of Aulnay-sous-Bois was "overturned" by a list of the United Opposition. In this center of traditional Communist strength—whose former mayor, Robert Ballinger, had been president of the Communist group in the National Assembly until he entered the Senate in 1981—9.3 percent of the voters gave their support to an unknown National Front candidate.[37] This election reaffirmed the strength that the National Front had demonstrated in the working-class Twentieth Arrondissement of Paris, but without Le Pen as a candidate. In December Le Pen attracted over 12 percent of the vote in a legislative by-election in Brittany (Morbihan), this time in a constituency with no significant immigrant population to which voters could react directly. After all, it seemed by the spring of 1984 that, as Raymond Barre said, "Le Pen is not a bogey-man."[38]

It is not surprising that with each of these symbolic victories, Le Pen and the National Front became the center of political interest and debate. Beginning in January 1984, Le Pen was invited by major radio and television stations to participate in a series of important programs, large extracts of which were routinely published by the press the next day. While the programs themselves gave journalists an opportunity to attack, accuse and criticize the leader of the National Front, they gave him the opportunity to present his most powerful issues and to "present himself as a scapegoat."[39] Perhaps more important, each time an established leader of the right appeared on an interview program, he was forced to define himself relative to Le Pen.

The result of the election victories, the media attention and the contorted statements by political leaders of the right was that fewer voters found it possible to remain indifferent to Le Pen and the National Front. The percentage of voters both sympathetic to him and the party and strongly opposed tended to increase during 1984, while relative opposition grew during 1985.[40] While the acceptance of Le Pen's "ideas" remained relatively strong, voters who identified with the established right reversed their support of an electoral alliance with the National Front, and, after November 1984, increasingly opposed such an alliance.[41] Five months before the leaders of the established right had come to the same conclusion, supporters of the RPR and the UDF had apparently concluded that there was real *party* competition to the right and not simply "attractive" issues.

Even after the European elections, political leaders of the established right flirted with the idea of dealing with Le Pen as a legitimate political actor. In late 1984 Raymond Barre confessed in a television interview that he had met with Le Pen because "he meets with everyone."[42] However, by the spring of 1985 there was a definite change of tone among opposition leaders. With the approach of the cantonal elections in March 1985, most of the important leaders who had approved the Dreux alliance and alluded to the possibility of future alliances with the National Front now moved sharply in the other direction. The RPR issued a formal proscription against alliances with the extreme right, "even at the local level," while Raymond Barre warned voters against the man who was no longer like any other politician.[43] This *cordon sanitaire,* said to have been encouraged by the Church and the success of antiracist movements, was also a recognition of the message of the European election that perhaps this was not simply a *poussée de fièvre,* but a more substantial party challenge. Nevertheless, the National Front was supported by 8 percent of the electorate in the cantonal elections and by 10 percent in those cantons where the party actually ran candidates.

POLITICAL SPACE AND THE STABILITY OF THE NATIONAL FRONT

The attempt to isolate the National Front did not preclude the continued validation of the issues on which the party had built its strength. Thus, the positions of the opposition on race and law and order, particularly those of the RPR, took on a tone and a substance that resembled those of the National Front. Party and personal "ostracism" did not mean that Le Pen did not continue to have a major impact on the terms of the political dialogue and debate.[44]

Without accepting all of the theses of the National Front, the UDF and the RPR share with it some common ideas: the particular contribution of immigrants to insecurity; the certainty that there are too many immigrants in France; the absolute necessity therefore to increasingly send them home; the affirmation that "naturally, if there were fewer immigrants, there would be less unemployment, fewer tensions in certain cities and certain neighborhoods, and a lower social cost" (Jacques Chirac in *Libération*).[45]

If the intensity of anti-immigrant sentiment was less pronounced in the 1986 election campaign than it had been in other campaigns since 1981, this was related to the integration into official statements and platforms of a number of familiar themes that had been popularized by the National Front. The strongest positions were taken by the RPR and the UDF, both of which called for stronger measures to encourage immigrants to return to their home countries and a reduction of payments of social benefits to resident immigrants. In addition, the RPR recommended a revision of naturalization legislation to make it more difficult for immigrants to gain French citizenship, and the UDF called for strong measures to deal with the "explosion of delinquency" among immigrants. The positions of the Socialists and the Communists were more muted, and both parties tended to focus on the need for stronger measures to control the frontiers of the countries to prevent the influx of illegal immigrants. In general, however, the overriding issue seemed to be the future of France as a multiethnic, multicultural society, with the parties of the established right committed to policies that would prevent this kind of evolution.[46]

The validation of many of the National Front issues, of course, could have attracted many of the voters who had moved from the established right to the National Front in 1983–85 back to their original parties. However, the results of the 1986 elections indicate that, while this may have happened in some cases (in Paris, for example), the net effect has been a solidification of the vote for the National Front nationally, a sharp increase in some areas, and a general validation of the political space within which the National Front is able to attract support.

BUILDING STRENGTH

There are a number of strengths that emerged in the National Front vote in 1984 that give us some indication of its durability. Perhaps the most obvious is that voters for the National Front share not only certain attitudes, but also geographic proximity in communities which can reinforce these attitudes. The National Front list, by previous standards, did well virtually everywhere in France. The list achieved over 5 percent of the vote in all but three (contiguous) departments in the Massif Central.[47] Nevertheless, the highest levels of support were concentrated in departments with large immigrant populations, and/or concentrations of *pieds–noirs* (former French North African settlers). Within departments, the votes for the National Front tended to be concentrated in the largest cities, particularly those with large immigrant populations. In 1984, 70 percent of the cities with more than 100,000 people registered support for the National Front at levels above the national average.[48]

The correlation between the vote for the National Front and the proportion of immigrants in the thirty-six cities with more than 100,000 people is clear and positive for the 1984 election (r = +.57) Pearson product-moment correlation at the 99 percent level). The association is stronger if we correlate the National Front vote with the proportion of North Africans (r = + .57 at the 99 percent level).[49] However, there is also evidence that in smaller communities, the issues around which the National Front has mobilized its electorate may not be reinforced directly by the presence of a large immigrant population. Among the thirty-one communes that comprise the Grenoble region, Pascal Perrineau found no relationship between the National Front vote and the proportion of immigrants in a commune. In this region, the centers of strength of the National Front are often areas in which immigrant communities are on the periphery, some distance from the center of town.[50] Therefore, it would seem that social realities often translate into values and political commitments in indirect and complex ways. Jérôme Jaffré also found that beyond the proportion of immigrants, support for the National Front in French cities (of over 30,000) also varied with the party of the mayor. Communist-governed towns generally resisted the Le Pen surge better than those governed by Socialists, and the Socialist-governed towns better than those governed by the opposition.[51]

The percentages and correlations, however, only give a general picture of the ability of the National Front to attract votes. For example, Communist-governed cities generally "resisted" the National Front, but not necessarily well. An average vote of almost 15 percent for the National Front in these cities in 1984, and an average vote in the Communist bastions (those cities over 30,000 governed by a Communist mayor for over thirty-three years) of 13 percent in 1986 is considerable. In several towns that had been Communist strongholds as recently as 1983, the National Front outpolled the Communists in both 1984 and 1986 (Poissy and Chelles), while in others (Aulnay-sous-Bois) the PCF just edged out the FN. In Marseilles, where Gaston Defferre just got by in 1983, the National Front came in second both in 1984 and 1986, increasing its vote from 19 to 24 percent (almost twice the PCF vote). Particularly in larger towns, with large immigrant populations, the National Front seemed to test the depth of party implantation in 1984, a test that was confirmed in 1986, perhaps with the exception of Paris.

Another indication of the strength of the National Front has been the kinds of social categories from which the party has been drawing its support. Far more than for any other party, support for the National Front increased with education in 1984.[52] The party has been supported most strongly by artisans and small shopkeepers, buy also disproportionately by those in liberal professions and the *cadres superieurs* (higher executives), as well as by voters with higher incomes. More than two-thirds of the National Front voters are not practicing Catholics, and 60 percent of its voters are male, far more than any of the other parties of the right (or left). Its voters are concentrated in the age group between thirty-five and sixty-five, although the National Front has attracted a large proportion of young voters as well. Finally, 23 percent of the National Front supporters claim to be very interested in politics, and another 49 percent a little interested (compared with 16 and 45 percent among the general electorate).[53] In short, at least in terms of education, age, income, sex and interest in politics, they are more likely than most voters to be stable and committed partisans.[54]

The initial successes of the National Front were achieved with little organizational support, but this is no longer the case. For some time before the 1983 takeoff, the party had both supporters and sympathizers among the militants and some leaders of the RPR and the more loosely organized UDF. The party also had some militants in small secondary groups, among a wider fellow-travelling audience. Aside from those militants directly associated with the party, probably the largest reservoir of militant strength has been the National Center of Independents and Peasants (Conseil national des indépendants et paysans, or CNIP), which has sometimes run National Front candidates under its label and has served as a party of transition for many ex-militants of the other party of the extreme right, the Parti des forces nouvelles (PFN), particularly after 1981.[55]

In 1984 one-quarter of the CNIP supporters voted for the National Front list, although the party was officially integrated into the Veil list. However, unlike the other parties that lost supporters to Le Pen disproportionately among their more marginal identifiers, the largest percentage of supporters for the National Front from CNIP came from those "closest" to the party.[56] Thus, there have been hidden reserves of militant strength for Le Pen in the more established parties, indicating the kind of acceptance by voluntary associations and mergers with other parties analyzed by Levite and Tarrow.

The process has become more visible since the local elections of 1983, with direct militant transfers of some importance. By September 1983 two-thirds of the militants of the local section of the UDF in the Twentieth Arrondissement of Paris (where Le Pen had run so well in March) had joined the National Front, and the president of the UDF section had become the National Front representative in the sector.[57] After the impressive Le Pen showing in Morbihan in December, a departmental federation was organized in Mulhouse led by a former militant of the Parti républicain, and a provisional departmental bureau was set up in Strasbourg directed by a former militant of the RPR. In important cities where the National Front electoral strength would be demonstrated in June 1984—Montpellier, Nîmes, Sète, Toulouse, Draguignon, Avignon, Narbonne and Roanne—large sections were organized in the winter of 1983–84, frequently based on defections from the established opposition. "It is the most activist militants of the right that rally to M. Le Pen, where the local notables of the parliamentary opposition have a tendency to cut themselves off from their base."[58]

After June 1984, the National Front demonstrated a capacity to expand beyond its more traditional front organizations. At the end of 1984, leaders of the party created the association Entreprises modernes et libertés, whose 800 or so members include small businessmen, doctors and lawyers. With four geographic sections in Paris, the organization announced its intention to have seven in the suburbs and thirty in the provinces by the end of 1985.[59] Naturally, success was not guaranteed, but one sure sign that the organizational expansion of the National

Front has had some impact has been the priority given by the RPR and the UDF to limit and/or forbid collaboration prior to the 1986 election, and to intensify their pressure on militants who may have been thinking of defecting.[60]

However, the most important indication of the expansion of the National Front has been its ability to present large numbers of candidates in 1985 and 1986. In the cantonal elections of March 1982, the National Front had difficulty finding 65 candidates to run in its name. Three years later, 500 candidates ran for the National Front, and in 1986 the lists of the National Front carried over 2,000 names. The heads of the departmental lists reflected the distance the party had travelled in just a few years. From a party of agitators, it had become a coalition of notables of the old traditional right, and right and extreme-right organizations: Pascal Arrighi, Frédéric Domenech and Edouard Frédéric-Dupont from the traditional right; Roussel, Chauvière and de Cornois from the UDF/RPR; Blachelot, Descaves, Vaysse-Tempé and Megret from different organizations. The influx of these notables was sufficiently disruptive to create a split in the organization with some of the older Le Pen loyalists in November 1985. However, the split seemed to have no impact on the National Front electoral showing in 1986, and it helped to alter the image of the party at the local level. Indeed, the party clearly made a strategic choice that would maximize not only its electoral appeal, but its ability to engage in coalition bargaining.[61]

In the process of expansion, the National Front appears to have attracted a relatively loyal following, who are party voters rather than loyal followers of a single man. From election to election increasing proportions of them are willing to make a commitment for the next election, a commitment more or less confirmed by the election results.[62] The success of the party in the legislative elections should be understood in the context of the efforts made by both the parties of the right and the press to isolate the National Front, as well as the accusations of bribery, having engaged in torture and suspect financial dealings, against which Le Pen was forced to devote considerable time defending himself, and finally, the split in the party in November 1985. It would appear from the results that, at least for the moment, the National Front has constructed an electoral following with a solid and growing organizational base.

Moreover, far from isolating the party, the new majority in the National Assembly may be forced to work with the new National Front parliamentary group in order to maintain their fragile majority. Indications of the relationship between the ''majority'' and the National Front emerged quickly as the National Assembly organized for its spring session. With the support of some government supporters, the National Front was able to secure two posts in the secretariat of the Assembly. In return, the National Front appears to have given its support to the candidates of the government in the four parliamentary committees where the ''majority'' does not have a majority; these votes were particularly critical in the defense and foreign affairs committees, where the National Front holds the balance of power. These votes indicate some areas in which the National Front will be able to maximize its bargaining power with the government.[63]

In addition, the right now depends on the support of the National Front in five of the twenty regions where it has formed a government, and both the new "majority" and the National Front appear to have begun to develop a working relationship in these regions.[64] Therefore there seems to be some question about the RPR/UDF maintaining their isolation of Le Pen's party. In fact, several leaders of the UDF have tentatively proposed collaboration with the National Front on the regional level, and the National Front has demanded real power in return.[65] All of this seems to mark another step in what Levite and Tarrow have called "the process of certification of the excluded party as a legitimate actor."

THE POLITICAL LIMITS

Certainly, with the help of conscious decisions by elites and groups within the political system, as well as through its own efforts, the National Front has come a long way toward establishing its legitimation. Nevertheless, there are political weaknesses of the party that are clearly related to its strength: issue voting. The issues of Le Pen and the National Front do not entirely coincide with those of large numbers of people who have voted for the party during the past three years.

The program of the National Front cannot be reduced to some kind of neo-*poujadism*, primarily because it goes well beyond simple categorical demands. Le Pen's political positions are rooted in the fundamentalism of the traditional political right in France, to which he has grafted some elements of *poujadist* populism. Thus, he has supported a variety of "people's capitalism," advocating the distribution of the capital of nationalized firms among *pères de famille,* and he has protested that "France has entered into a system of fiscal inquisition comparable to the gestapo." On the other hand, he has also supported European defense and the reentry of France into NATO as the only way to confront the Soviet Union effectively, despite his virulent attacks against foreigners, Europeans and Jews. Although he has criticized the "decadence" that has resulted from the policies of the state (particularly policies on immigration and abortion), he is by no means a neoliberal: "If there is in human beings an aspiration for harmony, it must be codified and guided by the authority of the national state . . . between good and evil, the government cannot remain neutral."[66] On the international level, he differentiates between countries in warm climates and those in temperate climates. In the temperate climates of Europe, intelligence has developed at the expense of unlimited sexuality, thus determining the superiority of Europe. From these primitive assumptions flow Le Pen's positions on the evils of immigration, the dangers of birth control and the need to return to traditional values.

However, support for the National Front comes far less from those who are most committed to traditional values of the past, and far more from those who are concerned with threats to the political community in the present. Voters for the National Front are generally in tune with Le Pen's focus on authority and

Table 7.5
Political Attitudes of the Electorates of the Opposition

	Support Nat. Fr.	Support RPR	Support UDF	Total Sample
Judge liberalization of abortion as progress	53	40	34	49
Give priority to respect for family, work and religion	35	47	47	33
Judge the word "Gaullism" positive	54	69	61	39
Wish that opposition would go beyond legality against the left	27	8	10	7
Think that once elected, politicians forget their promises	72	57	54	42
Want to reestablish the death penalty	88	71	61	57
Give priority to make the authority of the state respected	35	19	11	21
Give priority to put "the house of France in order"	62	54	49	37
Can justify fighting for the defense of an ally	56	48	46	35

Note: Among supporters of the National Front, 53 percent judge liberalization of abortion as progress.

Source: Ten surveys between September 1983 and January 1984. Results in SOFRES, Opinion publique, 1985 (Paris: Gallimard, 1985), p. 191.

order. More than other Frenchmen of either the right or the left, they are concerned with the priority of respect for the authority of the state, of "putting the house in order," of the importance of the death penalty. They are also passionately anti-left, and 27 percent believe that "the opposition should go beyond legal means in confronting the left." (See Table 7.5.) Of course this is an electorate that is concerned with immigration and law and order.

Still, relatively few of the supporters of the National Front are committed to other traditional values. There are fewer practicing Catholics, proportionately, than among supporters of the other parties of the right, many more workers, many more supporters of liberalized abortion (as "progress"), and far fewer people who believe that "respect for family, work and religion" is most important.

Subrata Mitra has found five distinct "types" of Le Pen supporters, based on a factor analysis of the responses to an Institut français de l'opinion publique (IFOP) exit poll on June 17, 1984. The largest group by far (38 percent of the National Front supporters) are the "xenophobes," whose vote is determined largely by attitudes toward immigration. These are also the group that appears to be most loyal to the party. Fewer than 30 percent of this group are practicing Catholics, compared with almost 40 percent in the general sample of National Front voters. For the next largest group in Mitra's analysis, the "idealists of the right" (28 percent of the sample), not a single respondent chose immigration as a priority issue. They *all* chose economic issues as the reason for their choice of Le Pen, while none of the xenophobes made the same choices.[67]

Therefore, it is not clear that the leadership of the National Front will be able to stabilize or augment its following in the long run, given the importance of issue voting for the party, and given the gap between the range of issues supported by the leadership and the basically nontraditional commitments of the largest group of its following. Indeed, this gap is greatest for the part of the National Front that is most committed to the party. Juggling contradictory political positions may be more difficult if the party gains real decision-making power.[68]

Beyond this, the system of proportional representation that has been highly favorable to maximizing the bargaining power of the National Front, as well as to the process of inclusion, will soon be changed. Even if the party is able to maintain its present level of electoral support, it is doubtful that the party would be able to secure more than a small token representation in either the National Assembly or the regional councils under a first-past-the-post system of *scrutin d'arrondissement*. The change in the electoral law may very well undermine the cohesion of the thirty-five-member parliamentary group, almost none of whom is likely to be reelected under the banner of the National Front.

CONCLUSION

Nevertheless, it is now clear that the process of political inclusion of the National Front has now reached a new stage. As a carrier of issues the party is in a highly advantageous position to bargain with and influence the governing majority, and to solidify its position within the electorate. How, then, can we understand its success? The issue of immigration has certainly been an important ingredient, but the case of the National Front demonstrates that political issues (as opposed to attitudes and values) do not emerge but are constructed as part of a political process. Anti-immigrant sentiment has ebbed and flowed at rela-

Table 7.6
Percentage Voting for the National Front in 1984 and 1986, by Group

	1984	1986
Men	13	12
Women	8	7
Occupation		
farmers	8	11
shopkeepers/artisans	15	14
professional/top mngm't	14	9
middle mngm't	} 10	10
white collar		7
blue collar	9	11
Religious practice		
regular churchgoers	11	8
occasional churchgoers	12	13
nonpracticing Catholics	11	11
Total	11	10

Sources: 1984: survey by SOFRES, Le Nouvel Observateur, June 22, 1984;
         1986: survey by Bull-BVA, Libération, March 18, 1986, and,
         for the results on religious practice, the exit poll reported
         by John Frears, "France: The Cohabitation Election," presented
         at the Annual Meeting of the British Political Studes
         Association, Nottingham, England, April 9, 1986.

tively high levels at least since 1968, and the National Front has been advocating anti-immigrant measures since it was founded in 1972. However, the ability of the party to mobilize 10 percent of the electorate around this issue was not evident until 1983–84.

The *alternance* of 1981, and the disappointment evoked by Socialist austerity, resulted in a party system that was more vulnerable to challenge. Voters on the margins of the established parties of the right (particularly the RPR) became less inclined to place their trust in these parties during a period of perceived economic crisis, and seized the alternative offered by Le Pen. The principal themes around which the National Front mobilized its electorate had been inserted into the national political debate by the Communist Party in 1980–81, and therefore were no longer simply the issues of the extreme right. By the time of the European elections of 1984, the problems of immigration, law and order and the link between the two had become well established in the national political dialogue, and had been legitimized and defined by all party elites.

The issues of immigration and law and order became the means through which the legitimation of the National Front was constructed through conscious decisions by party elites and groups within the political system. Elites of the right underestimated their own organizational vulnerability in 1983–84, as well as the ability of Le Pen to build an extensive political organization around defections of militants from the RPR and the UDF. By the time the National Front fielded 500 candidates in 1985, and over 2,000 in 1986, it was probably too late to establish a *cordon sanitaire*. They also underestimated the loyalty of National Front voters. By permitting collaboration with Le Pen, and by permitting Le Pen and the National Front to define the terms of the political debate on immigration, they undermined their own attractiveness among a significant percentage of their followers. Finally, the proportional representation election law, pushed through to preserve the flexibility of the president after 1986, also made it possible for the National Front to translate its electoral following into representation and bargaining. This position was reinforced by a similar process in the new regional councils. In this way, the legitimation and inclusion of the National Front was constructed during the post–1981 period.

NOTES

1. See Suzanne Berger, "Politics and Antipolitics in Western Europe in the Seventies," *Daedalus* 108, No. 1 (Winter 1979): 40.

2. This is one of the recurrent themes in the recent book by Edward Plenel and Alain Rollat, *L'Effet Le Pen* (Paris: Editions de la Découverte, 1984).

3. See Philip Cerny, "The New Rules of the Game in France," in Philip Cerny and Martin Schain, Eds., *French Politics and Public Policy* (New York: St. Martin's, 1980); Leslie Derfler, *President and Parliament* (Boca Raton: University Presses of Florida, 1983).

4. Frank L. Wilson, "The French Party System since 1981," *Contemporary French Civilization* 8, Nos. 1 and 2 (Fall/Winter 1983/84): 117.

5. Ibid.

6. See Berger, "Politics," and Jack Hayward, "Dissident France: The Counter Political Culture," *West European Politics* 1, No. 3 (October 1978).

7. Wilson, "French Party System," p. 117; Martin Schain, *French Communism and Local Power* (New York: St. Martin's, 1985), Chap. 5.

8. SOFRES, *Opinion publique, 1985* (Paris: Gallimard, 1985), pp. 28–29, 195.

9. Ibid., pp. 19, 26.

10. Jean Charlot, "Exposé introductif: l'évolution de l'image des partis politiques en France," presented at the Congress of the International Political Science Association, Paper, July 19, 1985.

11. See the survey done by SOFRES for *Figaro Magazine* (November 1983): 36.

12. Bruce Campbell, "On the Prospects of Polarization in the French Electorate," *Comparative Politics* 8, No. 2 (January 1976): 282–87.

13. Recalculated from tables in Gérard Grunberg, "L'Instabilité du comportement électoral," presented to the Congress of the International Political Science Association, Paris, July 15–20, 1985, pp. 21, 24.

14. Recalculated from results presented by Jérôme Jaffré, *Le Monde,* June 6, 1984.

15. The exit poll is cited by John Frears, "France: The 'Cohabitation' Election of 16th March 1986," presented at the Annual Meeting of the British Political Studies Association, Nottingham, England, April 9, 1986, p. 27.

16. See the survey by PID, published in *Le Matin,* June 21, 1984, as well as the SOFRES survey for the International League Against Racism and Anti-Semitism (LICRA), in November 1984, "Electorat de Jean-Marie Le Pen," pp. 4–5.

17. SOFRES, "L'Image de Jean-Marie Le Pen et de l'extrême droite à l'approche des élections Européenes," May 1984, pp. 4–6. SOFRES, *Opinion publique, 1985,* p. 178.

18. SOFRES, *Opinion publique, 1985,* p. 183.

19. LICRA survey, p. 2.

20. SOFRES, *Opinion publique, 1985,* p. 184, and SOFRES survey published in *Le Monde,* October 17, 1986.

21. SOFRES, *Opinion publique, 1985,* p. 214.

22. See, for example, the comments by Jérôme Jaffré in the article by Alain Rollat, *Le Monde,* March 7, 1986, p. 6.

23. See *Le Monde,* October 17, 1985.

24. Pascal Perrineau, "Le Front national: un électorat authoritaire," *Revue Politique et Parliamentaire,* No. 918 (July–August, 1985): 30.

25. Ariel Levite and Sidney Tarrow, "The Legitimation of Excluded Parties in Dominant Party Systems: A Comparison of Israel and Italy," *Comparative Politics* 15, No. 3 (April 1983): 300.

26. Monica Charlot, "L'Emergence du Front national," presented to the Congress of the International Political Science Association, Paris, July 19, 1985, p. 11.

27. See *Le Nouvel Observateur,* June 22, 1984: *Le Matin,* March 18, 1986.

28. See Martin Schain, "Immigrants and Politics in France," in John Ambler, ed., *The French Socialist Experiment* (Philadelphia: Institute for the Study of Human Issues, 1985).

29. Quoted from a resolution submitted to and adopted by the 24th Congress of the PCF, February 1982, cited in Plenel and Rollat, *L'Effet,* p. 161.

30. See Schain, "Immigrants and Politics in France."

31. See *Le Monde,* March 11, 1983; March 23, 1983.

32. Thus a majority of the electorate agreed that "the left has done too much for the immigrants," and that among the most effective ways of dealing with unemployment would be "to send the immigrants home." See SOFRES, *Opinion publique, 1984* (Paris: Gallimard, 1984), pp. 125, 221.

33. See Françoise Gaspard and Claude Servan-Schreiber, *La Fin des immigrés* (Paris: Editions du Seuil, 1984).

34. Cited in Colette Ysmal, "Le RPR et l'UDF face au Front National: concurrence et connivences," *Revue Politique et Parliamentaire,* No. 913 (November–December 1984): 13.

35. Plenel and Rollat, *L'Effet,* p. 99.

36. *Le Monde,* September 11–12, 1983.

37. I would like to thank Nadia Michel, CNRS Paris, for sharing with me her data on Aulnay.

38. See the long article by Catherine Pégard, "Faut-il avoir peur de Le Pen?," *Le Point*, February 13, 1984.

39. Charlot, "L'Emergence," pp. 5, 6. Charlot briefly presents the content of these programs.

40. See SOFRES, *Opinion publique, 1985*, p. 183; *Le Monde*, March 7, 1986.

41. See the comments by Jérôme Jaffré, quoted in *Le Monde*, March 7, 1986.

42. Ysmal, "Le RPR et l'UDF," p. 14.

43. *Le Monde*, March 2, 1985.

44. See especially the interview with Jacques Chirac in *Libération*, October 30, 1984. We should also note that the position of the Socialist government on immigration has also hardened considerably.

45. Ysmal, "Le RPR et l'UDF," pp. 17–18.

46. The positions of the various parties on immigration were published in *Figaro*, June 4 and 6, 1985.

47. *Le Monde*, June 19, 1984.

48. See the results in *Libération*, June 19–20, 1984, and *Le Quotidien de Paris*, June 19, 1984.

49. These results were supplied by Catherine de Wenden, CNRS, Paris, from an article submitted to her anonymously for review: "The Move to the Right: Immigration and the Geography of the National Front in France," p. 11.

50. See Perineau, "Le Front national," p. 29.

51. *Le Monde*, July 1–2, 1984.

52. See the exit poll by SOFRES/TFI published by *Le Nouvel Observateur*, June 22, 1984, p. 28.

53. Charlot, "L'Emergence," p. 11; Perrineau, "Le Front national," pp. 25–26. In the 1986 legislative elections, the National Front increased its support among workers and seems to have lost some support among the *cadres superieurs*. See *Libération*, March 18, 1986.

54. See Colette Ysmal, "Stabilité des électorats et attitudes politiques," in Jacques Capdevielle et al., *France de gauche vote à droite* (Paris: Presses de la FNSP, 1981), chap. 2.

55. Plenel and Rollat, *L'Effet*, pp. 63–67 and chaps. 5–7.

56. SOFRES, *Opinion publique, 1985*, p. 229.

57. *Le Monde*, September 30, 1983.

58. Plenel and Rollat, *L'Effet*, p. 71.

59. *Le Monde*, August 3, 1985.

60. Ysmal, "Le RPR et l'UDF," pp. 15–16.

61. See Pascal Perrineau, "Quel avenir pour le Front national?," *Intervention*, No. 15 (January–February–March, 1986): 40–41; *Le Monde*, October 22, 1985.

62. See Perrineau, "Le Front national," p. 30, and "Quel avenir," p. 40.

63. See *Le Monde*, April 3, 1986; *Libération*, April 7, 1986.

64. See *Le Monde*, March 21, 1986; *Liberation*, April 5–6, 1986.

65. *Le Monde*, March 21, 1986.

66. Plenel and Rollat, *L'Effet*, p. 32. Much of this section relies on material from Plenel and Rollat, Section 1, "Le Discours."

67. Subatra Mitra, "Structure et positionnement de l'électorat de l'extrême droite: une

analyse des électeurs du Front national aux élections Européenes, 1984,'' IFOP, January 1985, pp. 15–17.

68. Gérard Le Gall, ''Radiographie de l'image du P.C.F.,'' *Revue Politique et Parliamentaire* (January–February 1985): 19.

The Communist Party: Out of the Frying Pan

D. S. BELL AND BYRON CRIDDLE

The most important development in French politics in the 1980s was the apparently sudden and allegedly irreversible decline of the Communist Party. It was a decline that coincided paradoxically with the party's incorporation in government for only the second time in its sixty-year history. The paradox, however, was more apparent than real, for the two developments—Communist decline and *la gauche au pouvoir*—were closely interconnected, the first being a necessary condition of the second. Until the Communist Party lost its dominant position on the left, the left as a whole was unelectable, and the slump in the Communist vote as registered in the first ballot of the presidential election in April 1981 created the conditions for Mitterrand's success at the second ballot in May and for the near doubling of the Socialist Party's electorate from 5 to 9 million in the subsequent parliamentary election in June.[1] Communist decline, both absolutely and relatively, served to deradicalize the image of the left and thereby break the traditional advantage enjoyed by the right in French politics for the greater part of the postwar era.

The statistics of Communist electoral decline are simply stated. From the party's high-water mark of 28 percent in 1946 it survived the Fourth Republic with an average vote of 26 percent, and the Fifth Republic—until 1978—with an average of 21 percent. By 1981 it had fallen from 20 percent (1978) to 16 percent (1981 parliamentary election); by 1984 to 11 percent (European assembly election) and by 1986 to 9.8 percent (parliamentary election). The 1986 result represented the third successive slide in support in five years. Such figures reveal not merely the loss of two-thirds of the party's electorate since 1946, but in the space of eight years, from 1978 to 1986, the desertion of the party by fully half of its supporters. The scale and depth of the demise are demonstrated in Table 8.1. In 1978 the party polled over 20 percent of the vote in half (forty-five) of

Table 8.1
Communist Share of the Vote by Departments, 1978–1986

	1978[1]	1979[2]	1981[1]	1984[2]	1986[1]
25 percent and above	23	20	12	0	0
20–25 percent	22	22	13	5	3
15–20 percent	27	29	17	15	8
10–15 percent	15	19	24	31	27
10 percent and below	9	6	30	45	58
Total	96	96	96	96	96

[1] National Assembly election.

[2] European Assembly election.

Source: Adapted from Le Monde, Dossiers et Documents: Les élections législatives du 16 mars 1986.

the country's ninety-six departments, and in only nine did it fall below 10 percent. By stark contrast, in 1986 it was scaling 20 percent in a mere three of the ninety-six departments and polling under 10 percent in as many as fifty-eight.

Electoral decline was paralleled by losses in other areas, such as the share of the vote gained by the Communist-led CGT in workplace elections from over 50 percent to 30 percent between 1966 and 1984;[2] the decline of party membership and of activist participation; the falling circulation of the communist press; and the declining image of the party.[3] By 1986 the party had all the appearances of a marginalized political force, its electoral support a mere percentage point ahead of the extreme right *Front national* and occupying in parliament the same number of seats (thirty-five) as that party; with only six fewer seats the Communists would have lost their parliamentary group status.

It was in anticipation of this decline that the party had decided in 1977 to break its programmatic alliance with the Socialists, in an attempt to shore up an electoral base that showed signs of sliding to the Socialists, and in the hope of preventing a victory of the left simply because that victory would not be one the Communists could control. This wrecking tactic worked initially; the left was beaten in the election of 1978, but it failed in 1981 when François Mitterrand unexpectedly won the presidency and then deftly engineered a coattails victory in a precipitated parliamentary election. These two elections of 1981 highlighted the Communists' problem: their own decline alongside the Socialist Party's resurgence. Mitterrand outran Georges Marchais, the Communist leader, by 26 percent to 15 percent in the presidential poll, and the PS outran the PCF by 37 percent to 16 percent in the parliamentary election, figures serving to confirm both Communist decline and, importantly, loss of dominance on the left.

The history of the current position in which the PCF finds itself goes back to Nikita Khruschev's speech of 1956 and the subsequent strategy of left unity. Western Communist parties had previously adopted postures of radical hostility to "bourgeois" political systems, postures which, while not insurrectionary, did not allow for participation, alliances or electoral strategies. Khruschev's secret speech revealing Stalin's crimes and the strategy of peaceful coexistence opened up new possibilities for Communist parties in Western Europe. The PCF, like other parties, began to seek a place within the system mainly by hoping to persuade the Socialists to join an alliance, but during the Fourth Republic the weak non-Communist left shied away from any involvement with a dominant Communist Party. Attitudes changed, however, with the advent of the Fifth Republic and de Gaulle's creation of a large center-right coalition which could only be rivaled by a countervailing left-wing alliance of the sort first assembled in 1965 by François Mitterrand in his bid for the presidency against de Gaulle. For their part, the Communists, having to woo reluctant partners, were prepared to make major concessions, for example accepting Mitterrand's very moderate platform in 1965. In this sense, the origins of closer Communist Party cooperation with the non-Communist left may be traced to Khruschev, for his promotion of "de-Stalinization" and peaceful coexistence, and to de Gaulle, for his inauguration of a presidential system of government and a bipolarized system of electoral competition involving rival alliances of right and left.

There was, however, a basic difficulty: no left coalition could succeed electorally if the Communists were its dominant element. A victory for the left had as its precondition a non-Communist party which was clearly dominant over the Communists. This was broadly a consequence of the electoral system and presidential power—both highly uncongenial to a party regarded with as much suspicion as the PCF. The French Communists had failed to confront the dilemma of being a pro-Russian party on the one hand and seeking an electoral road to power on the other. The Communist Party most successful in parliamentary elections, the Italian Communist Party, resolved this dilemma by simply becoming less Communist—by abandoning the structures and dogmas of Marxism-Leninism. The inevitable result of an assiduously pursued strategy of left union was the growth of a credible, attractive Socialist Party which in the 1970s came to outgrow the Communists electorally. To this situation the Communists reacted initially along two lines. First, they tried to compete with the Socialists by presenting an "updated" model of "Socialism in French colors," which was more attractive, more open and less "Eastern." Second, they opened up attacks on the Socialist Party itself, thus compromising the viability of the alliance and its electoral prospects. Neither tactic worked: the liberalization was a case of too little too late, and the Socialist competitor continued to inflate, eventually at Communist expense.

In 1977, when it became clear that the Socialists could poll some 30 percent of the vote to the Communists' 20 percent, the Communist Party broke the alliance and moved into outright attack on the Socialists. As in the more sectarian of its phases, the PCF rejected left unity "at the summit" in preference for unity "at the base," a euphemism for Communist mobilization of its own resources in the cause of self-preservation and the curtailing of Socialist growth. An anti-Socialist campaign was waged through the elections of 1978 (legislative), 1979 (European) and the presidential elections of 1981. In the latter, Marchais ran a vigorously anti-Mitterrand campaign along the classic lines of portraying the Socialists as objective allies of the right. But the result was a disaster for the Communist leader, the severest setback for the party since 1958, with the party's share of the vote lower, at 15 percent, even than in that Gaullist landslide year. Within two days of Marchais' rout the PCF was calling on its supporters to vote for Mitterrand at the second ballot, on the eve of which the Communist leader made clear his party's wish to enter government as part of the new majority. Before this was conceded the Communists lost half their seats in the parliamentary elections and were obliged to sign an agreement with the Socialists which included reference to Russian withdrawal from Afghanistan, democratization in Poland and a commitment to a government alliance of "flawless solidarity."[4]

The nature of the problem for the Communist Party in 1981 was that the triumph of *la gauche au pouvoir* was in fact no more than *le parti socialiste au pouvoir,* with presidency, premiership and parliament all securely in Socialist hands. The parliamentary arithmetic summarized the extent of Communist marginalization: the Socialists had 285 (or 58 percent) of the seats, the Communists a paltry and ignorable 44 deputies. Over 1 million Communist voters had deserted their party for Mitterrand and the Socialists on the basis of casting a *vote utile,* and so strong was the demand among its own electorate for a new left government that the PCF, vanguard of the proletariat, was left with no choice but to follow where its voters led—into government with four strategically unimportant and thus purely token ministerial portfolios, the more significant of the four ministries, transport, even having its responsibility for capital investment programs removed to another *Socialist*-occupied ministry.

In government, the Communist Party proceeded to present two faces, the first of which being that of a conventional governing posture, with the four ministers (Charles Fiterman at transport, Anicet Le Pors at administrative reform, Marcel Rigout at job training and Jack Ralite at first health and then labor) observing collective responsibility. At times the commitment was patchy, as when Politburo member Roland Leroy announced in the autumn of 1981 that the party was "*in* the government but not *of* it." But self-interest decreed that the party hold ranks behind the Socialists so as to safeguard Communist positions in local government—crucial to the party's wealth and influence—due for renewal in the spring of 1983 and where alliance with the Socialists had delivered substantial gains in the previous municipal elections. To this end, at least until the second turn of Finance Minister Delors' austerity screw in spring 1983, the Communists were involved in only relatively minor breaches of solidarity, as for example when Administrative Reform Minister Le Pors made known his dislike for the deindexing of civil service pay. Nor was there significant evidence of Communist abuse of power, of "white-anting" in the Communist ministries by the infiltration of "sleepers." Care was in any case taken by the government to counterbalance Communist and non-Communist influence, for example in public corporations. Thus the Paris Metro, in which non-Communist unions were strong, was put under a Communist head, whereas the SNCF, where the PCF-led CGT is dominant, was not.

But the respectable ministerialist face of communism did not appear to pay off. Communist influence in government was negligible: the party's opposition to deflation was ignored as Mitterrand backed his finance minister in taking the strategic decision in favor of *rigueur* in 1982. Nor did its electoral slide abate; in both the local elections of 1983 and the European Assembly elections of 1984 further significant losses were registered, giving the party in mid–1984 little choice but to leave government to pursue a new strategy—that of *reculer pour mieux sauter*. The "new" strategy was in fact a reversion to the orthodoxy of 1977–81, attacking the Socialists for their bourgeois, class-treacherous characteristics, for their mere management of the capitalist crisis, their backsliding toward the right.

This was merely an overt expression of the second, alternative face of French communism as presented after entry into government in 1981.[5] Between 1981 and mid–1984 it was largely for internal consumption, for activists and *permanents*. At that time it was a stance of no more than grudging support for the Socialist government and the hope indeed that it would fail. The more visible evidence of this internal Communist distaste was found in the actions of the CGT, which was used by the party as a proxy, albeit a restrained one, in launching campaigns against the deflationary strategy and its consequences—industrial closures and job shakeouts. Before 1984 hostility was not taken so far as to jeopardize Communist participation, though the final year (1983–84) saw a mounting volume of Communist criticism of *rigueur* (austerity) and *modernisation* (closures) as the government adapted its strategy and vocabulary to encourage enterprise, competition and profit. In this closing phase the strain began to show, with *L'Humanité* criticising the PCF parliamentary group in April 1983 for voting a tougher austerity package, and with opposition to job cuts being reflected in the resignation of the Communist head of the state coal industry in November 1983 and the presence of George Marchais at a steelworkers' demonstration in April 1984. The latter incident was the more serious, coming only four months after a meeting of Communist and Socialist leaders, held at the latter's insistence, to "verify" the governing alliance.

POLICY

Even in opposition before 1981, and notwithstanding the so-called Common Program of 1972–77, the Communist and Socialist parties were far apart on most policy questions. In office, with the Socialist government adopting conventional social democratic remedies across the board, the gulf between the parties widened. The widest gulf was over foreign policy, where the PCF was, for obvious reasons, most suspect in its position on the Atlantic Alliance, the European Community, the French nuclear force and policy in relation to Chad and Lebanon. Despite the reference to "democratization" in Poland in the agreement between the two parties in June 1981, it was not long before the Communist Party was showing its indifference toward the imposition of martial law in Poland in December 1981 and to the fate of Solidarity. *L'Humanité* presented a very positive image of the Jaruzelski regime and dealt with Solidarity by pretending it no longer existed. In 1984 CGT delegations visited Poland—meeting official regime-approved union representatives—and Bulgaria, emphasizing the real loyalties of the party. The Soviet view, as expressed by V. Zaglandin in *The Soviet Peace Philosophy* (1981) was endorsed by the PCF, as by other Western Communist parties: the world being seen as divided into two camps, imperialist and progressive, with campaigns launched around the "peace" issue and with alliances involving governing "to manage the crisis" shunned.

This was a negation of the so-called Eurocommunist period of the 1970s (1975–78) when the PCF had appeared to dilute its commitment to "proletarian internationalism" as expressed in fealty to Moscow, and to mirror the revisionist path of the Italian and Spanish parties. During the 1970s criticism of the Soviet Union and Eastern-style systems was a tactical necessity in the party's competition with the resurgent Socialist Party; hence "Socialism in French Colors"—the slogan of the twenty-second party congress (1976), and attacks on Soviet labor camps and the treatment of dissidents. During this period routine meetings of French and top Soviet party officials had been suspended: Soviet Communist Party (CPSU) representation at PCF congresses was assigned to lower-ranking officials, and in 1976 Marchais missed the CPSU congress.

This phase of "estrangement" opened with Jean Elleinstein's *Le phénomène stalinien* (1975) and closed with A. Adler's *L'URSS et nous* (1978). By the time of the publication of the latter book, the PCF had already reverted to proclaiming the record of the Soviet system as *globalement positif,* thus setting itself apart from the more critical Italian and Spanish Communist parties. Thereafter, the party held loyal to the Socialist system and avoided consideration of the roots of Stalinism and other inherent difficulties in the Eastern bloc. The collapse of the left alliance in 1977—an alliance of which the Russians had to all appearances disapproved—facilitated a rapprochement between the PCF and the CPSU and the elimination from the party press and discourse of all criticism of the USSR; the twenty-fourth PCF congress (1982) saw world peace as guaranteed only by Soviet military might.

In the 1980s PCF foreign policy concerns came to be dominated above all by "disarmament," on which the party ran several campaigns, all lacking real resonance. One reason for the failure of such campaigns was the party's mere repetition of Soviet demands, for example the call in July 1983 for French and

British nuclear forces to be included in the talks on limiting intermediate range missiles in Europe—a position entirely at variance with the posture adopted by President Mitterrand. The PCF was also behind *L'appel des cent*, which in October 1984 held a demonstration calling for a reopening of negotiations and a pseudo zero option involving destruction of existing arms stocks. *L'Humanité* was particularly keen to promote the disarmament issue and made frequent references during 1984–85 to the peace campaigns elsewhere in Europe against "Star Wars." The party took special exception to Socialist Defense Minister Charles Hernu's "Rapid Intervention Force" (FAR) which, it argued, would put France into direct confrontation with the Warsaw Pact forces and increase the risk of conventional war. The PCF was thus, once again, barely nuanced in its alignment with the strategic interests of the Soviet Union.

It was, however, domestic policy considerations that determined the Communist Party's decision to leave the government in July 1984 when Mitterrand changed prime ministers, exchanging Pierre Mauroy for Laurent Fabius. The party, as distinct from its four ministers, and the CGT frequently spoke out against government policy as soon as that policy—from early 1982—began to reflect the government's commitment to a deflationary strategy, to cuts, closures and redundancies, which hit the PCF in its fiefdoms in the old heavy industrial sector. While foreign policy attitudes reflecting a sycophancy toward the Soviet Union were unpopular, implication in the domestic policy disappointments of the Socialist government was far more damaging to the electoral prospects of the party, which had survived nationally since the 1940s as a party of protest (as Georges Lavau's tribunitial party) and not as a party in power during a recession. From a modest stance as internal critic in the first year of government (1981–82) during which time the PCF called for more redistribution (viz., a higher minimum wage) it accelerated to a high decibel assault on deflation, opposing the wage freeze (1982) and using its deputies in this breach of solidarity by getting them to abstain. Cutbacks in social policy provision after 1982 were criticized by Marchais, and by 1983 *L'Humanité* had settled into a familiar groove of identifying the Socialist deflationary policies as indistinguishable from the austerity of Raymond Barre's government before 1981; of asserting that government by the left in fact meant administration by the right. Participation in government in the face of such realities was justified at the twenty-fourth (1982) congress only with the claim that the party was the guarantor of the workers' interests, guarding against Socialist concessions to business and ensuring "the honoring of the commitments of 1981."

The main vehicle for this role as caretaker of workers' interests was the CGT. Initially the Socialist government offered advantages to the unions, including the Communist-led CGT (for example, easier access to government), but it soon became clear that union influence remained weak—not least because of *Communist* control of the largest union confederation. While the program of nationalizations inaugurated in 1981 was derived from the largely tactical concession to the PCF in the Common Program of 1972, the 1982 measures were introduced without reference to union interests. Equally, the wage freeze and the shedding of labor in 1982 were also effected without prior consultation with the unions. In addition to the traditional weaknesses of French unions—their low weight in numbers and their ideological fragmentation—the government's deflationary strategy worked against effective union power. Moreover, the two main confederations—CGT and CFDT—mirrored in their rivalry and antagonism the hostility of the PCF and the PS, with the Socialist leader of the CFDT, Edmond Maire, identifying the Communist head of the CGT, Henri Krasucki, as likely if ever in power to present democratic trade union leaders with the choice of going underground or entering psychiatric hospitals.

As a Communist party proxy, the CGT had been kept on a tight rein until the late 1970s, but after the *rupture* in the left alliance in 1977 it was aligned more closely with the party and after 1981 used as the more muscular agent of Communist complaint, staging protests against rising unemployment in the coal, steel and motor industries, where CGT membership was traditionally concentrated. Yet the Communist unions were constrained in their effectiveness by the general air of demobilization among French workers. There was no upsurge of interest in industrial protest as in the days of the Popular Front of 1936; worker militancy in fact was low as acquiescence became the main response to recession. In any case, the CGT's own share of the vote in workplace committee elections had been declining for many years, from 50 percent in 1966 to 29 percent in 1984, and in labor tribunal elections there had been a fall from 42 percent to 37 percent between 1979 and 1982. With a vested interest in resisting job reductions in industrial sectors of traditional CGT strength, the confederation at times acquiesced in downwardly adjusted shakeout totals, as at the Talbot Roissy plant in 1983, where the Communist labor minister, Jack Ralite, was involved in the decision. But by 1983 it was clear that the lyrical illusion that the older industries would be cushioned by higher investment was no longer tenable, and the CGT broke most of its links with government.

After the PCF left office in 1984, Krasucki and other CGT leaders were arraigned for their spinelessness and lack of opposition to industrial "reconversion," and a new policy of all-out opposition was introduced. It is likely that CGT leaders such as Louis Viannet and Michel Warcholak were instrumental in the decision to pull the PCF out of government in 1984 in order to resist more vigorously the huge contractions being proposed in the auto industry, such as the proposed loss of 25,000 jobs at Renault plants. In 1985 a violent clash occurred at the SKF engineering plant, where the Socialist interior minister, Pierre Joxe, used the CRS riot police, and thus brought to mind a similar action by the Communists' *bête noir*, Socialist minister Jules Moch, in the late 1940s. Yet Communist attempts to capitalize on discontent over government cutbacks met with little popular response and, rather than proving the necessity of Communist support for the government, demonstrated that it could be dispensed with. Thus the CGT revealed the Communists' failure to come to terms with the France of the 1980s, where their strongholds in heavy industry were sociologically in decline and where their position had been eroded by new labor laws which obviated the need for union intermediaries of the kind the CGT had been in the 1940s and 1950s.

Moreover, CGT action had been political in the sense of the strategy between 1981 and 1986 being determined by *political* considerations and the strikes of 1984–85 (and 1979–81) being part of a *political* imperative. The political nature of CGT action was underlined by the use of the unions to stage "days of action" in the autumn of 1985 and in the run-up to the 1986 election. Such actions merely served to confirm the ineffectiveness of political syndicalism in the 1980s; for good or ill, the workers failed to exhibit the sort of militancy sought by the Communist Party in its effort to mobilize so as to retain its identity and force in the political arena.

ORGANIZATION

The decline of the party involved a growing organizational malaise. Despite the democratic centralist essence of the party, there had always been, even in the most confident periods, problems within the apparatus. Maurice Thorez had inherited the Resistance generation, which after 1945 he sought to purge; the Servin-Casanova, Marty-Tillon and Lecoeur affairs all testified to this organizational problem. But the union of the left of the 1960s and 1970s brought an influx of members enthused by a popular line and by a cause—left unity—which had not been a traditional Communist theme. The organizational dislocation of the 1980s could be traced from the brusque change of direction in 1977, from the rejection of the alliance with the Socialists and resort to a new sectarianism largely alien to the recruits of the previous ten years. A process of expulsions, which the party had in the heyday of the union of the left sworn to forgo, was begun against intellectual dissidents. Louis Althusser's articles in *Le Monde* in April 1978 touched a sensitive nerve in their denunciation of democratic centralism and *La langue de bois*. The twenty-third congress (1979) was accompanied by various attacks, and in 1979–80 the Paris federation, which under Henri Fiszbin's leadership had particularly favored left unity and had made the running in liberalization, was accused of opportunism and dissolved. Fiszbin wrote up the affair in *Les bouches s'ouvrent* (Fayard, 1980), founded the group *Rencontres communistes* and was expelled from the party in October 1981. In 1986 he was elected with Socialist support to the National Assembly.

The Communist campaign of 1981, concentrating its fire on Mitterrand and the Socialist Party, also created difficulties in the organization. The party lost many sympathizers, for example longstanding supporters such as Hélène Parmelin and activists who were demobilized by the disruption of the union of the left. Reliable membership figures were not easily come by: the figure of 700,000 claimed at the 1982 congress referred to cards distributed to the federations rather than to fully paid-up members. It passed credulity that the membership should have remained at the figure of 700,000 also claimed at the height of left unity in the 1970s, while the party's *vote* had been halved over the same period (1978–86). There had probably been a decline proportionate to that in the sale of *L'Humanité* and attendances at the annual *fête de l'Humanité*. Thus a figure of some 350,000 was more plausible, reducing the party closer to its Leninist core of professional revolutionaries and paid functionaries, though even this figure was still likely to be an exaggeration.[6]

In the approach to the 1982 congress the orchestrated tribune in *L'Humanité* was largely hostile to participation in government, in contrast to Communist *voters*, only a third of whom, as late as March 1984, wanted the party to withdraw. When the time came to withdraw in mid–1984, a dispute erupted over the new line which by implication condemned the record of the four Communist ministers. The dissent of Politburo member Pierre Juquin and ex-minister Marcel Rigout was reflected in *L'Humanité*'s exceptional publication of the account of the Central Committee meeting in October 1984 where rival views were expressed. But the intention seems to have been to draw attention to the isolation of the critics rather than to encourage dissent in the run-up to the 1985 congress. That congress nevertheless reflected the continuing force of a strong current of *rénovateurs* who rejected the party's abrupt about-face on leaving office in 1984, and who included three of the four former ministers. In October 1984 six Central Committee members abstained on the congress motion, and *L'Humanité* gave space to some of the critics (notably Juquin) to oppose the official congress motion—criticism which included the party's attitude to Eastern Europe, democratic centralism and its "recent errors"—the last being an implicit attack on Marchais. There may even have been an attempt to depose Marchais at this time, in favor of the most popular of the former ministers, Fiterman, but "antiparty" factionalism of this sort is well-nigh impossible and, in any case, Fiterman had avoided critical references to the party's strategy.

But that the *rénovateurs* had plucked a resonant chord was evident from the problems encountered in getting the federations to vote the 1985 congress motion unanimously. While difficulties had been encountered in the past, in the run-up to the twenty-third and twenty-fourth congresses, in 1985 9 percent of the delegates voted against the official motion in preliminary federation congresses, as compared with a mere 1.5 percent before the previous congress in 1982. Moreover, and hitherto without precedent, three federations voted to reject the resolution, including Haute–Vienne, one of the party's traditional bastions, led by the most critical ex-minister, Rigout. Yet, predictably, the 1985 congress reaffirmed the leadership's control by demoting critics such as Juquin from the Politburo (though not from the Central Committee) while Marchais' nominees were promoted, for example J.-C. Gayssot to the secretariat. Whereas the *rénovateurs* remained an important force after the 1985 congress, and while the leadership's control of the machine did not end the grumblings from ex-ministers and problems in certain federations, the prospects for the critics' future were not good. Democratic centralism, while not guaranteeing against the factionalism it is designed to crush, remained the leadership's key weapon over recalcitrant elements in the party.

The leadership's considerable resources were mobilized after 1984 to impose the new strategy of "unity from below," this time baptized *le nouveau rassemblement populaire majoritaire*. The strategy of undercutting support for social democratic parties by running campaigns around mobilizing issues was as old as the Third International, and the 1985 congress consecrated this theme. The annual *fête de l'Humanité* in September 1984 proclaimed the new "revolutionary" line; the party's leading economist, Philippe Herzog, produced *L'Economie nouvelle à bras le corps,* intended to show that the crisis was not inevitable and that it should be "refused." The twenty-fifth congress (1985) rehearsed familiar themes, including a defense of the Eastern bloc, attacks on U. S. foreign policy, and the ill-treatment of the party at the hands of the media. Newer themes included attacking the presidentialism of the Fifth Republic and the weakness of parliament, and demands for a return to full proportional representation—the only electoral system from which an isolated Communist party can prosper. The strategy of left unity "from the top" was designated a mistake, and the Socialist Party dismissed as a mere reflection of the right. From such a strategic retreat into its ghetto, the party turned to face the voters in 1986.

THE ELECTION OF MARCH 1986

Although the party explicitly denied the accusation, the Communist campaign for the legislative election of 1986 was very anti-Socialist until the Central Committee changed its line and began to attack the right as well. The headlines in *L'Humanité* before January 22, 1986, were anti-Socialist in a ratio of 49 to 3, but thereafter the line changed to one proclaiming that "the Communist vote is the anti-right vote." The election campaign continued on these twin tracks: that, on the one hand, the effective, authentic economic policy of the left was Communist and that, on the other hand, Socialist government had been a disaster and that the Socialists were preparing, through cohabitation, to govern with the right. The Communist campaign, in which *rénovateurs* such as Pierre Juquin played a vigorous role, also included demonstrations, CGT days of action (all abortive) and a campaign against the Socialist flexible work time bill, which was considered by the Senate in February 1986. Communist difficulties with the sectarian line may have reflected the hesitations in their electorate which, although the most left-wing in the sense of its hostility to the right, was by no means anti-Mitterrand. In the run-down industrial areas the unrealistic contention that no jobs need be lost was incompatible with the views of the electorate, even in hard-hit areas such as Nord, Pas de Calais, Moselle and Lorraine.

L'Humanité put a good face on the results by proclaiming "a party which counts" on the day after the elections, but the result was another in the long line of worsening votes. At 9.79 percent (2,724,381 votes) the party came only just ahead of the Front national. It was back at the level of its first ever elections in 1924 (9.5 percent) and only half of its 1978 result (20.6 percent). It had fallen below its European election result of 1984 (11.2 percent), which the party had blamed at the time on a low turn-out and on the presence of its ministers in the Socialist government.

There was very little relief for the party leadership in a decline which was uniform and which deprived the party of all but a token presence in many parts of France: the party had become in every sense marginal to mainstream politics. In geographical terms it retained over 20 percent of the electorate in only three departments—Cher, Allier and Haute–Vienne—and only in Cher (where it was led by the popular mayor of Bourges, Jacques Rimbault) did the party stem its decline, polling 7 percent more than in 1984, and 4 percent more than in 1981. In eight other departments, including industrial Pas de Calais, Aisne, Seine Saint Denis and Val de Marne, it polled over 15 percent, and these few were now all that remained of the fiefdoms where the party was once dominant. Even then, in Seine Saint Denis the vote had fallen from 36.3 percent in 1981 to 18.7 percent, leaving the party trailing in the heart of the red belt behind both the Socialists (29.1 percent) and the Gaullists (22.4 percent). The same was true in the Val de Marne, where in 1981 the party polled 36.3% but in 1986 dropped to 18.7 percent and was overtaken by the Socialists (25 percent) and Gaullists (23 percent). These were the constituencies respectively of J.-C. Gayssot, seen as a potential party leader, and of Georges Marchais.

Other former strongholds of the party suffered in the same way: in Seine Maritime, Nord, Pas de Calais and Haute–Vienne the party's leaders, Roland Leroy, Gustave Ansart, Rémy Auchède and Marcel Rigout, were unable to prevent the general movement downwards. But it was also noteworthy that the *rénovateurs* were equally impotent when it came to stopping the decline: Marcel Rigout, former minister, saw the vote fall from 33.4 percent to 20.9 percent in Haute–Vienne, and in Meurthe et Moselle Colette Goeuriot was only 390 votes ahead of the Front national and down by 6 percent on 1981 (to 10.2 percent). There was evidence, however, of a small but appreciable *notable* effect in the regional elections held at the same time. In these the party polled 10.21 percent. In Seine Saint Denis the regional list led by former minister Ralite polled 20.4 percent, but was still third. Party organization and the work of local *notables* often counts for a 1.5–2 percent difference between local and national elections in France.

A Bull-BVA exit poll published in *Libération* painted a pessimistic portrait of the Communist electorate in 1986. To start with, it was not a young electorate: only 4 percent of students supported the Communists, and only 6 percent of those under twenty-five. In only one occupational category—manual workers— did the Communists poll significantly over 10 percent, and even here their 20 percent of industrial workers and 15 percent of service workers was overshad- owed by that of the Socialist Party (34 percent and 31 percent, respectively) and the right (29 percent and 40 percent, respectively). Even the share of the unemployed (13 percent of whom voted Communist) was barely above the national level and well below that of the Socialist Party (33 percent) and the right (33 percent). The poll revealed that the increased turnout (up 11 percent on 1984) did not profit the Communist Party, only 5 percent of those who abstained in June 1984 voting Communist in 1986.[7]

The senior party leadership was strangely absent from the TV screens on election night. The party's response was that the vote had gone up (from the European elections, when there was a low turnout) and that with 10 percent the party was still a major force. But the other reaction was to reemphasize the sectarian line of the twenty-fifth congress, rejecting alliance with the Socialists and exalting the role of "mass organizations," particularly the CGT, but also fronts such as the peace and youth movements and unemployed and retired workers' organizations. The *L'Humanité* postelection editorial declared that the "influence of a revolutionary party cannot be measured merely by the number of votes it polls on election day; it is also a matter of its capacity for mobilization." Thus (as witness Laurent's election postmortem to the Central Committee entitled "Rally and Agitate in the Line of the Twenty-fifth Congress") it was not conceded that the alleged hard line or the leadership were responsible for the electoral setbacks since 1981.

The wave of criticism of the party and its leadership unleashed by the 1986 election results was not novel: there had been vocal criticisms of the party before (in 1978, 1981 and 1984). The novelty in 1986 arose from the predominance of locally elected Communists—their positions under threat—among the critics. But if bad election results changed the leadership, Marchais would have departed in 1981. With democratic centralism things are not so simple: postelection promotions such as that of Gayssot—a bureaucrat of the first stamp—underlined the weakness of the critical elements. Despite survey evidence that three-quarters of PCF voters were sympathetic to the *rénovateurs* and that half the Communist electorate wanted Marchais to resign,[8] he stayed; as Althusser had observed, when crises arise, instead of electing a new leadership, the leaders elect a new party.

PROSPECTS

The decline of the party in the 1980s had its roots in social, institutional and political sources. In social terms, the Communist Party suffers, as indeed its leaders came to acknowledge,[9] from the transformation of French socioeconomic structures, notably from the erosion of class barriers, and a decline in class consciousness—particularly working-class consciousness, most damaging for a party with so *ouvriériste* a persona. Self-analysis at the 1982 congress had revealed the leadership's acknowledgment of the failure to accommodate the reality of social change, of the rise of the white-collar salariat, the contraction of the blue-collar class and the flaws in the pauperization thesis. The growth of service sector employment at the expense of the manufacturing sector had much to do with the decline of the party in its Parisian red belt heartland in the 1970s.[10]

Institutional forces served clearly to marginalize the party. Presidentialism and bipolarity both imply a subordination of the Communist Party to its social democratic competitor, there being no prospect of a Communist presidential candidate being taken seriously or of a second ballot Communist representative of the left being as electable as a Socialist candidate. Bipolarization further involved the creation of alternative *governing* alliances, whereas it had always been the PCF's forte to be a party temperamentally suited to opposition and the articulation of protest.

Yet political sources of decline were equally important. The new institutional constraints of the Fifth Republic need not necessarily have marginalized the party as they did. It was in the power of its leaders to follow the Italian road to a social democratization of the party where the Leninist ideologies and structures were diluted, and where support held solid—in the Italian case around some 30 percent of the vote. The French party's persistent endorsement of Soviet postures was a folly, at a time when the evidence for voter hostility to the USSR was undeniable and when the Soviet Union was seen as a threatening power, an ineffectual economy and an illiberal society.[11] Survey evidence reveals that when closest to Mitterrand and distanced from the Soviet Union, as in the mid–1970s, the PCF secured its most favorable rating, with only 40 percent perceiving it unfavorably; by 1985 the "unfavorable" rating had reached 70 percent.[12] Yet the PCF chose to remain an orthodox party and to present itself essentially as a *mouvement de refus*.[13] In this sense, it has itself to blame for ignoring the electorate's—its own electorate's—declining sense of exclusion from the wider liberal democratic society from which the party has sought to isolate it. The decline of the Communist press and of its vote in working-class areas confirm the loss of its representational function at the very point at which it sought to define its *raison d'être*.

Politically too the party was outflanked by the Socialist Party, a party which had been boosted by social and institutional changes and by the astute leadership of François Mitterrand. By the 1980s Communist leaders were seeing as a tactical blunder the decisions to support Mitterrand's presidential candidacies in 1965 and 1974, thereby lending credence to the impression that the party had no choice in a presidential system but to be self-effacing and subordinate, and thus effectively to connive at its voters' casting a *vote utile* for Mitterrand in 1981 at the first ballot and thereby contributing to the further marginalization of the party. Presidential elections by the 1980s had become the least favorable to Communist candidates, and it was unfortunate for the party that the next election it was required to face after its humiliation of 1986 was a presidential election.

It has been argued that some of the sources of Communist decline are reversible,[14] notably those described here as political. Different strategies might have been pursued, had the leadership not opted for recidivist postures. Equally, the party could hope, as it did in the mid–1980s, for the eventual breakup of the Socialist Party in the post-Mitterrand era, when factional rivalries might rage without the steadying hand of *le patron*. Yet such hopes were probably no more than wishful thinking; the experiences of 1958 and 1981, when the Communists suffered large electoral reverses, seemed not to be reversible. Nor did the emergence of the FN as a rival, and because overtly nationalistic, more potent, protest party augur well for the PCF. Meanwhile, for an effective defense of its financially and politically important positions in local government, the party required the help of the Socialists: the return to the ghetto for a party that had in reality become *un parti d'élus*[15] made little sense, and it was not impossible to foresee a fracture between the electoralist and orthodox elements of the party as prefigured in Fiszbin's passage to the Socialists. It has to be remembered that Communist leaders, when faced with the prospect of relinquishing control of the apparatus in order to share it with critics, have preferred to split the party on the principle that it is better to reign in hell than to serve in heaven.

NOTES

1. "L'échec électoral du parti communiste," in D. Boy et al., *1981: les élections de l'alternance* (Paris: Presses de la fondation nationale des sciences politiques, 1986), p. 69.

2. J. Ranger, "Le Déclin du parti communiste français," *Revue Française de Science Politique* (January 1986): 46–62.

3. See G. Le Gall, "Radiographie de l'image du P.C.F.: double divorce avec la société et les sympathisants," *Revue Politique et Parlementaire* (January–February 1985): 16–27.

4. See R. Tiersky, *Ordinary Stalinism: Democratic Centralism and the Question of Communist Political Development* (London: Allen and Unwin, 1985), pp. 155–66.

5. See F. Hincker, "The Communist Party and the Government of the Left in France," in S. Williams, ed., *Socialism in France from Jaurès to Mitterrand* (London: Pinter, 1983), pp. 165ff.

6. See Ranger, "Le Déclin."

7. *Libération*, March 18, 1986.

8. SOFRES survey, *Le Monde*, July 10, 1986.

9. See M. Kesselman, "The French Communist Party: Historic Retard, Historic Compromise—or New Departure," in P. Cerny and M. Schain, eds., *Socialism, the State and Public Policy in France* (New York: Methuen, 1985), pp. 42–59.

10. T. Pfister, *Le Monde*, June 20, 1979.

11. See Le Gall, "Radiographie."

12. See Ranger, "Le Déclin."

13. H. Le Bras, "PC: un déclin inexorable," *Le Point*, March 31, 1986.

14. J. Baudouin, "L'Échec communiste de juin 1981: recul électoral ou crise hégémonique?," *Pouvoirs*, No. 20 (1981): 45–54.

15. T. Pfister, *A Matignon au temps de l'union de la gauche*. (Paris: Hachette, 1985), p. 299.

The Parti Socialiste in 1986

PATRICK McCARTHY

This chapter looks at the PS as it evolved from 1981 to 1986 and as it appears after five years of rule and an electoral defeat. It is suggested that these years changed the Socialists: the party of Metz, hard-line in opposition, and the party of Valence, exultant in victory, gave way first to a troubled, self-interrogating party of 1983 and 1984 and then to the party of government—wiser or more resigned—of 1986. The *tendances* drew closer on policy but continued their guerrilla war for power.

Meanwhile French opinion turned sharply against the PS in government but hesitated to embrace the right and allowed the Socialists to perform well in 1986. They were driven from power but remained France's largest party.

From a postelection vantage point one may attempt a first assessment of the Socialist government: how did it steer France through the depression and how did it deal with the structural problems of French society?

This chapter is divided into four parts. The first and longest traces the PS' course during the years of power, while the second casts a brief glance at the RPR-UDF during the same time. The third section makes a preliminary analysis of the 1986 election, the fourth attempts to synthesize the preceding chapters and to draw conclusions.

SPLENDORS AND MISERIES OF GOVERNING

As stated in Chapter 1, the Socialists began governing on the Epinay-Metz line. At Metz they had asserted that "the market will not regulate the economy as a whole. . . . The so-called economic laws, which the right presents as eternal, similar to the laws governing the movements of the planets, are in fact merely the principles on which the capitalist system rests."[1] Now the break with capitalism was supposedly made. At the Valence congress of October 1981 there was talk of "heads rolling,"[2] while even Pierre Mauroy denounced the "château dwellers." This was also the period of honeymoon between government and country, for in a June 1981 poll 71 percent expressed confidence in Mitterrand.

Why did the honeymoon not last? Raymond Aron's answer was simple: "The left thought the French had turned Socialist. But the left was mistaken."[3] Another observer points out, however, that most of the PS' early measures were popular: 50 percent of people wished to preserve the Auroux laws and only 18 percent favored repealing them; even the number favoring denationalization of the newly nationalized industries reached only 37 percent as opposed to 43 percent who wanted them to remain nationalized.[4]

Yet it seems hasty to conclude that the Socialists failed in the area of politics rather than policy because, when the switch of public opinion began in 1982, it coincided with a deterioration of the economic situation. Moreover, certain aspects of the Socialists' project—like the union of the left—had worn out their appeal before 1981.

In January 1982 four by-elections were won by the right, which also made gains in the cantonal elections of March. Here the left's total of 49.7 percent was approximately level with the right's, but it was 2 percent less than Mitterrand had won on the second round. A more severe blow was struck by the wage and price freeze. The party grumbled and Mauroy was obliged to explain away the freeze as a temporary interruption rather than what it became, namely, a new policy. It was impossible to hide the sad fact that the Socialists were contradicting themselves, and an August poll showed that many people felt that the government had no economic policy.

The Socialists had alienated groups who had from the start opposed them, like the Employers Association (this was perhaps inevitable) and the doctors, who were enraged with the Communist minister of health, Jack Ralite. Divisions within France were growing wider and the tone of political debate more heated precisely when the Socialists were also losing segments of the population who had supported them. In 1982 the phrase "people disappointed with socialism" made its way into the media, and on September 16 Giscard appealed to them on television.

The first watershed in the Socialists' five years arrived in March–April 1983. These months saw a series of interwoven events: the left suffered a defeat at the polls from which it never fully recovered; the PS made a second and decisive choice of economic rigor; the CERES leader left the government but was unable to offer a convincing challenge to rigor. These episodes were to shape the PS' life until the autumn of 1985.

In the elections of March 6 and 13 the left lost thirty-one towns with a population of over 30,000 (the PS fifteen and the PCF sixteen) and held only twelve of the thirty-six towns with over 100,000 inhabitants. When the first round is compared with the second round of the presidential elections, the losses are striking: the left's share of working-class votes declined from 72 percent to

62 percent, white-collar votes went from 62 percent to 48 percent and upper-level managers' votes from 45 percent to 22 percent. These statistics may be misleading, but they reveal losses in all social groups, heavier among middle-class groups but, as one observer has insisted, not overwhelmingly so.[5] Overall the right won 50.89 percent, the governmental majority won 39.7 percent, and 9.35 percent may be considered uncertain. Among the towns lost on the first round, two were especially significant: Roubaix, which sits amid the old industries of the Northeast and had long been a bastion of the left, and Grenoble, a town with modern industries which had been represented in parliament by Mendès France.

Yet the left's electoral situation was far from hopeless. If the right won 53.64 percent in towns with over 30,000 inhabitants it was partly because their abstention rate was higher than the average, reaching 35.54 percent in Marseilles. The left had a pool of potential votes, some of which it tapped in the second round. It held onto Marseilles, where Gaston Defferre remained mayor, and to Belfort, where Jean-Pierre Chevènement became mayor. Moreover, a poll taken after the elections showed that in a legislative election the left would win 49 percent of the vote to the right's 49 percent; the PS-MRG would win 31 percent, the PCF 15 percent, the far left 2 percent and the diverse left 1 percent.[6]

After ten agonizing days the government was reshuffled: Mauroy was reconfirmed as prime minister, Chevènement was replaced as minister of industry, and Jacques Delors' position was strengthened. The third devaluation and the second plan of rigor were preceded and followed by a debate within the party, which set supporters of the plan against antagonists who favored maintaining an expansionist policy, letting the franc float and introducing certain protectionist measures. The debates, so reminiscent of arguments within the British Labour Party during the 1970s, were conducted partly between the CERES and the other three *tendances* and partly within the Mitterrand tendency, where men like Pierre Joxe and Christian Goux resisted rigor.

The decision set the tone for the next three years, when the PS elaborated on internationalism and rigor. The battle within the party will be discussed below, but one must stress here that the supporters of the alternative policy were decisively defeated. The dreams of a break with capitalism were abandoned, measures to help business were taken, and Mitterrand began to sound ever more like a "latter-day Guizot."[7] If the party's economic task was to reduce the inflation rate, break the cycle of wage indexation and repair the public finances, its political task was to convince itself and its voters that rigor could be a societal project: a fruitful experience rather than a brutal necessity. Although it was not fully successful, its relatively strong performance in 1986 stemmed from its ability to present itself as a responsible party of government.

Rigor aroused hostility in the country, where right-wing opposition took many other forms. Medical students protested against Alain Savary's university reform and doctors against changes in the organization of hospitals. Some of these were no more than the anarchistic, corporatist flare-ups so traditional in France. No self-respecting government would wish, for example, to rule without provoking demonstrations by Breton farmers, as was the case in April 1983. But there was a more serious loss of support by the left, and by October only 31 percent of those polled retained confidence in Mauroy, 63 percent having no confidence. As Volkmar Lauber has pointed out, the "negative image" of economic policy that had been formed would not be shaken off.

Moreover, the government's decision to take "quick" rather than "gradual" action to promote restructuring weakened its political position. Since it had at first made the war on unemployment the chief criterion of its success, the blow to its credibility was all the greater. Public awareness of the issue grew with unemployment itself, and an *Express* article was characteristic of this period: "Over the next months the explosion of unemployment will perhaps replace inflation and balance of payments problems . . . companies, large and small, are obsessed with laying off workers."[8] Having claimed Giscard as a victim, the depression was now to claim the Socialists.

Competition with the revived RPR-UDF was only one of the PS' many problems. Another, analyzed by Martin Schain, was the rise of the FN, which made its strong showing at Dreux in this same autumn. Equally important were strains within the extended family of the left, namely, with the PCF, the unions and left-wing intellectuals.

David Bell and Byron Criddle have traced PCF-PS relations as the Communists saw them. The Socialists' aims were to keep the PCF in the government in order not to be outflanked from the left, to be perceived as playing fair in order to attract disaffected Communist voters, and to allow the PCF as little influence as possible over industrial policy and none at all in foreign affairs. At Bourg-en-Bresse Lionel Jospin—like Mitterrand before him—did not seek to hide the differences between the two parties. Chevènement warned of a split: "Do not let us repeat '47," he declared, alluding to the Communists' departure from the government and the start of the Cold War.[9]

But, while the PS did not want the Communists to leave, it was not prepared to sacrifice its economic policy. Bell and Criddle have explained that the PCF left because of strategic considerations that stemmed in part from real differences of policy. Indeed, it is hard to see how the self-appointed spokesman for the traditional working class could any longer have countenanced the harsher policy of rigor that Lauber describes, and it is easy to agree with George Ross that this policy damaged the other spokesman, the unions, which began to move back into opposition.

When the government's spokesman, Max Gallo, lamented the lack of support from left-wing intellectuals (*Le Monde,* July 27, 1983), he unleashed a long debate. In part the replies he received reflected a change in French intellectual life, for the generation that believed in commitment had long since vanished (its leader had been Jean-Paul Sartre who had, however, despised the PS and the Common Program). The next generation was, if Michel Foucault be taken as an example, more skeptical. Suspicious of ideologies and of proposals for global change and concerned above all to "reproblematize" institutions, Foucault pointed out the inconsistencies in the PS' position. It had as ally a PCF that remained faithful to the USSR, and it had proclaimed one economic faith only to switch after a year to another. It was demanding of left-wing intellectuals "a discourse to mask the changes it had undergone."[10]

The issue here was different: the PS was not losing support because of rigor but because it had pretended it could dispense with rigor. Nor was Foucault alone in thinking that the PS wanted "to make use of intellectuals";[11] as if to confirm this one Socialist leader condemmed them as "weak."[12] The paradox was that the PS was being criticized as a church precisely when it was ceasing to be a church. The fight to win back intellectual support was led by Jack Lang, who was innovative and pragmatic in his cultural policy.

Meanwhile the Socialist rank and file was demoralized. In part this was because the regime was as presidential as any that had preceded it during the Fifth Republic. While Mitterrand's early career was marked by a distrust of authority in the tradition of left-wing Republicanism, his decade as leader of the PS had taught him how to make himself obeyed. This left his followers to wonder what they were supposed to be, and one melancholy answer was that the PS, which had already been "a party to elect a president," had turned into the "president's party."[13] This had pernicious effects on both sides, for Mitterrand could be described as "isolated from the public and even from the party that is his creation,"[14] while the rank and file, whom Chevènement had exhorted at Valence to become the government's footsoldiers, had no heart for the battle.

It would be simplistic to exaggerate the party's lack of influence. If its role in foreign policy was slight, it exerted some influence on domestic issues. It was able, for example, to protect the bottom one-third of wage-earners from paying the supplementary tax to finance the social security system. In November 1982 the Socialist group in parliament, all too ably led by Joxe, harassed the government over the amnesty for the Algerian generals. In general, however, the party leadership took easily to the corridors of power, while the rank and file and even the parliamentarians conducted an "almost unreal" discourse of opposition.[15]

The gap was widened by class differences within the party. As explained by Partick Hardouin and others, the PS is a pyramid with a working-class base, a white-collar middle and a heavily upper-class leadership. Engineers and upper-level *cadres* made up 6 percent of the party and 52 percent of the ministerial cabinets; workers were 16 percent of the party and 0 percent of the cabinets; middle-level *cadres* were 10 percent of the party and 33 percent of the cabinets.[16] As already suggested, this made it easier for the PS to impose austerity but harder to persuade the membership to accept it.

Moreover, this seems to be an experience that each left-wing party must undergo for itself. Once more the British Labour Party comes to mind and, while the PS was less subject to pressure from unions, its culture was even less a culture of government.

In 1984 the PS was dispirited and the right exultant. Michalina Vaughan has analyzed the campaign against Savary's law, and one need only add that Savary became the scapegoat for anger that was directed at the left as a whole. Indeed, it seems to this observer that the abuse heaped on the Socialists is not to be explained either by the verbal excesses of Valence or by their policies. This was the necessary ideological catharsis that had to take place before the left could be accepted as a legitimate force of government.

The European elections of June 17, 1984, were a fresh disaster. The PCF went down to 11.2 percent and the PS to 20.75 percent, whereas in 1979 the PCF had won 20.5 percent and the PS 23.5 percent. The two parties were able to garner little more than 30 percent, and their only consolation was that the RPR-UDF, harassed by Jean-Marie Le Pen, reached only 42.9 percent. The low voter turnout—abstentions climbed to 43.27 percent—was a sign that many left voters had stayed home. In July a poll showed that only 25 percent of people had confidence in Mitterrand.

However, the president maneuvered cleverly. In a defensive ploy he withdrew the Savary law and caused its architect to resign; taking the offensive, he confused his opponents with a proposed referendum on public liberties. In a change of government Mauroy was replaced by Fabius, who was identified with "modernization." Out went the PCF and back came Chevènement.

In retrospect this was the second watershed of the five years, and it led to the Socialists' partial recovery. But in January 1985 *Le Monde* could write that "the government seems to have no future." Fabius' discourse of modernization was a facade behind which lay the failure to combat unemployment; the left was an abnormal 20 percent behind the right in the polls, and the PS was governing with no more than 20 or 25 percent of the electorate.[17] Nor did the cantonal elections of the spring bring respite: the RPR-UDF share of the vote went up to 49 percent out of a total right-wing vote of 58 percent, while the left attained only 41 percent, of which the PS' share was 26.5 percent.

So Mitterrand's April decision to opt for proportional representation was sensible. Although it was the pretext for Michel Rocard's resignation, the change in the electoral system registered unavoidable facts. A new Communist-Socialist pact would be obviously fraudulent and would not save the left from the fate that had overtaken the right in 1981. The only solution was for the PS to face defeat while saving as many seats as possible.

The form of proportional representation chosen—the departmental list, the 5 percent minimum and the "highest average"—favored the large parties. This allowed the PS to set itself an ambitious but realistic target of 30 percent. The RPR-UDF majority would be cut by the FN and would be small enough to prevent them from driving Mitterrand from power. Indeed, he could hope they would have no outright majority, which might leave him free to piece together a coalition government or to influence the choice of prime minister.

The choice of proportional representation was politically successful (even if morally dubious since it helped to legitimize the FN), and despite fresh setbacks in 1985 like the Greenpeace affair, which did no lasting electoral damage, the PS made a comeback. The main reasons were that, as Volkmar Lauber has pointed out, the results of rigor were growing clear and also that the party succeeded in convincing itself and many voters that rigor was part of a societal project. The "unprecedented" wage restraint[18] was defended on the grounds that French industry had to be restructured. This historic task had been evaded by the right and now fell to the left, which would execute it while protecting the poorer segments of society.

Painfully, the PS was acquiring an identity that seemed new even if it had been dimly present in the mid–1970s. Fabius' emphasis on Socialist efficiency appealed to centrist voters, as did Chevènement's rhetoric. It is intriguing that, whereas Michalina Vaughan stresses the continuity between Savary and Chevènement, the political projects they advocated were so different. By talking of effort and merit, Chevènement appealed to voters who were not favorable to socialism but believed in the Republican tradition. The PS' foreign policy and the "banalization" analyzed by Michael Harrison further contributed toward this evolution.

The Socialists' changed view of themselves was exhibited at the Toulouse congress of October 1985, which demonstrated that "the hour of Bad Godesberg" had come.[19] All the currents rallied behind the policies that had been adopted in 1983. For better or worse the PS was ceasing to be a party of opposition and was becoming a party of government. From being a "Socialist" party it was turning into a "Republican" party. A modernized version of an old French tradition, it identified with the nation and smoothed over social conflicts.

And voters responded. By October 1985 an *Express* poll gave Mitterrand only a 37 percent approval rating as opposed to 50 percent who disapproved, but it awarded Fabius a 45 percent approval to a 38 percent disapproval. The figures were to change, but as Fabius' ratings declined, Mitterrand's improved. A *Le Point* poll of January 1986 showed that 50 percent had a good opinion of him and only 42 percent a bad one.

To understand these developments one might glance again at the role of the *tendances*. To sum up, the CERES mounted the only serious challenge to rigor and was defeated in 1983, while the Rocardians, who had been proved right by the adoption of rigor, made a bid for power in the party two years later. Mitterrand's current split as his younger followers began vying—perhaps prematurely—for his succession.

The defeat of the CERES marks a change in the PS and the emergence of greater unity on policy. In 1983 a pessimistic observer wondered whether the PS could hold together after Mitterrand since it was united only by "a vague set of common references that were more or less mythical."[20] By 1986 the experience of governing had drawn the party together and the *tendances* were no longer groups with varying histories and divergent world views; they remained, however, armies organized behind leaders to fight for power.

Valence was a display of unity where the Rocardians were welcomed—albeit with reluctance—back into the fold, but in 1983 Chevènement, who had supported the 1982 wage freeze, led the CERES into opposition. "It is best to leave," said one of his henchmen, "We will not be part of a government that is not of the left."[21] In preparation for Bourg-en-Bresse the CERES rallied 18 percent of the party behind an alternative motion that called for the maintenance of buying power at the expense of letting the franc float. The policy of rigor, claimed the CERES, would lead to electoral disaster and a fourth devaluation— "the only issue is to know when the next readjustment will take place."[22]

The intriguing feature of this dispute was not that the leaders of the other *tendances* united against the CERES motion or that Jospin derided it as a magic solution, but rather that the CERES did not press its attack. When Chevènement rose to speak on Saturday afternoon at Bourg-en-Bresse the hall was tense, but an hour later the drama had vanished. For he did not spell out an alternative policy and in the end accepted a synthesis that contained very few corrections of the majority text. Chevènement was emulating the grand old Duke of York.

The simplest explanation is that he recognized already that "the union of the left in its 1972 version has exhausted its energy."[23] It surely did not escape him that Mitterrand's adherence to the Epinay-Metz line had been more a matter of legitimacy than of economic conviction, that the Communists were a declining, unreliable ally and that the PS could not be won over even to a limited protectionism. The CERES too had exhausted its energy, and its role as the catalyst of left-wing union was finished.

Although it was ironic that Chevènement should return to the government as the PCF was leaving, it was not a coincidence. Nor was it—as argued in Chapter 1—mere opportunism that led him to don the robes of Jacobin nationalism. Yet it is not clear in 1986 whether the CERES is a bankrupt current or a spearhead of the new republicanism.

On the opposite edge of the party the Rocardians pursued a different course. Despite the snubs their leader received and despite the early departure of two of their ministers, J.-P. Cot and Louis Le Pensec, they muted their criticism of the expansionist policy. The switch to rigor was, in their eyes, a proof that they had been right and that the PS was finally "telling the truth." At Bourg-en-Bresse the Pau alliance was reformed.

An intriguing feature of this congress was the defection—perhaps tactical— of Alain Richard, a dissident Rocardian who won 5 percent of the party to a motion that went beyond supporting rigor and argued that social progress was not primarily a matter of buying power. Behind this formula lurked the theses of *autogestion* which the Rocardians had been neglecting. Certain PS innovations could be seen as forms of *autogestion*: the freedom of expression section of the fourth Auroux law. But Jacques Julliard criticized Rocard for ignoring the need for redistribution of power: "Economic realism makes no sense unless it is accompanied by social initiatives . . . in a word by the participation of citizens in decision-making."[24] However, the Rocardians' neglect of *autogestion* may be yet another sign of the PS' break with its past.

Their agreement on economic policy brought no alliance between Mitterrand and Rocard, whose insurmountable differences are matters of culture as well as of personality and power. Where Mitterrand is steeped in literature and history, his rhetoric containing echoes of Chateaubriand and his Epinay speech phrases from Charles Péguy, Rocard is an economics and administration expert. Such differences are in part—like the differences between Fabius and Mauroy—a matter of generation.

Indeed, Rocard and Fabius have much in common, which explains Rocard's resignation: Fabius was usurping his role. Being proven right had not benefited the Rocardians, for the shift in economic policy was not accompanied by a shift of power within the party. The Mitterrandists were stealing Rocard's policies while continuing to snub him. His resignation was the start of a campaign to become the party's presidential candidate in 1988.

Rocard's strength lay in the polls, and the January 1986 *Le Point* poll gave him 26 percent of the vote to Fabius' 8 percent, or 22 percent to Mitterrand's 16 percent. But, since he needed to win over the party, his *tendance* presented its own motion at Toulouse and won 28 percent of the party. That it then agreed to a synthesis with the other currents was both a gesture to party unity and a sign that policy was not the issue. To protect himself on his left, Rocard has criticized liberalism, suggesting that "the myth of laissez-faire has collapsed" and that "a strong state is needed to fix the rules of the economic game."[25] Such statements were characteristic of the PS leadership.

Rocard's Toulouse motion contained criticisms of the first two years of Socialist rule, so it was not designed to restore the Metz alliance with Mauroy. After resigning, Mauroy reaffirmed that the PS must be a recognizably left-wing party and not the cold-hearted agent of modernization. In this lay a strategic concern: the need to cull Communist votes. Despite the fratricidal struggle that long divided Communists and Socialists in the Nord, Mauroy's current could be a pole of attraction for discontented PCF supporters.

This was an issue among the Mitterandists, whose unity was strained in 1985 by the Fabius-Jospin dispute.[26] Although it began as an argument about who was to conduct the election campaign, it was also a disagreement about the role of the PS. In calling for the "broadest possible *rassemblement,*" Fabius was opening toward the center and was ready to merge the party into a looser grouping that might constitute a "Republican front." As party secretary Jospin could not let the PS be downgraded. Instead he asserted that the campaign be led by the party officials and that it be based on the "union of popular forces." Like Mauroy, Jospin was arguing that the PS must be anchored on the left: "We must offer direction to Communist voters at a time when the crisis of the PC offers us the opportunity of creating one big party of the left."

Initially Fabius had the upper hand because his strategy was more in harmony with the PS' economic policy. Then a series of misfortunes befell him: the Greenpeace affair; an October 27 debate with Chirac, who dominated him; and the Jaruzelski incident. Practical considerations were still more important: since the Socialists were certain to lose seats, they had few to distribute to centrist dignitaries capable of forming a plausible republican front. Jospin recovered ground and reaped credit for the PS' strong showing in March 1986.

In the intraparty struggle differences of policy did then exist. But they were far less sharp than in the 1970s, when the dispute about relations with the PCF as well as about *autogestion* or defense issues plagued the PS. The catch-all factor—to the degree that it still existed—was an advantage. Ex-Communists could be drawn by Mauroy, centrists by Fabius; Chevènement incarnated tradition, Rocard modernization. The threat to party unity continues, however, because of the way rivalries so easily assume organizational forms.

For the election the party united around a platform that was described as "very prudent."[27] The foreign policy section differed from the right's platform in two areas only. On "Star Wars" the PS declared: "We cannot offer support to the American SDI project which seems to us unrealistic and utopian."[28] Elsewhere the document called for defense of the "European identity against the superpowers and against the technological domination of the US and of Japan." This is also the theme of Régis Debray's recent book, *Les Empires contre l'Europe*.

On domestic issues the platform reiterated the key themes of PS policy since 1983. At a time of depression French industry must be restructured, but the salaried classes must be protected: "only the Socialists can reconcile modernization with social progress." So reduction of working time was advocated but was linked to a more efficient use of machine time. A fresh attempt would be made in labor relations, and the right of expression in the fourth Auroux law would be extended to small enterprises. Prudent as such proposals might be— *Le Monde* complained that there was little to "mobilize people"[29]—they were an attempt to define a left-of-center stance for the late 1980s.

The platform contained a few bold ideas: the establishment of a minimum income for each individual and the suggestion that the costs of economic modernization be borne by the collectivity rather than by the individuals displaced. The section on immigrants was weak, and the possibility of their voting in local elections "will have to be examined."

Few promises were made because too many had been made in 1981. This was a defensive document and, preparing to go into opposition, the PS warned against the "two-tiered" society the right would create. In particular it picked out the repeal of the "administrative authorization for dismissals" as an issue around which to rally the salaried classes. The contrast between the platform and Mitterrand's *110 Propositions* reflected the distance the PS had travelled.

THE RIGHT IN TRANSITION

The tale of the right's journey from 1981 to 1986 has as one of its themes Jacques Chirac's partially successful attempt to impose his leadership and policies on a thriving but confused political area. If René Rémond's categories explain the situation of 1981, they are more difficult to apply in the years that follow.

In 1985, for example, Rémond dismissed the FN as a "virulent protest that will quickly subside."[30] In fact, Martin Schain has demonstrated that the FN is well rooted in local life and may not just go away.

Second, the wave of liberalism that swept the right in the early 1980s and the greater caution which reigned before the elections contributed, each in its own way, to blurring the Orleanist-Bonapartist distinction. Rémond has argued that the mood of Bonapartism is one of "drama," whereas Orleanism seeks to "explain and reassure."[31] But in 1986 the RPR's brand of cohabitation was specifically designed to reassure. Similarly, the "liberalism" of the 1980s is different both from Giscard's emphasis on reconciling the social classes and from the Bonapartist belief in state intervention. It thus pushed most of the RPR and the PR in the same direction, one that was different from their previous paths. This is not to conclude that Rémond's analysis has exhausted its usefulness, for the two families he distinguishes may well reappear in clearer forms as the right continues to rule.

The RPR's quest was to strengthen the right while allotting to the UDF the role of junior partner. Once more Martin Schain points out that the task was difficult because, while the RPR was consistently stronger than the UDF, the two parties' share of the vote remained obstinately low. In consequence the electoral victory of 1986 would be narrow indeed. Yet Chirac did succeed in establishing himself as leader of the right, in imposing the strategy of cohabitation to prepare for the presidential elections of 1988 (or earlier) and in devising a blend of liberalism and centrism that provided the right with a basis—however shaky—on which to govern.

As stated in Chapter 1, the RPR was in a stronger position than the UDF in 1981 and was able to present itself as the dominant opposition force. This attracted money and members, membership growing from 670,000 in 1981 to 800,000 in 1986. Younger men pushed their way into leadership positions: Alain Juppé, Philippe Séguin, Michel Noir and the new mayor of Grenoble, Alain Carignon.

In March 1983 the RPR's share of cities with more than 9,000 inhabitants rose from 82 to 158 and it won 23 percent of the vote to the UDF's 21 percent. However, the European elections, where the right presented a joint list led by Simone Veil, were disappointing because the RPR-UDF gained 42.9 percent, a smaller figure than it had hoped. If this could be explained away as the price that had to be paid for unity, it was all the greater a setback because Chirac had spent the previous year taking a more pro-European stance on the economic and institutional aspects of the European Community (EC) as well as on defense. The cantonal elections of 1985 were more successful, for the RPR gained 192 seats, but this victory was overshadowed by Mitterrand's decision to opt for proportional representation in the legislative elections.

Chirac's policy of unity with the UDF was a neat reversal of his strategy in the 1970s, which had helped bring about Giscard's defeat. It was all the more necessary after 1985 because Mitterrand's decision was designed not merely to allow Le Pen to cut into the right's share of the seats but to offer the UDF and its various components the possibility of standing alone.

The FN represented a further problem. As Martin Schain has shown, the RPR was at first willing to use Le Pen as an ally against the left, and then—after his initial success—it sought to isolate him. As well as legitimizing the FN, this forced the RPR to adopt a tougher stance on immigrants.

In his policies Chirac continued to dilute the Gaullist legacy by his concessions on Europe and his kind words for the United States. How much of this was rhetoric is unknown; Michael Harrison has suggested that some of it was.[32] Chirac also rode the wave of liberalism which he had anticipated during his 1981 campaign.

The new liberalism rejected the view that the state should intervene to reconcile and tame social and economic forces. This was a philosophy stressing individual initiative, entrepreneurial values and distrust of the state. Liberalism found its intellectuals in France, and one example among many is constituted by J.-F. Revel's book Le Rejet de l'état (1984). Formerly a man of the center-left, Revel propagated the thesis that statism of all kinds was evil.

Such views seem inimical to French political traditions of whatever ilk, and one may wonder whether they are—in their more extreme forms—merely part of the ideological catharsis. However, the wave of liberalism divided both the RPR and the UDF, opposing Alain Juppé to Philippe Séguin and Alain Madelin to Roger Chinaud. Although such a philosophy clashes with Bonapartism, the point at which the two meet is that both are aggressive world-views. Thus liberalism was part of a more general RPR stance which stressed anti-Communism and law and order. The aggressive mood was apparent in the years 1983–1984 when Charles Pasqua led the campaign against the Savary law. In calling, for example, for denationalization not only of industries nationalized in 1981 but of those nationalized at the Liberation (by de Gaulle) or in demanding competition within the social services, the RPR was taking positions that broke with the right's past.

It was not to be expected that such positions would be fully maintained, as the comeback of the PS demonstrated that there was still a large middle ground in French politics. So Chirac staked out the RPR's terrain on the right but closer to the center, as an examination of his campaign document will reveal. This was a difficult tightrope, and one observer has written that the RPR has "not succeeded in developing a more centrist identity but it has succeeded in leaving an empty space on its right."[33] Nor did Chirac promote his standing in the polls. As late as January 1986 the Le Point poll revealed that only 15 percent of voters favored Chirac for president, as compared with 8 percent for Giscard and 31 percent for Barre. These figures helped shape Chirac's conciliatory stand on cohabitation.

The UDF was described as "holding together by the force and habit of inertia."[34] This may be misleading, however, because two of its main components—the PR and the CDS—are solidly rooted in local life. Their strength lies not in party organization—where the RPR is far superior—but in their quota of *notables* and their ability to gather votes in regions of provincial France like Brittany, which is Pierre Méhaignerie's territory, or the Auvergne, which is Giscard's. Moreover, the UDF too threw up a new generation of leaders: such men as Jean-Claude Gaudin, president of the parliamentary group, and François Léotard, the secretary of the PR. While the last five years demonstrate the superiority of the RPR, they offer no reason to think that it can absorb the UDF.

However, the UDF has been plagued by splits, of which the most important has been the Giscard-Barre rivalry, which has both divided the PR from the CDS and the Radicals, among whom Barre has much support, and perturbed the PR, where Barre has followers like Charles Millon, who demanded as early as 1984 that Barre be named the UDF's presidential candidate.

Although this rivalry is primarily one of ambition, it had repercussions on policy and strategy. While Giscard endorsed the new liberalism, Barre attacked significant aspects of it. He denounced supply-side economics, declaring that taxes could not be cut unless government expenditures were first reduced, criticized the Reagan administration for its budget deficit and warned against the inflationary consequences of "global economic expansion."[35]

It was the failure of the left's expansionist policy that rehabilitated Barre and made him—along with Rocard—the most popular politician at the polls. Barre incarnated a more "traditional" view of the economy than the liberals Chirac and Giscard.

But Giscard's strategy was superior. By playing the card of right-wing unity he delayed Barre's rise within the UDF and enlisted Chirac as an objective ally. The PR took an independent stance within the UDF and presented itself as the true voice of liberalism. Yet Giscard failed to restore his own position. Not only did he deliver up the UDF to the RPR, but the PR leadership under Léotard became a force in its own right and sought to be more liberal than Giscard. "Every state, even Giscard's, is dangerous," proclaimed Léotard.[36]

The result of this maneuvering was that Barre was denied a position of strength within the UDF and a role in the right-wing government to be formed after 1986. He took an intransigent stand on cohabitation, which he denounced as "wheeling and dealing among the parties such as took place under the Fourth Republic."[37] This Gaullist language marked his bid to establish himself as de Gaulle's legitimate successor, as did his stand on East-West relations, where he tended to rebuke Chirac's pro-Americanism and to distance France from the cruise missile controversy.

This strategy might have succeeded in a presidential race (and may still succeed) but, when the right was bidding for parliamentary power, a stance of contempt for parties could hardly be useful. The inconsistency in Barre's position lay in the blend of centrist economics—where his views were not so very different from those of the post–1983 Socialists—and political aggressivity—where he demanded a complete break with them.

The splits within the RPR-UDF alliance diminished its ability to galvanize opinion when it was strongly anti-Socialist, allowed the PS to make its comeback and left an opening for Le Pen. Pessimistic comments flowed from the right's spokesmen: "We have less than a year to go from a majority based on the refusal of the left to a majority of support for the right" (Giscard, June 1985); "The opposition has not succeeded in explaining its project, in convincing people that it will bring about change" (Léotard, January 1986). Informed by an interviewer that "a majority of French people remain skeptical about opposition unity," Chirac could find little to reply.[38] Skepticism about schemes to combat unemployment grew as the 1980s wore on. Moreover, the very certainty of the right's victory probably reduced its size.

In looking beyond the personal struggles and inconsistencies of the two parties one may suggest that the way to understand the right in the last five years is to use the antithesis of "liberalism" versus "tradition" or of "aggressivity" versus "conciliation." The right was engaged in a debate about how radically it wished to reverse the Socialists' policies and its own previous period in office. The debate was confused because, as Rémond has pointed out, each segment of the right compels other segments to distort their positions in order to compete: Barre's political aggressivity drove Chirac to be prudent. But behind the distortions the two options for the right were clear.

A glance at the RPR-UDF platform reveals that a compromise was reached. The right would, as one observer puts it, "preserve much of the Socialist legacy,"[39] but it also promised to undo parts of it and of its own legacy.

The first pages contain a declaration of liberalism: the right would unleash "individual initiative in economic, social and cultural life."[40] The section on the economy was entitled "Breaking with Interventionism" (a phrase reminiscent of previous breaks with capitalism). Denationalization of the banks and industries nationalized in 1981 was promised, while "in the long term" the Liberation nationalizations were to be reversed too. The section on public finances called for reduction in the budget deficit and reduced taxation, especially for companies. Perhaps because of Barre's criticisms, the two were to run parallel.

The strategy for combatting unemployment was very different from the one adopted in 1981. Competitiveness was the key, so concessions to employers included modifications in their social security payments and the possiblity of changes in the minimum wage. A special effort—stressed during the campaign—was to be made in the area of youth unemployment. The TUC were to be replaced by incentives for companies to hire young people at wages that might be below the official minimum wage and with reduction of social security payments.

The right was gambling on investment and growth: "France must once more enjoy a growth rate as high as her neighbors, one that will create jobs." Further concessions were made to employers in the field of labor relations. Ending the "administrative approval for dismissals" was designed to promote flexibility in the labor market, modifications were to be made in the Auroux laws, and the thresholds at which companies were obliged to create shop stewards and works councils were to be "suspended." Regulations on the use of part-time and temporary workers were to be loosened.

Such policies mark the shifts toward liberalism, but they were less drastic than they might have been. The state would continue to help sectors in difficulty— "with temporary encouragement"—and the high technology area—with "support for key projects." The Auroux laws were not to be dismantled, and even the "administrative approval" may be more a political than a labor issue.

While the right's spokesmen insisted on political transformation, they were cautious on economics, Michel Noir admitting that the state would continue to be a "catalyst."[41] *Le Monde* concluded that "the RPR was moving away from pure liberalism" and even that "an economic policy based on consensus was being mapped out."[42] Certainly there were areas of agreement between the Fabius government and the RPR-UDF opposition, but there was also a maximalist and minimalist reading of the right's economic program which might become an issue once it took power.

In other areas the break with the left was clear. The Quilliot law was to be repealed in the belief that the restrictions it placed on owners discouraged real estate investment. On law and order the right fixed its guns not on Pierre Joxe's law but on its favorite target, Robert Badinter, who had created a "lax legal context." A reference to "restoring the police's self-confidence" set a different tone.

Consensus between the PS and the opposition was—as Michael Harrison has shown—evident in foreign policy. The right was, however, kinder toward the United States: defense cooperation was to take place "in close consultation with our American ally," and France was to consult Britain and Germany on the Strategic Defense Initiative (SDI), which appeared to mean that France might take a more favorable view. But because of the degree of consensus, foreign policy played little role in the elections.

HOW GREAT WAS THE SOCIALISTS' DEFEAT?

The election was fought under a version of proportional representation. Promised both in the Common Program and in the *110 Propositions,* proportional representation was introduced as a defensive maneuver. In 1981 the PS-MRG had won 59 percent of the seats with 38 percent of the vote. Had majority voting been used in the European elections the RPR-UDF, with 42.9 percent, would have won 60.8 percent of the seats. Conversely, if proportional representation had been used in 1981, the Communists would have held the balance in parliament. In 1986 proportional representation worked as expected for, had majority voting been used, the RPR-UDF would have had 358 seats, 66 more than they won via proportional representation.

There are many kinds of proportional representation, and the Socialists chose a system that helped them. First, a party that failed to obtain 5 percent won no

Table 9.1
Parliamentary Election Results, March 16, 1986

Party	Percent of Vote	Number of Seats*
Extreme Left	1.53	0
Communist party	9.78	35
Socialist party	31.04	206
Union of the Left	0.20	2
Radical left	0.38	2
Various left	1.03	5
Ecologists	1.21	0
Regionalists	0.10	0
RPR (independent lists)	11.21	76
UDF (independent lists)	8.31	53
UDF/RPR (joint lists)	21.46	147
Various right	3.90	14
National Front	9.65	35
Extreme right	0.20	0

Socialist party through Various left: 32.65 — 215 Socialist group

RPR (independent lists) through Various right: 44.88 — 290 new majority

* Omits 1 seat to PS in Saint-Pierre-et-Miquelon and 1 seat to RPR in Wallis-et-Futuna.

Source: Information Service, French Embassy.

seats at all, which eliminated small groups like the far left or the Ecologists. Second, by choosing the *département* as the unit the PS damaged larger but still minor parties like the PCF, which wasted votes—even if it went over 5 percent— in *départements* with few members of parliament. Finally, by adopting the principle of the "highest average" rather than the "largest remainder"[43] the PS further helped large parties. A purer proportional representation system, like the Italian, would have weakened both the PS and the RPR-UDF.

All these factors, however, not merely helped the RPR-UDF but compelled it to unite to form the largest electoral grouping. If it had presented joint lists everywhere it would have won still more seats, but this would have prevented the RPR from demonstrating its superiority over the UDF. So some of the lists were separate, and in these regions the RPR outpolled the UDF by 11.21 percent to 8.31 percent (see Table 9.1).

Proportional representation did nothing, then, to break down the right-left split and create centrist parties. Even if *Le Monde* could detect a consensus in economic policy, the Fifth Republic remained divided down the middle; the RPR-UDF bloc faced the PS with the PCF and the FN on the wings.

The French hostages in Lebanon cast a shadow over the campaign, and the government's inability to get them released probably weakened the PS and helped Le Pen, even if the parallel with President Carter and the Iran hostages is superficial. Aside from this the campaign was anticlimactic, which indicates that the storms of 1983 and 1984 were waning. The Socialists ran posters with a headline "Help, the right's coming back," while the RPR posters displayed an ostentatiously casual Chirac in shirtsleeves and the slogan "On to tomorrow." Since the results were preordained by the polls, the only speculation was the size of the right's majority and the issue of cohabitation.

As in 1978, when it appeared that the left might win, the French discovered that the domination of the president was not enshrined in the Constitution, which allowed, as Michel Debré has pointed out, for parliament to rule.[44] Indeed, the texts indicate that the prime minister is to have the upper hand, and the power exerted by the presidents stemmed from personal charisma or from their role as head of a clear parliamentary majority.

While the president is responsible for the "orderly functioning of public powers" (Article 5), the prime minister "determines and conducts the policies of the nation" (Article 20). The president appoints the prime minister, but the prime minister cannot operate without a parliamentary majority, which limits the president in his choice. The president may refuse to sign the government's decree, but he must promulgate its laws. He can dissolve the assembly, but he cannot on his own call referenda. Even the reserved domains of defense and foreign affairs are more custom than constitution. While Article 5 calls the president "the guarantor of national independence" and a decree of 1964 gives him a degree of control over the use of nuclear weapons, there is nothing in the Constitution that grants him the right to run foreign affairs.[45]

Cohabitation was of absorbing interest to the political class—UDF parliamentarians even noted that the Elysée Palace had no budget to keep the lights on or cut the grass and threatened to leave Mitterrand in the dark and surrounded by a wilderness—but the ground rules were laid down during the campaign by Mitterrand and Chirac. Although Mitterrand made ambiguous statements, declaring now that "my role could change" and now that "there is no question of my becoming a cut-rate president," he recognized that 1986 would bring a change of regime. Meanwhile Chirac agreed to cohabitation on condition that the prime minister have the support of the majority, that he have the right to execute his program and that Article 20 be observed.

So the issue that had not been faced in 1981 was faced in 1986, and a resolution of sorts was found. At the time of writing there is no way to tell how long cohabitation will last and what its outcome will be. But, if the Fifth Republic's institutions have demonstrated a certain flexibility, it is because flexibility suited both sides. Mitterrand wished to finish his seven years as president, to reserve the possibility of being a candidate again and to retain some institutional power for the PS, while Chirac wanted to avoid an early presidential election when Barre had a large lead over him in the polls.

As for voters, a *Libération* poll showed that 50 percent felt Mitterrand should stay and 44 percent felt he should go, but this is not conclusive, since 87 percent of PS voters thought he should stay and 72 percent of RPR-UDF voters thought he should leave. Chirac and Mitterrand were probably correct in believing that voters did not want a further election, a constitutional crisis and possible economic chaos.

The elections brought two mild surprises and confirmed trends that were reshaping French politics (see Table 9.1). The first surprise was that the FN vote was higher than opinion polls had suggested, although Martin Schain's chapter explains why this was so. The second was that the PS did not merely pass the 30 percent barrier but reached—with its satellites—32.65 percent. It followed that the RPR-UDF result was less good than it had hoped—40.98 percent. This figure translated into 277 seats, so the 3.9 percent and 14 seats won by the diverse right would be needed to obtain an outright parliamentary majority.

The narrowness of victory stemmed logically from the RPR-UDF's failure to create a popular dynamic, but Barre was made the scapegoat, and the Rhône results might indicate that the voters were punishing him for rejecting cohabitation. The PS list, led by Hernu (who actually profited from the Greenpeace scandal), won 29.28 percent to Barre's 22.67 percent. In Lyons itself Barre was overtaken by Michel Noir, 23.45 percent to 24.19 percent. In fact, there are other reasons for this, notably that Barre has no roots in Lyons; but the result was to eliminate—for the moment—right-wing opposition to the cohabitation strategy.

This made Chirac's immediate task easier. Mitterrand seems to have been tempted by the narrowness of the victory to split the RPR by naming Jacques Chaban-Delmas as prime minister but, once this plan was thwarted, Chirac could assume office. In the long run, however, his task remained to gather around himself the bloc of the right's votes including the nearly 10 percent that had gone to Le Pen.

The election confirmed the RPR's supremacy over the UDF and also the nature of the two parties. In Paris the RPR outpolled the UDF by 35 percent to 11.8 percent, while the UDF fared better in solidly provincial areas like the Côtes du Nord, where it won 25.46 percent to the RPR's 18.49 percent, and Ille et Vilaine, where Méhaignerie thrashed the RPR by 36.64 percent to 16 percent. In the Bouches du Rhône the UDF eclipsed the RPR, which was devastated by defections to the FN: the UDF won 21.64 percent, the RPR 9.47 percent and the FN 22.53 percent. In Paris the UDF was Le Pen's prey and lost support in the western parts of the city. In general the RPR and the UDF patterns of voting do not differ much from earlier elections. The PR remains a party of *notables,* and Léotard's attempt to turn it into a mass party like the RPR has yet to be realized. However, the PR was the strongest of the UDF's components, with sixty members of parliament to the CDS' forty-one and the Radicals' six.

On the left the PCF continued what Bell and Criddle consider its historic decline, while the Socialists were justified in maintaining that their performance was a success. In many parts of the country the decline from the "extraordinary" score of 1981 was merely a few points: in Finistère, where the PS had won 39.37 percent, it now won 38.06 percent, while in Ille et Vilaine, where it stood at 38.49 percent, it reached 34.87 percent. If one measures the results by the Mitterrand-Crépeau score on the first round of 1981, they seem even better: in Belfort, for example, Chevènement's list drew 42.46 percent compared with Mitterrand-Crépeau's 35.43 percent, while in Paris the PS scored 31.94 percent compared with Mitterrand-Crépeau's 26.7 percent. Indeed, Paris represented a strong comeback after the 1983 local elections for the PS won several marginal arrondissements like the Thirteenth and the Eighteenth.

The geographical splits in France are still present: the right maintains its hold on the east and the Massif Central. In the Haut-Rhin, for example, the PS-PCF won a mere 31.57 percent compared to the RPR-UDF-FN total of 60.05 percent. Yet the PS is now solidly present in regions of the west, and in the Vendée, ancestral home of counterrevolutionaries, it won two seats to the right's three.

A keenly watched area was the Nord, where the unemployment rate is 13 percent, rising to 18 percent at Roubaix, where immigrants represent 30 percent of the population. The FN duly made its breakthrough with 21.18 percent in Roubaix, where it became the second party behind the PS with 29.15 percent. Throughout the region the Socialists held 30.01 percent compared with 27.29 percent for Mitterrand-Crépeau, while the PCF slid to 13.74 percent from the 21.44 percent who had voted for Marchais in 1981. These figures would seem to indicate that Mauroy's strategy may be working and that the PS can hold its position in a region of smokestack industries by winning votes from the PCF.

Sociologically, the election confirmed known trends. Regularly practicing Catholics voted 67 percent for the RPR-UDF and only 16 percent for the PS, while those without religion voted 47 percent for the PS (and 20 percent for the PCF) and only 17 percent for the RPR-UDF. Among age groups, the PS performed far better than its rival among those under twenty-five—40 percent to 38 percent compared with 32 percent to 42 percent overall—while for the group aged fifty to sixty-four there was a gap of 24 percent in favor of the right (see Table 9.2). The sexual differences indicate that the PCF and FN are the "chauvinist" parties.

The PS was stong but not overwhelmingly so among manual workers. The statistics here are interesting because the PS does only approximately 3 percent better than its national average. Moreover, the PS-PCF share of the working-class vote is a mere 54 percent compared with 64 percent in 1973, 63 percent in 1978 and 68 percent in 1981. The big battalions of the PS come among white-collar workers, where the PS got 12 percent more than its national score, and among middle-level managers—6 percent more. Here the difference between the public and private sector is significant and helps explain the right's zeal to denationalize.

Table 9.2
Who Voted for Whom, March 16, 1986 (by percentage)

	PC	PS	RPR/UDF	FN	Other
Total	10	32	42	10	6
By Sex					
Men	12	30	40	12	6
Women	7	34	45	7	7
By Age					
Under 25	6	40	38	9	7
25-34	12	41	30	8	9
35-49	10	33	40	9	8
50-64	9	25	49	12	5
Over 65	10	23	53	9	5
By Profession					
Farmers	7	21	54	11	7
Shopkeepers/Artisans	5	14	61	14	6
Liberal prof. } Upper-cadres }	4	32	49	9	6
Middle-cadres	9	38	36	10	7
White-collar	12	44	33	7	4
Workers	20	34	29	11	6
Service pers.	15	31	40	6	8
No prof.	11	29	45	9	6
By Status					
Unemployed	13	33	33	14	7
Salaried private sector	11	31	39	12	7
Salaried public sector	12	46	28	7	7
Self-employed	6	21	53	13	7
Students	4	41	43	5	7
Housewives	6	26	52	8	8

Source: Libération, March 18, 1986.

Conversely, the PS' support is weakest among shopkeepers and artisans, where the FN does as well and the RPR-UDF—expecially the RPR—is overwhelmingly strong, as it is among farmers. The self-employed best resist the blandishments of the PS (which helps explain the right's determination to scrap the "administrative authorization for dismissals"), as do housewives, although not working women. The unemployed vote for the party only slightly more the nation does, while the liberal professions and upper managers follow the national average.

These results confirm the picture that Etienne Schweisguth, Patrick Hardouin and others have painted of the PS as the electoral machine of the salaried classes. They also confirm that the travail the party went through in 1983 and 1984 may have changed its policies and culture but not its electoral character. Since its strengths are among the young and in the expanding segments of the population, it may legitimately hope to grow. The goal of 40 percent may be less utopian than it seems.

One may respond to the question posed at the head of this section by affirming, then, that the PS' defeat in 1986 was not a grave one, but two questions arise from the election. The first is that the PS must either continue to absorb the PCF's voters or else renew the alliance with a reformed PCF. The Communists cannot be ignored, for their 10 percent of the vote is vital to a left-wing victory. The second question is that the PS' strong showing in 1986 must not blind us to the left's poor performance: 44 percent, which is 8 percent fewer than in the presidential election of 1981 and 11 percent fewer than in the parliamentary election. The present gap of 11 percent between left and right is wider than in de Gaulle's period. So the PS' proud claim to be France's largest party may not mean very much and will mean even less if the right becomes a solid bloc. The PS must expand on its right and its left if it is to become "the large majority grouping which . . . will on its own . . . offer an alternative to the right."[46]

CONCLUSIONS

After the elections cohabitation began to work as Mitterrand and Chirac had decided it must. Power passed to the prime minister, who set about his program of denationalization, changing labor law to favor employers and restoring the old system of majority voting. Concessions were made to the president over the choice of foreign and defense ministers. By the time these pages were written in June 1986 strains were already appearing as Mitterrand refused to sign governmental decrees denationalizing the industries nationalized at the Liberation or repealing the administrative authorization. Conversely, Chirac insisted on accompanying the president to the Tokyo summit, thus demonstrating that foreign affairs were not a reserved domain.

Alfred Grosser perceives in this development a shift in the practice of the Fifth Republic, with the president becoming little more than the guardian of national unity.[47] It will surely not be lost on the political class that the decisive election in France is now the parliamentarian and not the presidential election, and this may influence the 1988 elections. However, at the moment the president is not a symbolic head of state like the Belgian king but retains formidable power. This may be exerted to shape policy where consensus exists between president and government, as with the refusal to allow U. S. planes to fly over France on their way to bomb Libya. More important, power may be used negatively to delay and complicate the implementation of policies—like the administrative authorization—with which the president disagrees.

This negative power (Mitterrand is proving to be a master in the art of making himself a nuisance) guarantees the opposition a position within the state, while at the same time offering it an opportunity to appeal to public opinion over the government's head. In the case of the administrative authorization, Mitterrand was emphasizing that the repeal could increase unemployment, and he was thrusting onto the right responsibility for a measure that may prove politically damaging.

So one might modify Grosser's thesis to state that the Fifth Republic has indeed entered a new phase but one where the president retains a certain kind of power. However, this situation is itself unstable and unlikely to last. The Fifth Republic has always demonstrated that institutions do not exist in a vacuum, and the present arrangement will last only until the next presidential election. After that the possibilities are numerous: a victory for Chirac would restore the presidential domination exercised by de Gaulle and Pompidou; were Barre to win, he might find himself in the same state as Giscard did. Nor would a Mitterrand triumph perpetuate the present situation, since his strength would be increased by his reelection and conflict with the government would surely grow. Then there is the possibility of a Rocard or a Fabius victory with further complications that are hard to predict. One may simply note that the Fifth Republic's institutions, while clumsy, have proved both in 1986 and 1981 that they can be adapted to new developments and also that these institutions may now be modified without traumas. Dedramatization has taken place in this area.

It is probable that students of French politics will now concentrate on the right, but this book will conclude with a glance at the PS. Here again the future is uncertain. Is the blend of modernization and solidarity sufficient to offer the party a stable identity? Can the currents continue to work together without—or with—Mitterrand? Will the party be able to recover centrist voters while continuing to gain Communist votes? Instead of speculating one might turn back to the years of power and ask three questions: How did the PS deal with the international depression? How did it grapple with specifically French problems? How well did it execute the tasks that left-wing parties set themselves?

The answer to the first question is that after a disastrous start the PS coped fairly well. Volkmar Lauber notes that a left-wing government succeeded where the right had failed in halting wage indexation and the progression of public spending. Even the nationalizations may be justified pragmatically as a necessary infusion of cash. Thomson is already a success story, and Lauber suggests that with the passage of time the Socialist record may be even more favorably viewed. That the PS failed to reduce unemployment is not—in this context—a condemnation since other European countries deploying different policies have fared no better.

Unemployment aside, one feature of the present depression is that the structures of each country's economy have not altered and the measures each has taken have been in harmony with its history. Thus Italy has had the greatest difficulty with inflation and Britain the most bitter labor disputes. It seems well nigh inevitable that France should resort to a strong dose of state intervention. This occurred not merely in 1981 but even in the PS' more "liberal" phase because, as Lauber and Ross have pointed out from different perspectives, rigor was imposed and not agreed on; in 1983 the government took scant heed of other social actors.

This brings us to the second question, for Stanley Hoffmann has long argued that, while the state has been the motor of economic modernization in France, it has also paralyzed civil society, rendering group action futile and provoking silly, anarchistic protests. The Fifth Republic, Hoffmann wrote during the last years of Giscard's presidency, may have worsened matters since to Gaullism "the state is the sole definer or diviner of the national interest."[48] Hoffmann distinguished four related problems: efficiency—the state causes and must then supplement the inefficiency of other social forces; inequality; the legacy of an authoritarian past; authority itself and hence the legitimacy of government.

Of the first issue it has been argued that the PS itself grew more efficient in government but was largely unsuccessful in helping others to become more efficient. At least it was aware of the problem, as it demonstrated in different ways by helping unions with the Auroux laws and by showing a belated comprehension for business. Greater equality was a prime Socialist goal pursued by a range of policies from the early increases in the minimum wage to educational reform. The latter was largely a failure, and the way the *grandes écoles* succeeded in having themselves exempted from Savary's university law is a textbook example of how French society resists change. One shall return to inequality, but here one might stress that what Hoffmann calls "the desire for rapid collective social promotion" was one reason why the Socialists, spokesmen for an important segment of the working and salaried middle class, came to power. Disappointment with the pace of such promotion was bound to bring disillusionment with them.

In their concept of the state they were racked with contradictions. Even as they nationalized and increased the role of civil servant technocrats, they sought to decentralize. Indeed this was, as Vivien Schmidt has argued, the most obvious achievement of the five years. Yet here again contradictions appear. If decentralization was successful, it is because a leading party and governmental figure took hold of the issue and pushed through reform before opponents were able to organize. Conversely, Michalina Vaughan explains that Savary's university law failed because he consulted too well and too long. The paradox, which is merely apparent, is that state power was necessary to accomplish a reduction of state power.

The PS' greatest contribution toward the problem of legitimacy was quite simply to govern for five years, thus ending the exclusion of one-half of the population from government. Unlike the Popular Front, it took and left office without traumas; it may also hope to be recalled soon. Moreover, by adopting the Gaullist model of foreign policy it legitimized not merely itself as a national party but the policy as a national policy.

In this and in—as Michael Harrison suggests at the end of his chapter— proposing new developments of Gaullism, the PS was an agent of modernization in Hoffmann's sense of the term. French politics are less of a religious war than they have ever been. One should not speak too rashly of the end of extremism because the decline of the PCF is compensated by the rise of the more virulent National Front. Moreover, the flamboyant ideologies that flourished in the past were more theatre than reality (the PCF has long been a "revolutionary" party in name alone), and they exercised a conservative function—dreams of revolution replacing concrete change. But because of this the greater consensus that has emerged in the last two years may be regarded as a sign of modernity. After the polarization of 1983–84 nearly 80 percent of the electorate voted for "lay" parties with fairly moderate programs.

Does this mean that the French are growing more like everyone else? In part yes, as the influence of the international economic order increases. But it has already been suggested that each European country is drawing on its own traditions as it seeks to restructure its economy, so it is not surprising that the PS helped perpetuate some of the traits that Hoffmann considers obstacles to his kind of modernization. After all, its own modernizers like Rocard and Fabius are products of the education system that so cleverly resisted change.

No French institution has changed more than the PS itself, even if it has, like France, drawn on its traditions and chosen to become more like the old Republican left. The question of how successful it was as a left-wing party may now be posed, and here again the answer is mixed.

The PS professed to offer what has been called "socialism of a different kind."[49] It was neither a Leninist nor a social democratic party but rather offered a third way: society was to be run by *autogestion*. Alas, the five years of power have revealed few traces of *autogestion* and overwhelming evidence that the PS has no new vision of socialism.

It does, however, have a slogan and even a vision of solidarity, and here the complementary assessments of Lauber and Ross are important. Lauber points out that except in the period 1983–84 the PS did offer some protection to the weakest groups in society. This is not an achievement to be lightly dismissed, especially if one compares France with Britain, where the policies of the Thatcher government have widened the gulf between employed and unemployed or between regions of old and new industry. By attempting to increase the minimum wage and to combine flexibility of the labor market with job protection, the Socialists were trying to restructure French industry while preserving the standard of living and rights of the working class. They were anxious to avoid the trap of "social technocracy" of which one of their own intellectuals had warned them.[50]

Ross' more pessimistic assessment is also valid. The crucial decisions of 1983 and 1984 were made to promote the international competitiveness of French industry, and little account was taken of working-class interests. Moreover, the five years as a whole brought no great shift of power toward that class. On the contrary, working-class identity was weakened, and the integration of the class into the national community has been accomplished because it has accepted a subordinate role. In this context the severe judgment of Bell and Criddle on the PCF is well founded: by its willful stupidity the party rendered that process easier.

As a left-wing party the PS was unable to escape the fate of the Western European left in general. That it could do so by becoming a "social democratic" party is too simple a solution because social democracy—as the history of the British Labour Party and of the German Social Democrats (SPD) reveals—flourishes in periods of economic growth and not harsher climates like the 1980s. The PS tried—like the Italian Communists in the period of national solidarity (even the language is similar) from 1976 to 1979—to use the acceptance of austerity to buy greater working-class power, but they were no more successful. Certain historical options have been closed but surviving the depression, helping modernize the French economy and encouraging solidarity will stand as the hallmarks of the Socialists in power.

NOTES

1. "Motion finale de politique générale, Congres de Metz," *Le Poing et la Rose,* No. 81 (May 1979).

2. The phrase was uttered by Paul Quilès, who was nicknamed "Robespaul."

3. Raymond Aron, "La Reconquête," *Express,* March 18, 1983, p. 47.

4. Frank L. Wilson, "Socialism in France," *Parliamentary Affairs* 38 (Spring 1985): 165.

5. Etienne Schweisguth, "Les Couches moyennes salariées sont-elles socialistes?" *Intervention,* Nos. 5 and 6 (August 1983): 65.

6. SOFRES poll, *Nouvel Observateur,* April 1, 1983.

7. Volkmar Lauber, "Reinventing French Socialism," *Parliamentary Affairs* 38 (Spring 1985): 55.

8. Yves Guihannec, "Chômage: l'inévitable explosion," *Express,* October 28, 1983, p. 63.

9. J.-P. Chevènement, quoted in *Le Monde,* November 1, 1983, p. 7.

10. Michel Foucault, "Le Souci de la vérité," *Magazine littéraire* (May 1984): 22.

11. Jacques Julliard, "Réflexions d'après le prochain congrès," *Intervention,* Nos. 5 and 6 (August 1983): 9.

12. J.-P. Chevènement, quoted in *Express*, April 1, 1983, p. 43.

13. Gérard Grunberg, "Le PS, machine à fabriquer des présidents," *Intervention*, Nos. 5 and 6 (August 1983): 37.

14. Wilson, "Socialism," p. 177.

15. Hugues Portelli, "La Doctrine du PS depuis 1945," *Intervention*, Nos. 5 and 6 (August 1983): 27.

16. Patrick Hardouin, "Un Parti d'intellectuels," *Intervention*, Nos. 5 and 6 (August 1983): 68.

17. Jean-Marie Colombani, "Les Socialistes à mi-septennat," *Le Monde*, January 3, 1985, p. 1.

18. *European Industrial Relations Review* (January 1985): 13.

19. Maurice Duverger, "L'Heure de Bad Godesberg," *Le Monde*, October 8, 1985, p. 1.

20. Pascal Perrineau, "Adolescence et maturité précoce du PS," *Intervention*, Nos. 5 and 6 (August 1983): 29.

21. Didier Motchane, quoted in *Express*, April 1, 1983, p. 43.

22. J.-P. Chevènement, quoted in *Financial Times*, May 31, 1983, p. 1.

23. J.-P. Chevènement, *République Moderne*, No. 1 (June 1985): 5.

24. Julliard, "Réflexions," p. 8.

25. M. Rocard, "Ce qui menace le monde," *Nouvel Observateur*, January 10, 1986, p. 32.

26. See *Le Monde*, June 20–22, 1985.

27. *Le Quotidien de Paris*, December 16, 1985.

28. "Plate-forme du Parti socialiste pour les élections législatives du 16 mars 1986," *PS Info*, January 4, 1986.

29. *Le Monde*, December 21, 1985, p. 6.

30. René Rémond, "D'ou viennent les cavaliers," *Express*, November 1, 1985, p. 40.

31. René Rémond, *Les droites en France* (Paris: Aubier, 1982), p. 346. This is a new edition of *La Droite en France* and goes up to 1981.

32. Michael Harrison, "France in suspense," *SAIS Review* (Winter–Spring 1986): 111.

33. William R. Schonfeld, "Le RPR et l'UDF a l'épreuve de l'opposition," *Revue Française de Science Politique* 36, No. 1 (February 1986): 21.

34. *Le Point*, January 26, 1986, p. 37.

35. Raymond Barre, quoted in *Le Monde*, June 11, 1985, p. 8.

36. François Léotard, quoted in *Le Monde*, December 7, 1983, p. 2.

37. Raymond Barre, quoted in *Le Monde, Dossiers et Documents: Les élections législatives du 16 mars 1986*, p. 57.

38. Giscard d'Estaing, *Le Monde*, June 11, 1985; Léotard, *Le Point*, January 26, 1986; Chirac, *Express*, March 4, 1986.

39. Simon Serfaty, "The French Fifth Republic," *SAIS Foreign Briefs*, February 15, 1986, p. 13.

40. RPR-UDF, "Plate-forme pour gouverner ensemble," January 16, 1986, p. 1.

41. Michel Noir, quoted in *Le Monde*, December 12, 1985, p. 1.

42. Eric le Boucher, "Le RPR s'éloigne du libéralisme pur et dur," *Le Monde*, December 12, 1985, p. 1.

43. The system works by the allotment of a certain number of seats, based on pop-

ulation, to each *département*. After the votes are counted they are added together and divided by the number of parties having more than a 5 percent share. The result of this calculation establishes the "electoral quotient." Each party or coalition of parties that has reached the quotient then receives one seat. The remaining seats are divided by the method of the "highest average." An imaginary seat is added to each party's score and the sum of the party's votes is divided by the number of seats it has. That number will be 2 for parties that already have a seat and 1 for those that do not. When the sum is divided by 1 or 2, the party with the highest score obtains another real seat. This process is continued until all seats are allotted. A simulation published by *Le Monde* (April 5, 1985) indicates how the "highest average" favors large parties more than the "largest remainder" does.

44. Michel Debré, "Introduction," in *The Fifth Republic at Twenty*, edited by William G. Andrews and Stanley Hoffmann (Albany: State University of New York Press, 1980), p. 15.

45. For one of the many analyses of cohabitation see *Express*, March 21, 1986. For the statements by politicians see *Le Monde, Dossiers et Documents: les élections* du 16 mars 1986, pp. 52ff.

46. Max Gallo, "Les Atouts du PS," *Le Matin*, March 18, 1986, p. 2.

47. Alfred Grosser, "Le Déclin du president," *Le Monde*, April 13, 1986.

48. Stanley Hoffmann, "Conclusion," in *Fifth Republic at Twenty*, p. 457.

49 See Bernard E. Brown, *Socialism of a Different Kind* (Westport, Conn.: Greenwood Press, 1982). The author was already benign but skeptical about *autogestion*.

50. Paul Bacot, *Les Dirigeants du Parti socialiste* (Lyons: Presses universitaires, 1979), p. 221.

Selected Bibliography

The literature on the French Socialists is enormous, and only a small sample can be given here. This bibliography is divided into sectors: the first lists general works on the Parti socialiste, while the following sections refer back to Chapters 2 to 8. This method is designed to provide the reader with precise sources of supplementary information. In general no work is listed twice, although clearly many works are useful for more than one chapter.

Some French publications regularly contain valuable information on the PS; these include the *Revue Française de Science Politique* (RFSP), *Revue Politique et Parlementaire, Projet, Faire* and *Intervention* as well as party newspapers like *Le Matin*.

GENERAL REFERENCES

Ambler, John, ed. *The French Socialist Experiment*. Philadelphia: ISHI, 1985.
Attali, Jacques. *La Nouvelle Economie française*. Paris: Flammarion, 1977.
Bacot, Paul. *Les Dirigeants du Parti socialiste*. Lyons: Presses universitaires, 1979.
Bell, D. S., and B. Criddle. *The French Socialist Party*. Oxford: Clarendon Press, 1984.
Bizot, J.-F., et al. *Au parti des socialistes*. Paris: Grasset, 1975.
Brown, Bernard E. *Socialism of a Different Kind*. Westport, Conn.: Greenwood Press, 1982.
Cayrol, R. "Les Militants du Parti socialiste." *Projet* 88 (September–October 1974): 929–40.
———, and C. Ysmal. "Les Militants du Parti socialiste—originalité et diversités." *Projet* 165 (May 1982): 572–86.
Cerny, P., and Martin Schain, eds. *Socialism, the State and Political Power in France*. New York: Methuen, 1985.
Charlot, J. "Le Double Enchaînement de la défaite et de la victoire." *Revue Politique et Parlementaire*, No. 892 (May–June 1981): 15–28.
Chevènement, J.-P. *Les Socialistes, les communistes et les autres*. Paris: Aubier, 1977.

————. *Le Vieux, la crise, le neuf*. Paris: Flammarion, 1975.
Codding, G., and W. Safran. *Ideology and Politics: The Socialist Party of France*. Boulder, Colo.: Westview, 1979.
Evin, K. *Michel Rocard ou l'art du possible*. Paris: Simoën, 1979.
Giêsbert, F.-O. *François Mitterrand*. Paris: Seuil, 1977.
Hanley, David. *Keeping Left? Ceres and the French Socialist Party*. Manchester: University Press, 1986.
Hardouin, P. "Les Caractéristiques sociologiques du Parti socialiste." *RFSP* 28 (April 1978): 220–56.
Hurtig, C. *De la SFIO au nouveau parti socialite*. Paris: Armand Colin, 1970.
Intervention, Nos. 5–6 (Autumn 1983).
Johnson, R. W. *The Long March of the French Left*. London: Macmillan, 1981.
Machin, Howard, and Vincent Wright, eds. *Economic Policy and Policy-making under the Mitterrand Presidency 1981–84*. London: Pinter, 1985.
Mauroy, P. *Héritiers de l'avenir*. Paris: Seuil, 1968.
Mitterrand, F. *Le Coup d'état permanent*. Paris: Plon, 1964.
————. *Politique*. Paris: Fayard, 1977.
Nugent, N., and D. Lowe. *The Left in France*. London: Macmillan, 1982.
Perrineau, P. "Le PS, de l'affirmation à la crise d'identité." *Projet* 187 (July–August 1984): 796–801.
Pfister, T. *A Matignon au temps de l'union de la gauche*. Paris: Hachette, 1985.
————. *Les Socialistes*. Paris: Albin Michel, 1977.
Poperen, J. *La Gauche française 1958–1965*. Paris: Fayard, 1972.
————. *L'Unité de la gauche 1965–1972*. Paris: Fayard, 1975.
Portelli, H. *Le Socialisme français tel qu'il est*. Paris: P.U.F., 1980.
————. "Les Socialistes et l'exercice du pouvoir." *Projet* 168 (October 1982): 921–32.
Rocard, M., and Jacques Gallus. *L'Inflation au coeur de la crise*. Paris: Gallimard, 1975.
Roucaute, Y. *Le Parti socialiste*. Paris: Huisman, 1983.
Schonfeld, W. R. "La Stabilité des dirigeants de partis politiques: le personnel des directions du Parti socialiste et du mouvement gaulliste." *RFSP* 30 (June 1980): 477–505.
Viveret, P. "La Gauche piégée dans l'état." *Projet* 166 (June 1982): 666–74.
Williams, S., ed. *Socialism in France from Jaurès to Mitterrand*. London: Pinter, 1983.
Wilson, F. *The French Democratic Left 1963–69*. Stanford: University Press, 1971.
————. "Socialism in France: A Failure of Politics Not a Failure of Policy." *Parliamentary Affairs* 38 (Spring 1985): 163–79.

CHAPTER 2

Alexandre, Phillipe, and Roger Priouret. *Marianne et le pot de lait*. Paris: Grasset, 1983.
Beaud, Michel. *Le Grand Écart*. Paris: Syros, 1985.
————. *Le Mirage de la croissance*. Paris: Syros, 1983.
Blin, Maurice, Jean Chamant, André Fosset, and Henri Torre. *Rapport d'information* (on the newly nationalized industrial firms), annexe au procès-verbal du Sénat, séance du 3 Octobre 1985.
Boublil, Alain. *Le Socialisme industriel*. Paris: Presses universitaires de France, 1977.
Cahiers français, No. 212 (July–September 1983), "La politique industrielle."

Clerc, Denis, Alain Lipietz, and Joël Satre-Buisson. *La Crise*. Paris: Syros, 1983.
Estrin, Saul, and Peter Holmes. "French Planning and Industrial Policy." *Journal of Public Policy* 3, No. 1 (February 1983): 131–48.
L'Expansion. *Les Sept Crises*. Paris: Pluriel, 1984.
Fossaert, Robert. *La Nationalisation des chrysanthèmes*. Paris: Le Seuil, 1985.
Friend, J. W. "What Progress in French High-Tech." *French Politics and Society* 8 (December 1984): 15–19.
Grjébine, André. *L'Etat d'urgence*. Paris: Flammarion, 1983.
Haut Conseil du Secteur Public. *Rapport 1984*. Paris: La Documentation française, 1984.
Lauber, Volkmar. *The Political Economy of France*. New York: Praeger, 1983.
———. "Reinventing French Socialism: Economic Policy, Ideology, Political Strategy." *Parliamentary Affairs* 38, No. 2 (Spring 1985): 150–62.
McCormick, Janice. "Une Puce à l'oreille." *French Politics and Society* (December 1984): 20–23.
Maillet, Pierre. *La Politique industrielle*. Paris: Presses universitaires de France, 1984.
Mandrin, Jacques (pseudonym for CERES leaders). *Le Socialisme et la France*. Paris: Le Sycomore, 1983.
Mitterrand, François. *110 propositions pour la France* (election platform, 1981).
Morville, Pierre. *Les Nouvelles Politiques sociales du patronat*. Paris: La Découverte, 1985.
9ᵉ plan de développement économique, social et cultural 1984–1988. Paris: La Documentation française, 1984.
OECD. Economic Reports on France (series).
Programme commun de gouvernement du Parti communiste et du Parti socialiste. Paris: Editions sociales, 1972.
Projet socialist. Paris: Club socialiste du livre, 1980.
Rhodes, Martin. "French Government Subsidies for Information Technology." Paper, ECPR Joint Sessions in Barcelona, March 1985.
Rocard, Michel. *Parler vrai*. Paris: Le Seuil, 1979.
Simonnot, Philippe. *Le Grand Bluff économique des socialistes*. Paris: Lattès, 1982.
SOFRES. *Opinion publique*. Paris: Gallimard, 1984.
———. *Opinion publique*. Paris: Gallimard, 1986.

CHAPTER 3

Grosser, Alfred. *Affaires extérieures: la politique de la France, 1944–1984*. Paris: Flammarion, 1984.
Harrison, Michael. "Mitterrand's France in the Atlantic System: A Foreign Policy of Accommodation." *Political Science Quarterly* 99, No. 2 (Summer 1984): 219–46.
———. *The Reluctant Ally: France and Atlantic Security*. Baltimore: Johns Hopkins University Press, 1981.
Hernu, Charles, *Nous . . . les grands*. Lyon: Boursier, 1980.
Hoffmann, Stanley, *Decline or Renewal? France since the 1930s*. New York: Viking, 1974.
Howorth, Jolyon, and Patricia Chilton, eds. *Defense and Dissent in Contemporary France*. New York: St. Martin's Press, 1984.

Serfaty, Simon, ed. *The Foreign Policies of the French Left*. Boulder, Colo.: Westview Press, 1979.

CHAPTER 4

Archer, M. S. *Social Origins of Educational Systems*. London: Sage, 1979.
Aron, R. *Plaidoyer pour l'Europe décadente*. Paris: Laffont, 1976.
Baudelot, C., and R. Establet. *L'Ecole capitaliste en France*. Paris: Maspero, 1974.
Berger, I. *Les Instituteurs d'une génération à l'autre*. Paris: P.U.F., 1979.
Boudon, R. *Effets pervers et ordre social*. Paris: P.U.F., 1977.
Bourdieu, P., and J. C. Passeron. *Reproduction in Education, Society and Culture*. London: Sage, 1977.
Fraser, W. R. *Education and Society in Modern France*. London: R.K.P., 1963.
Howorth, J., and P. Cerny, eds. *Elites in France: Origins, Reproduction, Perpetuation*. London, Pinter, 1981.
Norvez, A. *Le Corps enseignant et l'évolution démographique*. Paris: I.N.E.D.–P.U.F., 1978.
Prost, A. *Histoire de l'enseignement en France, 1800–1967*. Paris: Colin, 1968.
Ringer, F. K. *Education and Society in Modern Europe*. Bloomington: Indiana University Press, 1979.
Schiff, M. *L'Intelligence gaspillée*. Paris: Seuil, 1982.
Suleiman, E. N. *Elites in French Society: The Politics of Survival*. Princeton, N.J.: Princeton University Press, 1978.
Touraine, A., et al. *Lutte étudiante*. Paris: Seuil, 1978.
Vaughan, M., and M. S. Archer. *Social Conflict and Educational Change in England and France: 1783–1848*. Cambridge, Eng.: Cambridge University Press, 1971.
Vaughan, M., et al. *Social Change in France*. Oxford: Martin Robertson, 1980.

CHAPTER 5

Abélès, Marc. "Les Chemins de la décentralisation." *Les Temps Modernes*, No. 463 (February 1985).
Bernard, Paul. *L'Etat et la décentralisation: du Préfet au Commissaire de la République*. Paris: Documentation française, 1983.
Caroux, Jacques. "The End of Administrative Centralization?" *Telos*, No. 55 (Spring 1983).
Crozier, Michel. *On ne change pas la société par décret*. Paris: Grasset, 1979.
Dosière, René, Jean-Claude Fortier, and Jean Mastias. *Le Nouveau Conseil Général*. Paris: Editions ouvrières, 1985.
Dupuy, François, and Jean-Claude Thoenig. *L'Administration en miettes*. Paris: Fayard, 1985.
Grémion, Pierre. *Le Pouvoir périphérique*. Paris: Seuil, 1976.
Mény, Yves. "Decentralization in Socialist France: The Politics of Pragmatism." *Western European Politics* 7, No. 1 (January 1984).
Ravanel, Jean. *La Réforme des collectivités locales et des régions*. Paris: Dalloz, 1984.
Rondin, Jacques. *Le Sacre des notables*. Paris: Fayard, 1985.
Schmitt, Dominique, ed. *La Région à l'heure de la décentralisation*. Paris: Documentation française, 1985.

Wright, Vincent, ed. *Continuity and Change in France*. London: George Allen and Unwin, 1984.

CHAPTER 6

Adam, Gérard. *Le Pouvoir syndical*. Paris: Dunod, 1983.

Aglietta, Michel, and Anton Brender. *Les Métamorphoses de la société salariale*. Paris: Calmann-Levy, 1984.

Bergounioux, Alain. *Force ouvrière*. Paris: Que sais-je?, 1982.

Boyer, Robert, et al. *La Flexibilité du travail en Europe*. Paris: La Découverte, 1986.

Gallie, Duncan. *Social Inequality and Class Radicalism in France and Britain*. Cambridge, Eng.: Cambridge University Press, 1983.

Kesselman, Mark, ed. *The French Workers' Movement*. London: George Allen and Unwin, 1984.

Landier, Hubert. *Demain, quels syndicats?* Paris: Pluriel, 1981.

Lange, Peter, George Ross, and Maurizio Vannicelli. *Unions, Change and Crisis: French and Italian Trade Union Strategies and the Political Economy, 1945–1980*. London: George Allen and Unwin, 1982.

Morville, Pierre. *Les Nouvelles Politiques sociales du patronat*. Paris: La Découverte, 1985.

Mouriaux, René. *La CGT*. Paris: Seuil, 1982.

———. *Syndicalisme et politique*. Paris: Anthropos, 1985.

———. *Les Syndicats dans la société française*. Paris: Presses de la Fondation Nationale des Sciences Politiques, 1983.

Reynaud, Jean-Daniel. *Les Syndicats en France*. 2 vols. Paris: Seuil, 1975.

———. *Les Syndicats, les patrons et l'Etat*. Paris: Editions ouvrières, 1978.

Ross, George. *Workers and Communists in France*. Berkeley: University of California Press, 1982.

Segrestin, Denis. *Le Phénomène corporatiste*. Paris: Fayard, 1985.

Sellier, François. *La Confrontation sociale en France, 1936–1981*. Paris: P.U.F., 1984.

Touraine, Alain, et al. *Le Mouvement ouvrier*. Paris: Fayard, 1984.

CHAPTER 7

Charlot, Monique. "L'Emergence du Front national." *Revue française de Science Politique* (February 1986).

Gaspard, Françoise, and Claude Servan-Schreiber. *La Fin des immigrés*. Paris: Editions du Seuil, 1984.

Le Pen, J.-M. *Les Français d'abord*. Paris: Editions Carrere-Michel Lafon, 1984.

Lorien, Joseph, Karl Ceiton, and Serge Dumont. *Le Système Le Pen*. Paris: Editions EPO, 1985.

Perrineau, Pascal. "Le Front national: un électorat autoritaire." *Revue Politique et Parliamentaire* (July–August 1985).

———. "Quel avenir pour le Front national?" *Intervention*, No. 15 (January–February 1986).

Plenel, Edward, and Alain Rollat. *L'Effet Le Pen*. Paris: La Découverte, 1984.

Schain, Martin. "Immigrants and Politics in France." In John Ambler, ed., *The French Socialist Experiment* (Philadelphia: ISHI, 1985).

SOFRES. *Opinion publique, 1984, 1985, 1986*. Paris: Gallimard, 1984, 1985, 1986.
Ysmal, Colette. "Le RPR et l'UDF face au Front national: concurrence et connivences."
    Revue Politique et Parlementaire, No. 913 (November–December 1984).

CHAPTER 8

The following sources are additional to those cited in the Notes:

Adler, A., et al. *L'URSS et nous*. Paris: Editions sociales, 1978.
Duhamel, O., and J.-L. Parodi. "Images du communisme." *Pouvoirs* 21–22 (1982).
Elleinstein, J. *Le PC*. Paris: Grasset, 1976.
———. *Le Phénomène Stalinien*. Paris: Grusset, 1975.
Herzog, P. *L'Économie nouvelle à bras le corps*. Paris: Messidor, 1984.
Jeambar, D. *Le PCF dans la maison*. Paris: Calmann-Levy, 1984.
Jenson, J., and G. Ross, *The View from Inside*. Berkeley: University of California Press,
    1984.
Lavau, G. *A quoi sert le Parti communiste français?* Paris: Fayard, 1981.
Platone, F. "Les Communistes au gouvernement: une expérience 'complexe' et con-
    tradictoire." *Revue Politique et Parlementaire* 914 (January–February 1985): 28–
    49.

Index

About the Contributors

D. S. BELL is Lecturer in Politics at the University of Leeds and was formerly Research Fellow at the University of Sussex. He is coauthor of *The French Socialist Party: Resurgence and Victory* (1984).

BYRON CRIDDLE is Senior Lecturer in Politics at the University of Aberdeen. He was Visiting Professor of Political Science at the University of Massachusetts, Amherst, in 1985–86. He is coauthor of *The French Socialist Party: Resurgence and Victory*.

MICHAEL M. HARRISON was, when he wrote this chapter, an Associate Professor at the Johns Hopkins University School of Advanced International Studies in Washington, D.C. He has also taught at Columbia University and at the Johns Hopkins Center in Bologna, Italy. He is the author of *The Reluctant Ally: France and Atlantic Security* (1981) and coauthor of *Italy: A Country Study* (1986), as well as numerous articles on West European and Atlantic affairs. In mid–1987 Dr. Harrison assumed the post of Associate Director of the Programme for Strategic and International Security Studies at the Graduate Institute of International Studies in Geneva.

VOLKMAR LAUBER is Professor of Political Science at the University of Salzburg. He holds law degrees from the universities of Vienna and Harvard and a Ph.D. in political science from the University of North Carolina at Chapel Hill. Before returning to Austria, he taught at the University of South Florida, West Virginia Wesleyan College, and the Johns Hopkins University Bologna Center in Italy. His publications include *The Political Economy of France* (1983) and numerous articles and book contributions on French politics, political economy, and energy and ecology politics in Western Europe.

PATRICK MCCARTHY, who was educated at Oxford and Harvard, has taught European literature and politics at Cambridge University, Johns Hopkins Bologna Center and Haverford College. He is the author of *Céline* (1976) and *Camus* (1982) as well as articles on left-wing politics in France and Italy.

GEORGE ROSS is Professor of Sociology at Brandeis University and Senior Associate at Harvard University Center for European Studies. He is the author or coauthor of *Workers and Communists in France* (1982); *Unions, Change and Crisis: France and Italy*, Volume 1 (1982), with Peter Lange and Maurizio Vannicelli; *The View from Inside: A French Communist Cell in Crisis* (1984), with Jane Jenson; *Unions, Change and Crisis: the UK, West Germany and Sweden* (1984), with Peter Gourevitch and Andrew Martin; and coeditor of *The Mitterrand Experiment: Continuity and Change in Socialist France* (1986).

MARTIN A. SCHAIN is Professor of Politics at New York University. He has edited two volumes with Philip Cerny: *French Politics and Public Policy* (1980), and *Socialism, the State and Public Policy in France* (1985). He is the author of *French Communism and Local Power* (1985), as well as numerous articles on the French trade union movement and immigrants and politics in France.

VIVIEN A. SCHMIDT received her B.A. from Bryn Mawr College and her M.A. and Ph.D. from the University of Chicago, all in political science. She has published articles on the philosophy of science and on its relationship to the social sciences, on administrative ethics, as well as on French politics and administration. She is currently at work on a book on decentralization in France entitled *Democratizing France: The Political, Administrative, and Economic History of Decentralization*. She teaches organizational theory and comparative administration at the University of Massachusetts at Boston.

MICHALINA VAUGHAN was born in Poland and attended primary school, *lycée* and Paris University as a refugee in France. Her qualifications include *doctorat (d'Etat) en droit, diplôme de l'Institut d'Etudes Politiques* (Paris) and diplomas of higher studies in sociology and in languages from the Sorbonne. Vaughan has served as Program Assistant at UNESCO (Social Sciences Department) in 1955–57, Lecturer in Sociology at the London School of Economics in 1959–72, and Professor of Sociology at the University of Lancaster (1972 to date). Her publications include *Social Conflict and Educational Change in England and France* (1971), with M. S. Archer; and *Social Change in France* (1980), with M. Kolinsky and P. Sheriff.